# Mind Your Business

Merging Meaningful Work with Financial Wisdom

JULIUS A. AUSTIN
JUDE T. AUSTIN II

Copyright © 2026 American Counseling Association. All rights reserved.

American Counseling Association
2461 Eisenhower Avenue, Suite 300
Alexandria, Viriginia 22314

Published in the United States of America

*Library of Congress Cataloging-in-Publication Data*

Library of Congress Control Number 2025044248
ISBN 9781556200090 (print)
CIP data requested but not available at time of publication

# Contents

Preface .................................................................................................i
1. The Counselor as Businessperson ........................................................... 1
2. Insights and Trends Within the Counseling Marketplace ..................... 15
3. Our Earning Potential ............................................................................ 35
4. Getting Out of the Hole ......................................................................... 49
5. Professional and Legal Considerations ................................................. 67
6. Traditional Business .............................................................................. 87
7. Nontraditional Business and Side Hustles in Counseling ................... 111
8. Administrative Duties .......................................................................... 135
9. Marketing Strategies for Counselors .................................................. 153
10. Taking Advantage of Counseling Innovation ..................................... 175
11. A Trainer's Paradise ............................................................................ 189
12. The Business of Supervision .............................................................. 203
13. Evaluating and Improving Your Business .......................................... 217
14. Generating Wealth Toward Retirement ............................................. 231
15. Having Money on the Mind and Not in the Heart ............................ 245
16. Doing Good Business ......................................................................... 255

    Conclusion ........................................................................................ 267

    About the Authors ............................................................................ 275

# Preface

We didn't set out to write a business book. We set out to answer a question we've been hearing in classrooms, conference halls, and late-night text threads: Can I actually make a living doing this work?

A few years ago, we were invited by Dr. Kent Butler, a mentor and past ACA President, to join a task force focused on supporting minority counselors. One of the themes we uncovered was that many students of color avoid the mental health field because they've heard—or seen—that counselors don't make money. When we shared what counselors can actually earn, especially in private practice or certain agency settings, people were stunned. And we got it. We were stunned once, too.

We came into this field planning to pursue sports psychology. When someone first mentioned community mental health, we scoffed. But the deeper we looked, the more we realized two things: (1) counseling can absolutely be a viable, even abundant, career; and (2) the business training out there wasn't speaking to people like us. Most of what we found was focused on private practice only—often tied to a gimmick or rigid model—and ignored the broader, messier reality of counselors trying to build a sustainable career.

This book is for the ones who feel called to help, even if it means overextending themselves. For the ones who were taught that financial struggle is part of the package. For the ones who've bought into the myth that you need five certifications, a business degree, and a flawless five-year plan before you even begin.

We're not offering a formula. We're offering perspective. Consider this book a back-pocket mentor. Something to pull out in between sessions, on a layover, or while sitting in your car wondering what's next.

We want you to feel encouraged, grounded, and equipped—not hyped up and overwhelmed.

We've made every mistake in the book (and probably a few that didn't make the cut). But we've given each other space to fail forward and try again. We've built practices with doctoral degrees, supervision credentials, and strong reputations—only to realize sometimes clients just like our profile picture. We've wrestled with what it means to build a business that supports our families, reflects our values, and serves our communities without losing ourselves in the process.

This isn't a call to start a private practice unless that's what you want. It's a call to start building a career that's aligned with who you are. That might mean moving slow. It might mean redefining success. But whatever it means, let it be yours.

We hope this book meets you exactly where you are. If you're a graduate student wondering if you've made a huge mistake, this book is for you. If you've just started a practice and you're barely breaking even, this book is for you. If you're an undergrad debating between counseling and corporate, just flip through a few chapters. There's a place for you here.

And if you're bringing your full self—your culture, your creativity, your questions—into a field that wasn't built with you in mind, we want you to know: you belong. You don't have to build your career the "right" way. You get to build it your way.

We're not ahead of you. We're walking beside you. Still figuring it out. Still adjusting. Still dreaming. Still building.

# 1

# The Counselor as Businessperson

If you're anything like us, you probably skipped the preface—you know, the part where we explain how to use this book, outline its purpose, and talk about the journey behind and ahead. No problem. Here's the shortcut: This book helps you build a career that's both meaningful and financially sustainable. We're not writing this to make you chase money. We hope this book helps you create a life and career that actually works for you and for the people you serve.

This chapter is the starting point. If you're reading this, you already have what you need to succeed. The goal isn't to become someone else—it's to take what you have and learn how to care for it, organize it, and put it to work in a focused, intentional way. With the tools this book offers, you can shift from seeing yourself only as a counselor to seeing yourself as the person responsible for your career. That means stepping into the role of CEO of your time, your energy, and your practice.

## Heart and Hustle

At the start of each academic year, we welcome a fresh crop of students—wide-eyed, eager, and ready to begin their journey into the world of counseling. I (Jude) teach a course on counseling theories to first-semester graduate counseling students. The class meets on Wednesdays, so they've already sat through Ethics on Monday and Psychopathology on Tuesday by the time they walk into my room. To make matters worse, they are often terrified they will get arrested for sneezing in session and convinced that the creators of the *Diagnostic and Statistical Manual of Mental Disorders* (5th ed.; DSM-5) read their personal journals.

Knowing this, I like to keep our first class conversational, inviting open questions, comments, and concerns. It doesn't take long before someone inevitably asks the big one: "Why are we doing this?" They don't mean just this class, but this whole career path. Every year, a student answers with, "I just want to help people."

If we stepped down from our high horses, we would acknowledge that wanting to help people isn't the full truth. Yes, it's noble and socially acceptable, but it's also incomplete. There's something deeper, messier, more human that draws us to this work. Maybe it's a desire to heal what we didn't heal in ourselves. Maybe it's a longing to learn something worthwhile from pain. Or maybe, just maybe, it's the fact that we get to do something profoundly meaningful and get paid for it. That last part, wanting to get paid? That's okay. In fact, it's healthy.

Too often, we separate passion from profit as if making a living somehow taints the purity of helping others. What if those two things could coexist? What if being a counselor doesn't mean choosing between heart and hustle? That's the idea we want to explore in this chapter and throughout this book.

## Public Perception

To see why many counselors find it hard to build successful businesses, we need to think about how people view the profession in our culture. Let's be honest, most of us didn't grow up seeing counseling offices on every corner or watching our neighbors proudly talk about their weekly counseling sessions. If you're like us, you came of age in a pre-internet, skinned-knees, streetlight-curfew kind of childhood. Mental health care wasn't mainstream. It certainly wasn't marketed. Most people had no idea what a counselor even did, other than the vague sense that "something must be wrong with you" if you needed to see one.

Counseling just wasn't common back then, at least not in a visible, normalized way. That cultural invisibility planted seeds that still shape how people see us today. We've made huge strides in reducing stigma and promoting access to care, but those early impressions still linger in the background. Counseling is more accepted now, but public perception continues to cast us primarily as helpers, healers, and empathetic listeners—rarely as professionals running businesses.

This image, while well-intentioned, is part of what makes it so difficult for counselors to fully embrace their business identities. According to Fall et al. (2017), mental health professionals are consistently rated as trustworthy and caring, but less often seen as competent in business-related domains. The public often admires the compassion of counselors while overlooking the fact that what we do is also deeply skilled, highly specialized, and deserving of fair compensation.

This perception has consequences. When you're told, directly or indirectly, that your job is "a calling" rather than a profession, it becomes harder to charge for your time. It feels awkward to talk about money. Setting firm boundaries feels like you're betraying the very heart of your work. Many counselors internalize these perceptions, developing what researchers call "self-stigma"—a subtle but powerful sense that we're somehow wrong for wanting to earn a good living from this work (Thornicroft et al., 2022). That internalized belief often shows up in everyday ways:

- You feel guilty about raising your fees.
- You hesitate to enforce your cancellation policy.
- You apologize when you bring up payment during intake.
- You overextend yourself, seeing just one more client again and again until you burn out.

You're not alone. These dynamics are part of a larger cultural issue. As Thornicroft et al. (2022) explained, stigma isn't just a personal problem; it's a social and structural one. Society often funds mental health care less than other health services. It views mental health as less than, and people who need support tend to be seen as "less capable" or "less reliable." Counselors get caught in that web, too, not just their clients.

The result is a cycle in which struggling clients see struggling counselors who see struggling clients. That's not sustainable. We cannot pour from an empty cup. To break this cycle, we need a new narrative that positions counselors as compassionate and financially empowered. We can set boundaries and serve our clients well, and we can run businesses without apologizing for it. That starts with reframing how we see ourselves—not just as healers, but as business owners with legitimate expertise, value, and economic agency. The truth is, you can help people and build a thriving business. You can do good and do well. That shift in perception starts with us.

## Empathy and Self-Sacrifice in Counseling

The counseling profession is inherently rooted in empathy and a profound commitment to client well-being. While these qualities are indispensable, they can lead counselors to rank clients' needs over their own, often resulting in compromised self-care. This tendency is exacerbated by societal expectations that idealize selflessness in helping professions, potentially fostering environments where counselors feel compelled to overextend themselves. Counselors, torn between their own well-being and that of their clients, often struggle to establish and maintain boundaries between their professional responsibilities and personal lives. This challenge is multifaceted, encompassing intrinsic motivations, ethical considerations, and external financial pressures. As noted by New Hope Mental Health Counseling Services (n.d.), unmanaged stress and exhaustion can contribute to mental health issues such as anxiety and depression, highlighting the importance of recognizing the link between boundaries and mental well-being.

### *Financial Pressures and Overextension*

Beyond intrinsic motivations, external factors such as financial strain significantly influence counselors' boundary-setting abilities. Many counselors deal with significant financial stress. They face high costs to start and run private practices. Educational debts add to the burden, and their pay is often lower than that of other helping professions, like physical therapy, occupational therapy, or nursing (U.S. Bureau of Labor Statistics, 2025). These economic challenges can compel counselors to accept additional clients or extend working hours beyond sustainable limits to achieve financial stability. Implementing financial boundaries safeguards counselors against potential exploitation and ensures a smoother workflow.

### *Ethical Considerations and Burnout*

Ethical frameworks in counseling emphasize unwavering dedication to client welfare. Yet, without appropriate boundaries, this commitment can lead to burnout. The *American Counseling Association Code of Ethics* (2014) makes clear that counselors have a responsibility not only to protect their clients but also to maintain their own well-being to ensure competent care. Practicing within one's boundaries of competence, seeking consultation when needed, and engaging in ongoing self-care are best practices and ethical imperatives. Counselor roles and boundaries should be established at the start of the counseling relationship and reinforced periodically, particularly at times when the client is experiencing high stress.

## Romanticized Perceptions and Recruitment

The counseling profession is often romanticized, attracting individuals drawn to the notion of being perpetual helpers. Empathy is important, but it can sometimes hide the need for practical skills and resilience. To foster a more balanced workforce, it is crucial to shift the narrative of counseling, showing that it requires analytical and strategic mindsets in addition to sensitivity and patience. In making this critical definitional shift, the career might start appealing to those who lead first with analytical and strategic mindsets, in addition to those who lead first with sensitivity and patience. By rounding out the population of potential counselors, the profession can ensure a more holistic approach to client care.

## Navigating Financial Realities

Financial pressures further complicate boundary-setting. Counselors often face substantial educational debts and operational costs, compelling them to take on more clients or extend working hours to achieve financial stability. This economic strain can lead to overextension and burnout, compromising both personal well-being and the quality of care provided. Implementing financial boundaries safeguards counselors against potential exploitation and ensures a smoother workflow. Balancing empathy with self-care, navigating ethical complexities, and managing financial pressures are critical for counselors striving to maintain effective boundaries. Recognizing and addressing these multifaceted challenges is essential for sustaining both counselor well-being and the efficacy of therapeutic practices.

## The Internal Conflict of Calling It a Business

There is a tension that lives in the hearts of many counselors. It is the quiet clash between the desire to become a counselor to help people and the desire to make a living. This tension shows up clearly after a tough session. When the energy is low, interventions don't work, and both the counselor and client feel uncertain about what happened and what was achieved—or not. In those moments, it can feel as though the counselor should be paying the client for wasting their time. That is when the discomfort sets in.

Often, there is a realization that you are profiting from someone's pain. That realization can feel particularly heavy—perhaps heavier than it might for other professionals. A dentist pulls teeth. A mechanic changes brakes. A real estate agent sells houses. Counselors sit with people in their most personal pain. They listen to stories of abuse, trauma, shame, grief, and loss. They hold space for people's darkest thoughts. And then, at the end of the hour, they say, "That will be $150. Please leave the payment on the table as you leave." That exchange can feel deeply personal—and slightly unsettling—as if being present with someone in their struggle should cancel out the right to get paid.

There is also a dissonance in language. Saying, "I am a small business owner," or "I run a private practice," often feels disconnected from the soul of this work. Counselors do not spend years in graduate school dreaming of LLCs or profit margins. They trained to help, to sit with, to listen. When business words pop up—revenue, scaling, branding—it can spark an identity crisis.

This discomfort intensifies when counselors compare themselves to traditional businesspeople. A car salesperson at a dealership and a realtor at a real estate agency both work for a business. A counseling practice does not feel the same. It feels more sacred and intimate. In many ways, it is, but it is also undeniably a business. That is the complicated task that many of us must grapple with: how best to expand our counselor identity without jeopardizing the heart of the work. The belief that financial success and ethical practice cannot coexist is a false dilemma. Business acumen is not about excelling at manipulation or exploitation. It is a trait that fosters sustainability. Having business acumen helps you design a life and career where you can continue doing meaningful, life-giving work without constantly teetering on the edge of burnout.

Research supports this reality. Many counselors experience discomfort or guilt when it comes to charging for their services, especially after sessions they perceive as unproductive (Clark and Sims, 2014). Others report ongoing conflict around the ethics of making money from deeply human struggles (Cummings, 2020). These internal tensions, when left unaddressed, are a contributing factor in burnout and premature departure from the field (Corey et al., 2023).

It does not have to be this way. Setting clear fees, enforcing no-show policies, and getting paid fairly for one's time are not only practical actions—they are ethical ones. According to the *ACA Code of Ethics* (2014), counselors are encouraged to establish fees that are fair and reasonable and to inform clients of these policies up front (Standard A.10.c). This transparency supports trust and professionalism. It also affirms the counselor's right to earn a living. Yes, it may feel strange at first to say, "I run a business." It may feel cold or impersonal, but there is nothing impersonal about a counselor who has built a sustainable practice that honors their time, energy, and worth. What is actually impersonal is being forced to leave the work because of poor financial planning or persistent undercharging.

Counselors do not need to become hard-hearted or detached, but they do need to stay afloat. They need to have enough left in the tank to show up for the next client. That means being willing to wear two hats: one as the compassionate counselor and one as the responsible business owner.

## Reframing the Money Mindset: Why Financial Success is Ethical and Necessary

At some point in their journey, most counselors must wrestle with this question: "Can I make good money doing this work and still be ethical?" The answer is a resolute "Yes!" Financial sustainability is part of ethical practice because it enables longevity, self-care, and excellence in service.

One common myth is that clients only benefit when counseling is low-cost or free. While affordability and access are vital, evidence has suggested that "skin in the game" can enhance commitment. For example, in examining the records of 269 fee-paying and non-fee-paying clients of a counseling training clinic, Sammons (2019) found that clients who paid fees were more likely to attend a planned termination session compared to non-fee-paying clients, even when controlling for counselor competence.

More broadly, meta-analytic work on mental health incentives has shown that financial contributions or incentives can improve treatment engagement and reduce dropout rates (Khazanov et al., 2022). This suggests that when clients invest—even modestly—they may psychologically assign greater value to the work and persist.

Charging a fair rate is not antithetical to ethics. It can actually support therapeutic efficacy and commitment, provided we offer sliding scales or subsidized spots to preserve equity.

## Understanding the Business Mindset

Learning the business side of counseling doesn't mean you are selling out; it means you're staying in. When we understand how to manage money, set boundaries, and build sustainable systems, we're protecting ourselves and creating space to keep showing up for the people who count on us. We don't have to lose our voice or our values. We get to build practices that reflect who we are, serve our communities, and still let us sleep at night.

## Cultivating a Healthy Business Mindset

Cultivating a business mindset involves embracing practices that support both your clients' needs and your professional longevity. Consider the following strategies.

- **Create a clear vision:** Define what kind of life you want to have, not what kind of career you want to have. Establishing clear life goals helps align your business strategies with your therapeutic mission (Adams et al., 2019).
- **Embrace entrepreneurial thinking:** Recognize that running a business—whether it's a private practice, a group practice, a nonprofit, or a shave ice stand—entails entrepreneurial responsibilities. This includes understanding market demands, adapting to changes, and seeking growth opportunities.
- **Invest in professional development:** Attend workshops and seminars to enhance both your clinical and business skills. Building a network with other professionals can provide support and insights into effective practice management.
- **Set appropriate boundaries:** Establish clear policies regarding fees, scheduling, and communication. Transparent boundaries foster mutual respect and professionalism in the therapeutic relationship (Knox et al., 2011).

By integrating sound business practices with your counseling work, you not only ensure the sustainability of your career but also enhance the quality of care provided to your clients. Embracing a balanced approach allows you to remain true to your unique style while building a thriving, ethical, and professional counseling career.

## Counseling Skills Are Business Skills

The competencies that define an effective counselor—such as active listening, goal setting, motivational interviewing, and alliance building—are transferable to the realm of business. By recognizing and leveraging these parallels, counselors can enhance their entrepreneurial endeavors while remaining authentic to their professional values.

In counseling, active listening involves fully engaging with clients to understand their experiences and concerns. Similarly, in business, attentiveness to market trends and client feedback is essential. By actively listening to the needs and preferences of their target audience, counselors can tailor their services effectively, ensuring relevance and responsiveness in a dynamic market. This approach fosters adaptability and innovation, both of which are key components in sustaining a successful practice (Schaefle et al., 2005).

Counselors collaborate with clients to set clear, attainable treatment goals, providing direction and measurable outcomes for counseling. This practice fits well in business. Setting clear, strategic goals helps guide growth and ensure sustainability. Defining goals like client acquisition targets, revenue milestones, or professional development aims enables counselors to monitor progress and make informed decisions (Cooper and Law, 2018).

Motivational interviewing empowers clients by exploring and resolving ambivalence, facilitating intrinsic motivation for change. In marketing, understanding the motivations and behaviors of potential clients is equally vital. By comprehending what drives individuals to seek counseling services, practitioners can craft messages that resonate, addressing specific needs and demonstrating the value of their services. This client-centered marketing approach enhances engagement and fosters trust (Kirk-Jenkins & Evans, 2022).

Establishing a strong therapeutic alliance, one characterized by trust, collaboration, and mutual respect, is foundational in counseling. Similarly, building robust relationships with referral sources—such as health care providers, community organizations, and fellow professionals—can significantly impact a practice's growth. Networking and fostering these connections can lead to a steady stream of client referrals, enhancing both the practice's reputation and reach (Mellin et al., 2011).

Effective marketing also requires a deep understanding of one's strengths, limitations, and unique offerings. Counselors' self-awareness enables them to authentically represent their services, ensuring that their outreach efforts align with their competencies and values. This kind of honest self-appraisal builds credibility and attracts clients who are the right fit, ultimately improving outcomes and satisfaction.

Finally, strong communication skills are essential for articulating the value of one's services, engaging meaningfully with professional networks, and collaborating with other providers. Whether it is explaining your approach to a physician or presenting at a community workshop, these interpersonal skills support both the business and clinical sides of practice (Stubbe, 2017).

Recognizing these parallels helps counselors approach business not as a separate identity but as an extension of the therapeutic work they already know how to do. Integrating counseling competencies into business strategies not only enhances professional growth but also ensures that empathy, authenticity, and client-centered care remain at the forefront of their entrepreneurial journey.

A business's identity doesn't define itself overnight. A counseling practice builds its identity over time. This includes its culture, reputation, values, and operations. It develops not just through formal planning, but also from daily experiences in running the practice. Sometimes, it sneaks in through late-night note writing or quiet moments between sessions. Other times, it comes with a crash—when the bills hit, the clients cancel, or you realize you don't know how to file a quarterly tax form. Tanner Garrett, Licensed Professional Counselor Associate (LPC-A) and owner of TSG Counseling, PLLC, in Arlington, Texas, shares what it looks like to dream big and then meet the reality of building something from scratch. His story captures the early tension of loving the work but learning the business.

## Voices from the Field

TANNER GARRETT

### Jumping In: The Harsh Reality of Starting Up

From the beginning of my schooling, the dream was always clear: I wanted to build a clinical practice I could call my own. That vision kept me going through my bachelor's and master's degrees. I remember sitting in a cubicle during my internship, imagining a full caseload, a waitlist, and a team of clinicians building something meaningful alongside me. I could see the office layout in my mind—a dedicated room with sand trays lining the walls from ceiling to floor. It was grand. It was romanticized. Most importantly, it kept me moving forward. Even now, as I grind through the early days of private practice, I still return to that dream. It reminds me of why I started.

When I received my LPC-A license, I jumped straight into launching my private practice. I had high hopes and a full-time job as a high school teacher. I began seeing a small number of clients after school hours. Very quickly, I realized that starting a business was far more demanding than I had imagined.

I had never started a business before and had only a vague understanding of what was required. I thought I needed an LLC, only to learn that I needed a PLLC instead. I tried to open a business bank account and realized that not all accounts are created equal. I started researching client-management tools and discovered an overwhelming number of electronic health record platforms.

My to-do list kept growing. I was learning and problem-solving on the fly, and with every step, I became more aware that being a counselor and being a business owner required two very different skill sets.

## Confidence in Clinical Work, Uncertainty in Business

I felt confident in my clinical skills. I knew I was still early in my journey, but I trusted that my training had prepared me to help people. That was the whole point. I wanted to help others through my own practice. Unfortunately, the dream that once carried me through school was starting to feel more like a fantasy than a reality.

I remember one particular call. A potential client reached out, and although I had already scheduled with a few people by then, each call still felt like a make-or-break moment. The call began well. She introduced herself and shared her reasons for seeking counseling, but when it came time for me to speak, I froze. My words tumbled out in pieces. I offered to schedule her first session, and she replied, "I'll let you know if I'd like to move forward."

I hung up and immediately ran to tell my wife about the "devastating" call. That moment was small, but it was pivotal. It confirmed what I had started to suspect: being a good counselor does not automatically make you a good business owner. Doubts I had been pushing down suddenly got louder. I found myself asking, again and again, "Can I actually build a successful private practice? Am I cut out for this?" I am now a little over a year into owning my practice, and I feel more grounded in my role as a small business owner, even if I am still learning every day. Phone calls no longer feel like do-or-die moments. Some clients schedule, some don't. That's all part of the process.

I've come to understand that marketing matters. Clinical skills don't mean much if no one knows how to find you. I've learned that I can do small business things, as long as I'm okay with making mistakes along the way.

That early dream is still alive. It continues to push me forward into the unknowns of ownership. I have been able to build a client base, even if I still worry about whether there will be enough new clients. I've also learned that I am not alone. Many clinicians walking this path have faced the same doubts, the same fears, and the same learning curve. Many of them have made it through.

Each new client helps quiet the doubts and strengthens my belief that my dream might actually be possible. Deep down, I believe I am capable of getting there.

Most of us walk into this profession with heart and have to build the hustle muscle over time. Tanner's honesty reminds us that it's okay to start with big dreams and small systems. The businessperson in you doesn't need to be perfect. It just needs to be willing to grow. And if you're reading this thinking, "I'm not there yet," that's okay. You're not behind—you're becoming.

# References

Adams, D. R., Williams, N. J., Becker-Haimes, E. M., Skriner, L., Shaffer, L., DeWitt, K., Neimark, G., Jones, D. T. & Beidas, R. S. (2019). Therapist financial strain and turnover: Interactions with system-level implementation of evidence-based practices. *Administration and Policy in Mental Health and Mental Health Services Research, 46*(6), 713–723. https://doi.org/10.1007/s10488-019-00949-8

American Counseling Association. (2014). *ACA Code of Ethics.* ACA. https://www.counseling.org/docs/default-source/default-document-library/ethics/2014-aca-code-of-ethics.pdf

American Psychiatric Association. (2013). *Diagnostic and Statistical Manual of Mental Disorders* (5th ed.). https://doi.org/10.1176/appi.books.9780890425596

Clark, P., & Sims, P. L. (2014). The practice of fee setting and collection: Implications for clinical training programs. *The American Journal of Family Therapy, 42*(5), 386–397. https://doi.org/10.1080/01926187.2013.857914

Cooper, M., & Law, D. (Eds.). (2018). *Working with goals in counseling and psychotherapy.* Oxford University Press. https://doi.org/10.1093/med-psych/9780198793687.001.0001

Corey, G., Muratori, M., Austin, J. T., II, & Austin, J. A. (2023). *Counselor self-care* (2nd ed.). American Counseling Association.

Cummings, D. (2020). When clients want to pay more for psychotherapy: Ethical issues and implications. *Ethics & Behavior, 30*(2), 150–160. https://doi.org/10.1080/10508422.2019.1641711

Fall, K. A., Holden, J. M., & Marquis, A. (2017). *Theoretical models of counseling and psychotherapy* (3rd ed.). Routledge. https://doi.org/10.4324/9781315733531

Khazanov, G. K., Morris, P. E., Beed, A., Jager-Hyman, S., Myhre, K., McKay, J. R., Feinn, R. S., Boland, E. M., & Thase, M. E. (2022). Do financial incentives increase mental health treatment engagement? A meta-analysis. *Journal of Consulting and Clinical Psychology, 90*(6), 528–544. https://doi.org/10.1037/ccp0000737

Kirk-Jenkins, A. J., & Evans, S. (2022). Utilizing counseling skills in the classroom to promote student well-being and success. *Journal of Counselor Preparation and Supervision, 15*(3), Article 12. https://research.library.kutztown.edu/jcps/vol15/iss3/12

Knox, S., Edwards, L. M., Hess, S. A., & Hill, C. E. (2011). Supervisor self-disclosure: Supervisees' experiences and perspectives. *Psychotherapy, 48*(4), 336–341. https://doi.org/10.1037/a0022067

Mellin, E. A., Hunt, B., & Nichols, L. M. (2011). Counselor professional identity: Findings and implications for counseling and interprofessional collaboration. *Journal of Counseling and Development, 89*(2), 140–147. https://doi.org/10.1002/j.1556-6678.2011.tb00071.x

New Hope Mental Health Counseling Services. (n.d.). Prioritizing wellness: A guide to self-care, healthy routines, and stress management [Blog post]. *New Hope Mental Health Blog.* Retrieved October 28, 2025, from https://www.thenewhopemhcs.com/prioritizing-wellness-a-guide-to-self-care-healthy-routines-and-stress-management/

Sammons, K. E. (2019). *Differences in treatment utilization between fee-paying and non-fee-paying clients in a counseling training clinic* [Doctoral dissertation, University of Northern Colorado]. Scholarship & Creative Works @ Digital UNC. https://digscholarship.unco.edu/dissertations/555/

Schaefle, S., Smaby, M. H., Maddux, C. D., & Cates, J. (2005). Counseling skills attainment, retention, and transfer as measured by the Skilled Counseling Scale. *Counselor Education and Supervision, 44*(4), 280–292. https://doi.org/10.1002/j.1556-6978.2005.tb01756.x

Stubbe, D. E. (2017). Competent communication in collaborative care. *Focus, 15*(3), 298–300. https://doi.org/10.1176/appi.focus.20170016

Thornicroft, G., Sunkel, C., Alikhon Alim, A., Baker, S., Brohan, E., El Chammay, R., Davies, K., Demissie, M., Duncan, J., Fekadu, W., Gronholm, P. C., Guerrero, Z., Gurung, D., Habtamu, K., Hanlon, C., Heim, E., Henderson, C., Hijazi, Z., Hoffman, C., ... & Winkler, P. (2022). The *Lancet* Commission on ending stigma and discrimination in mental health. *The Lancet, 400*(10361), 1438–1480. https://doi.org/10.1016/S0140-6736(22)01470-2

U.S. Bureau of Labor Statistics. (2025). *Occupational Outlook Handbook.* Office of Employment and Unemployment Statistics, U.S. BLS. Retrieved October 16, 2025, from https://www.bls.gov/ooh/home.htm

# 2

# Insights and Trends Within the Counseling Marketplace

The counseling profession is in the middle of a seismic shift. If you're not paying close attention, you will miss the signs until it's too late. This isn't the same field it was five, ten, or even two years ago. The marketplace is evolving at a pace that demands awareness, adaptability, and business literacy—not solely clinical skills. This chapter helps you understand and harness those changes before they become problems.

Mental health has evolved from a side conversation to a national priority. In the aftermath of the COVID-19 pandemic, demand for mental health services skyrocketed across nearly every demographic (Panchal et al., 2023). In some states, behavioral health service utilization more than doubled, and workforce shortages followed fast behind—straining systems already at capacity (Corlette et al., 2024). Counseling has moved from the margins into the mainstream. Counselors are now seen as essential professionals in clinics, schools, churches, workplaces, and digital spaces. That visibility, however, comes at a cost.

Clients are coming in with more complex needs, higher expectations, and shorter patience. Misinformation on social media has created a wave of DIY diagnoses and pop-psych assumptions that often distort what counseling actually is (Hendrikse & Limniou, 2024; Nguyen et al., 2023). Meanwhile, younger generations are bringing new fluencies in mental health language to their counseling sessions—but also a different relationship to vulnerability, boundaries, and healing timelines (Baral & Thapa, 2022). The gap between public perception and clinical reality is growing, and it's showing up in your counseling room.

At the same time, the systems designed to train and support counselors are under pressure. Graduate program enrollment is rising, but the availability of practicum placements and qualified supervisors hasn't grown in tandem (Schweiger et al., 2012). Licensure boards are backlogged, reimbursement models remain unpredictable, and tech-driven disruption is outpacing ethical infrastructure (Kaplan et al., 2014). Many new clinicians enter the field underpaid, underprepared, and overworked, only to land in burnout within a few years (Acker, 2012). If you're not factoring these shifts into how you build your practice, set your fees, choose your niche, and plan your career, then you're not leading your counseling business. You're reacting to it. So, let's name what's happening. In this chapter, we break it down into two parts:

1. **Insights**, or what we are learning from real counselors and real clients. These are patterns, behaviors, and cultural dynamics that affect how we show up and what clients expect from us.
2. **Trends**, or the bigger systemic movements that are reshaping our profession, such as policy shifts, educational bottlenecks, tech innovation, social media influence, and generational change.

Counselors who survive in this landscape will be those who understand the playing field: those who zoom out far enough to see what's coming and adjust accordingly. You can be clinically brilliant, deeply compassionate, and still fail to build a sustainable career if you don't read the room. Let's make sure that doesn't happen to you.

## Insights

### When the Numbers Don't Add Up

I (Julius) remember exactly when it hit me. It was a Thursday afternoon, and I was sitting in the school pick-up line. My phone had been buzzing all morning with emails, voicemails, and DMs from people looking for counseling. Business was moving. I had the full caseload, the waitlist, the weekly rhythm I used to dream about in graduate school. I sat in the car thinking about how I saw 23 clients during the week and was still barely covering overhead. There was no cushion. No margin. No way to scale. Just enough business to keep the lights on. I stared at my laptop and thought: Is this really what success looks like?

I (Jude) had my own wake-up call, but from the other side. I had partnered with a friend from graduate school and was seeing clients a couple of days per week out of her office. My practice was slim and simple—just me, two chairs, a clock, and clean, focused clinical work. It felt balanced and manageable, but life was still slipping through the cracks. Friends would invite me to hang out, and I'd have to say no. I remember one day with back-to-back sessions like always, when a client mentioned something about the Capitol being stormed. I hadn't heard a thing about that. I was literally getting breaking news from the counseling room—one fragment at a time. When I got home, I found out my son had used the potty for the first time. I had missed it. That night, on the phone with Julius, I asked myself a question that still echoes: "How much of my life am I willing to miss?"

Both of our stories point to the same truth: Something had shifted. In our practices, in the culture, in the demand for counseling—it was all moving faster. We weren't just seeing more clients. We were seeing a new kind of moment.

## *From Panic to Purpose*

When COVID-19 hit, our caseloads exploded. In the early months, anxiety and fear were hyper-present: clenching jaws, disrupted sleep, tight chests. I (Jude) felt like my entire schedule was one long, collective panic attack.

The data confirms it. A global review found a 25% increase in anxiety and depression during the first pandemic year (WHO, 2022). In the United States, telehealth usage for mental health surged from nearly zero to representing 40% of mental health and substance use outpatient care by mid-2020 (Cantor et al., 2022).

Then, something changed. As lockdowns dragged on, panic evolved into purpose. Suddenly, the question shifted from "Is this safe?" to "Is this good?" Clients began asking deeper questions: "Do I even like the life I've built?" "Is this marriage working?" "Have I been surviving instead of living?" Men, first-time clients, and people of color began showing up in greater numbers—like a dam had finally burst.

My caseload swelled and deepened. With this new depth came weight. I started asking myself: "How many people can I realistically help? What's the cost? How do I stay fully present for clients—and for my family?" This shift wasn't just anecdotal. A systematic review showed mental health services worldwide rushed to telehealth as face-to-face care dropped off (di Filippo et al., 2022), even as the prevalence of anxiety, depression, and stress remained elevated. Telehealth rapidly became a lifeline but also highlighted capacity limits and concerns of clinician strain (Cantor et al., 2022).

Our work didn't just intensify—it transformed. We moved from urgency to introspection. We began asking new questions, holding deeper space, and feeling a heavier kind of responsibility. We moved from panic to purpose, but purpose without boundaries isn't sustainable. We weren't the only ones waking up. As counseling deepened behind closed doors, something louder was happening out in the open. Mental health care, a previously private, individual journey, was becoming a cultural movement.

## Mental Health Is Having a Moment

Counseling is no longer whispered about behind closed doors or reserved for people in crisis—it is in your group chat, on your cousin's social media timeline, and in that one friend's Instagram bio where they proudly announce they're "in counseling and healing." While we are genuinely grateful that the world is finally catching up to what we've known all along—that tending to your mental health is powerful and necessary—we have also been trying to make sense of what this moment means for counselors. How do we meet the moment without losing ourselves in it? How do we serve more people without burning out? How do we protect the integrity of our work when the world is finally paying attention?

This moment isn't just cultural—it's structural. As counseling takes center stage in public conversation, the demand spills over into our systems, our schedules, and our stress levels. That kind of attention doesn't come without weight.

## The Boom and the Buckling

This moment has brought long-overdue legitimacy to counseling. Schools have started hiring counselors en masse (McLean et al., 2022), companies have rolled out Employee Assistance Programs, and churches have partnered with counselors. Clients have stopped side-eyeing counseling—instead, they started asking for friends' counselors' numbers. For counselors of color, this surge in visibility has been a breakthrough. Representation is becoming a reason clients reach out (McLean et al., 2021).

Like any growth spurt, this one comes with stretch marks. Graduate programs have scrambled to keep up with enrollment—often without enough practicum sites or supervisors (Maurya & DeDiego, 2023). State boards are overwhelmed. New clinicians, eager to serve, often set fees too low—believing compassion should come at a discount—only to burn out. The profession is booming, but parts of it are buckling under expectations that were never ours to hold. We're facing more referrals, more emotional intensity, and more public attention—and all of that is showing up in the room in ways that feel generational, cultural, and deeply personal.

## The Social Media Dilemma

This is when social media enters the mix. Suddenly, anyone with a ring light and trauma buzzwords can be a "mental health educator/coach." You can't scroll five minutes without seeing, "3 Signs You Have Anxious Attachment" or "How to Cut Off Toxic People and Reclaim Your Power." Some content is useful, but much of it is just loud. Sometimes, it is worse than loud; it's dangerous. People without any formal training are claiming authority in spaces where real harm can be done. On platforms with no guardrails, advice can spread faster than fact. Clients often expect counseling to be like TikTok—quick and catchy. They think it can be summed up in three steps. But real change needs more than just a trending soundbite.

In reality, clinical counseling with a licensed counselor is slow, messy, and full of detours and uncomfortable silences. Human nature demands that pace—real change and growth don't happen overnight. People who come in primed by "social media counseling" often don't understand that. When their first session doesn't match the polished energy of a podcast or a three-step TikTok, they ghost. That ghosting is frustrating and dangerous. Dropping out after one session cuts clients off from the very process that could actually help them. Research has shown that early termination in counseling is common, especially in telehealth, where nearly one in five clients don't return after the first meeting (Andersson et al., 2019). When clients expect quick fixes and walk away the moment counseling feels hard, they risk reinforcing hopelessness instead of healing.

Social media has become the new waiting room. Before clients ever step into your office—or log on remotely—they've likely scrolled through counselor posts, watched reels on attachment, or shared carousels on "emotional immaturity." On one hand, it's amazing: Counseling is showing up in barbershops, beauty salons, locker rooms, and group chats. On the other hand, much of what's out there is misleading—or worse.

Studies have shown that over 17% of TikTok videos labeled as mental health content contain misinformation, with fewer than 5% referencing credible sources (Hennessy et al., 2019). One of my (Julius) clients said,

"I think I'm emotionally abusive because I need space after conflict," after consuming content that pathologized healthy boundary setting—a classic case of misapplied counseling speak (Lorenzo-Luaces et al., 2023).

Some counselors may benefit from claiming space online to counter confusion. You don't need millions of followers; you simply need a clear, ethics-aligned voice to inject nuance into simplistic narratives (Nguyen et al., 2023).

Meanwhile, behind the scenes, the infrastructure is collapsing under strain. Challenges, including supervisor shortages, bottlenecked licensure, overloaded agencies, and counseling apps treating clinicians as gig workers, are not only frustrating but also dangerous. When good counselors are unsupported and overworked, clients and communities pay the price.

Research has reinforced this: Gig-based mental health workers report greater loneliness, financial instability, and psychological distress compared to traditionally employed mental health professionals (Al-Massalkhi & Ajonbadi, 2024). For new counselors, burnout often doesn't come from a lack of resilience but from being chronically set up to break under unsustainable conditions. Counseling platforms that promise to match a client with a counselor in 24 hours often prioritize speed and volume over clinical integrity. It's fast-food counseling—quick, convenient, and filling in the moment, but lacking the substance and nourishment that real, sustained counseling requires.

The demand for care is urgent and growing, but when systems sacrifice quality for speed, they rob both clients and counselors. That's a compromise the profession can't afford. Research has shown that social media mental health content often drives engagement and visibility, but also promotes superficial, misaligned expectations (Hendrikse & Limniou, 2023; Nguyen et al., 2023).

## *Different Generations, Different Languages*

We have both seen it in our practices and classrooms—working with Gen Z or Millennials versus Baby Boomers or Gen X is like switching between two radio frequencies. Same airspace, different sounds. Gen Z clients often come in fluent in emotional language, having absorbed blog posts, mental health reels, and counseling-adjacent content before ever booking a session. I (Julius) once had a 22-year-old begin her intake with, "I've been exploring my avoidant attachment style and how that relates to intergenerational trauma." It wasn't performative—it was part of her language. She had the vocabulary; she just needed help slowing it down and living it out.

Contrast that with older clients—Gen Xers or Boomers—who might say, "I don't know what to talk about," or "I was raised to keep things to myself." For them, counseling is unfamiliar territory—not due to a lack of insight, but because vulnerability was never modeled as strength. Studies have confirmed this generational divide: Younger clients report greater mental health literacy and are more likely to have sought counseling, while older adults still link counseling with weakness (Goodnight et al., 2019; Lorenzo-Luaces et al., 2023).

Stigma doesn't just shout—it also whispers. I (Julius) hear it when an older client says, "I know you're busy. I don't want to waste your time." Or, "I know others have it worse." That's shame wrapped in politeness. Gen Z's stigma wears a different outfit: "Is this normal?" or "Why am I not healed yet?" They've checked every mental health box. They journal, meditate, and hydrate. When their lives don't feel perfectly aligned, they wonder if they're broken (Peachey Counselling, 2024).

We must meet both ends of the spectrum with a steady presence. We affirm, normalize, and gently untangle internal messages. Healing doesn't require perfection. It just requires permission.

## *Staying Rooted in a Shifting Field*

Let's take a breath. You've seen how much the counseling field is shifting from telehealth and TikTok counseling to policy waves and platform burnout. In times like this, it's easy to feel lost, or worse, irrelevant, but don't check out. Instead, reconnect with your identity, your values, and your voice. We get it: Many counselors hear the word marketplace and instinctively tense up. You didn't enter this profession to chase profits; you came to help. The truth is, just because you're not in it for the money doesn't mean money won't affect your work. If you don't understand the market, you will be shaped by it whether you intend to be or not (Reese et al., 2013). Knowing the trends doesn't make you greedy—it makes you prepared. It helps you anticipate client needs, advocate for your community, and build a practice that can actually last.

When we teach counselor development, we teach ethics and the business side by side. Every business decision is also an ethical one: how many clients you take, what you charge, and how you protect your own capacity. Ethical entrepreneurship means building a visible, accessible, and sustainable practice that is aligned with your values and vision (Chang & Rieple). More than ever, your identity as a counselor matters. Professional identity gives you stability when the landscape shifts and connects your daily clinical choices to the long-term impact you hope to make (Ibarra, 1999; Gibson et al., 2010).

The research is detailed: When counselors integrate their values into both their clinical work and their business decisions, burnout decreases, and client outcomes improve (Merriam & Tisdell, 2016). So no, this isn't about selling out. This is about being rooted—knowing who you are, what you believe, and how you want to practice. Because in a landscape that keeps evolving, the most grounded counselors won't be the ones who know everything. They'll be the ones who stay aligned and keep their minds open to new pathways.

Now that we've looked inward at the cultural, emotional, and clinical realities shaping our day-to-day, it's time to zoom out. While your insight grounds you, trends shape the terrain you're walking on. Let's take a look at what's happening around us: the systems, policies, technologies, and training structures that are redefining what it means to do and sustain this work.

## Trends

### The Pipeline Problem and the Professional Bottleneck

You've noticed the surge in demand and realized it's time to grow—maybe hire a clinician, build a group practice, or refer clients elsewhere. That's when the bottleneck hits. More students are entering counseling programs than ever, yet there's nowhere near enough supervision capacity or timely licensure processes to match. That's the pipeline problem.

Supervision shortages are real: Over half of trained supervisors report that time constraints and full caseloads impede their ability to take on new supervisees (Berg et al., 2018). Clinical placement sites are tapped out, leaving new graduates stuck in limbo (ChangeLab Solutions, 2024). Even when internships are complete, licensure boards drag. Many candidates wait months for board decisions, fingerprint clearance, or jurisprudence exams (ChangeLab Solutions, 2024). What should take six months often stretches into a year, stalling careers and stalling your growth plans.

On the business side, these delays aren't minor. Hiring provisionally licensed counselors becomes unpredictable. Insurance credentialing is delayed. Your projected revenue stalls. Meanwhile, licensed clinicians pick up the slack. They experience higher caseloads, fewer breaks, and no space for creativity. It's a burnout loop fueled by systemic slowdown (National Conference of State Legislatures, 2023).

Outside the profession, people wonder why there aren't more counselors available. The reality is that they exist, but they're gridlocked in our system. As counselor-entrepreneurs, you must build realistic timelines for hiring, credentialing, and billing plans, and advocate for streamlined licensure, increased supervision funding, and better onboarding infrastructure. Demand without capacity is a recipe for failure. Your clients and your business deserve better.

## Policy Winds: Follow the Money

Let's shift focus. If the previous section was about traffic jams inside the profession, this one looks up at the roadblocks and ramps being built above us. Demand is soaring, but money moves the work, and money follows policy. Even the most compassionate, competent counselor can't build a sustainable practice without understanding how funding flows. These funding streams show up in different ways, through insurance laws, Medicaid expansion, temporary grants, and state budgets, and each carries its own opportunities and pitfalls.

- **Law versus practice in mental health parity:** The Mental Health Parity and Addiction Equity Act mandates equivalent coverage for mental and physical health (U.S. Dept. of Treasury et al., n.d.). Unfortunately, reimbursement remains inconsistent: Networks are narrow, rates are low, and claims are tangled in administration (Barnett et al., 2018). If you plan to bill insurance, assume delays, denials, and hidden costs are inevitable.
- **The cautious opportunity of Medicaid expansion:** When a state expands Medicaid, access opens, but the jobs that follow are often underpaid and overburdened, with reimbursement lower than private insurance (Wang et al., 2022). Clinicians are hailed as frontline heroes, but many burn out under unsafe caseloads. Treat expansion as an opportunity to explore, but not the only door open to you.
- **Grants as fuel, not foundation:** Grants can spark programs for youth mental health, trauma-informed schools, and crisis response, but they are temporary. Programs built solely on grants can collapse when the funds end. Use them strategically—as accelerants, not as anchors.

- **Budget as a business owner:** Policy is momentum. Whether it's K–12 behavioral health allocations, rural incentive programs, or new tax credits—these are your signposts. Track your state's budget like a stock ticker and align your strategy accordingly. When funds flow, opportunities grow. When they recede, pivot fast. Understanding policy isn't politics—it's a survival strategy. By grasping these funding currents, you position your practice at the confluence of mission, ethics, and sustainability.

## *Disruptions You Need to Know About*

If policy shows the direction of the wind, these disruptions reveal what the weather feels like on the ground. They're reshaping how counseling is practiced, paid for, and perceived. Some are empowering, others uncomfortable, but all demand our attention.

The pandemic accelerated telehealth's rise from necessity to norm. Counseling through a screen evolved from an acceptable option to an expected feature. For clients with anxiety, mobility issues, or caregiving responsibilities, virtual sessions offered unprecedented access (Pierce et al., 2020). But with wider reach comes new considerations: scheduling, privacy, and digital presence. If telehealth is part of your plan, you must understand the technology's potential and its limitations.

Meanwhile, wellness influencers and unlicensed "coaches" are filling a gap in people's minds and hearts. They offer fast access, relatable language, and self-care shortcuts that feel appealing yet can lack rigor (Kim & Kim, 2022). Rather than dismiss them, we can learn from them: sharpen your clinical edge and communicate with clarity and warmth. Credentials matter, but so does connection.

Insurance remains a thorn. Reimbursement rates keep slipping while the administrative burden rises (Barnett et al., 2018). Whether you're in-network or out, billing—or deciding not to bill—requires awareness of hidden costs and cash flow implications. If insurance is in your business mix, build in systems that protect margin from day one.

Finally, group practices offer shared supervision, referrals, and infrastructure—at the risk of crowding out solo practitioners. Solo counselors aren't obsolete; they just need clarity. What's your niche? What do you offer that no group practice can replicate? Your strength isn't size—it's distinction.

None of these shifts spells disaster, but they do demand adaptation. The counselors who thrive recognize early, respond intentionally, and build practices that align with both their values and the world they live in.

## Education Is Changing, Too

Behind the frontlines of telehealth and coaching, another major transformation is underway: how counselors are being trained. Gone are the days of fixed classrooms and physical practicum sites—today's pathways are more flexible, but also more fragmented. The way people enter, prepare for, and grow within this profession is shifting quickly. From graduate programs to continuing education, the learning landscape looks very different what it did even a decade ago. Here are some of the key ways these changes are showing up.

- **Online Council for Accreditation of Counseling and Related Educational Programs (CACREP) programs:** These programs have democratized access—opening doors for those in rural areas, working parents, and career changers (Snow et al., 2018). But not all online experiences are created equal. Without solid mentorship and real-world exposure, some trainees finish with credentials but not confidence. It's not a critique of distance education—it's a reminder that support systems matter more than ever.
- **More graduates, more workers, more gaps:** With program growth comes a flood of fresh professionals. But not all are prepared: Some walk into the field well-equipped; others lack real experience with trauma, grief, or anger in the room (Moh & Sperandio, 2022). That variability needs to be accounted for in hiring, onboarding, and supervision.
- **Faculty shortage in counselor education:** Behind every counselor is a teacher. Many counselor educators are overworked, underpaid, and under-resourced, leading to burnout and turnover (Coaston & Cook, 2017). Considering teaching—even part-time—can be a vital way to ensure next-generation counselors are not just licensed but ready.
- **CEUs and certifications:** For seasoned professionals, ongoing training is necessary and strategic. Counselors who added EMDR training, trauma certification, or equity-focused continuing education units (CEUs) reported enhanced client engagement, stronger referral streams, and renewed purpose (Morris & Chen, 2023).

## Innovation, Platforms, and the AI Question

The counseling marketplace has transformed. Technology is driving much of the shift. This isn't about hype. It's about purposefully learning to use new tools while holding on to what fundamentally matters.

The pandemic accelerated telehealth into a standard offering—clients now expect flexibility and accessibility (Pierce et al., 2020). Virtual sessions are no longer a compromise but a lifeline for many. Telehealth also reduces burnout: recent studies have found that clinicians offering online counseling report lower levels of emotional exhaustion and depersonalization compared to those working exclusively in person (Békés & Aafjes-van Doorn, 2020).

At the same time, artificial intelligence (AI) is moving into mental health spaces. Chatbot companions like Wysa (2025) reach millions and have shown meaningful reductions in depressive symptoms in real-world data studies (Yonathan-Leus & Brukner, 2025; MacNeill et al., 2024). Some users even report perceiving a bond or alliance with the agent, though it is weaker and less stable than the bond with a human counselor (Denecke et al., 2021). But these systems lack relational depth, emotional nuance, crisis management, and ethical accountability—all critical elements a human counselor provides (Moylan et al., 2025).

Digital platforms like BetterHelp (2025) and Talkspace (n.d.) represent another form of disruption. These platforms offer built-in infrastructure, client volume, and faster cash flow, but often tilt incentives toward quantity over depth. Users of BetterHelp have shown symptom improvement in studies (Marcelle et al., 2019), yet many report inconsistent therapeutic depth, boundary challenges, and variable quality. These aren't inherently bad options—they're choices with trade-offs. To use them wisely means understanding your limits, setting intentional boundaries, and planning for what's next.

Tech is not your enemy; fear is. Thriving in this next era means integrating tools with intention, aligning them with your values, your clinical integrity, and your well-being. Start small. Try a mood-tracking app, explore telehealth if you haven't, or learn the digital ethics behind AI tools. You don't need to be a tech expert. You just need to stay awake. The future of counseling won't belong to the biggest tech whiz—it will belong to the clinician who can weave tools, insights, and human presence into a unified practice.

The counseling field is shifting culturally, technologically, and structurally. The rules of engagement are changing faster than most of us were trained for. But here's the truth: You don't need to know everything to move forward. You just need to be willing to pay attention.

Pay attention to what your clients are bringing into the room, and where they're getting their expectations. Pay attention to your state's policies, your professional identity, and the business models you're quietly building every day with your choices. Pay attention to the platforms you're on, the hours you're working, the people you're mentoring, and the values you're translating into action. At the end of the day, the work beneath the work is learning to adapt without losing yourself. The most powerful counselors in this new marketplace won't be the loudest voices online or the ones with the most certifications. They'll be the ones who keep doing honest, human work on purpose, with presence and a plan.

When people talk about "market trends," they often think of insurance policies, telehealth platforms, or billing software. But there's another current running beneath the counseling profession that's shaped by laws, policies, and culture wars. These shifts affect who enters the field, how we train future counselors, and who gets served. In this contribution, Dr. David Julius Ford, Jr., Department Chair and Associate Professor of Professional Counseling at Monmouth University, calls our attention. He invites us to think bigger than revenue and regulations and reflect on the soul of our profession: advocacy, justice, and cultural humility.

## Voices from the Field

DR. DAVID JULIUS FORD, JR.

In 2025, the counseling profession finds itself at a critical crossroads. We are navigating a political and social climate marked by intensifying anti-Blackness, homophobia, xenophobia, transphobia, and Islamophobia. These forces are directly shaping both policy and practice. Recent legislative shifts have eroded protections for marginalized communities (Human Rights Campaign, 2024; Southern Poverty Law Center, 2024).

Women's rights are under renewed threat, particularly through restrictive abortion laws that disproportionately impact the health and safety of Black women (American College of Obstetricians and Gynecologists [ACOG], 2023; VandeVusse et al., 2024). Anti-immigrant sentiment continues to rise, with mass deportation policies and enforcement surges disproportionately affecting Latinx and Muslim communities (Gelatt, 2024).

At the same time, states across the country are rolling back Affirmative Action (Crusto, 2023) and dismantling diversity, equity, and inclusion (DEI) initiatives in higher education and health professions (Bryant & Appleby, 2025). Perhaps most concerning, new laws in several states permit helping professionals to deny services to individuals whose identities conflict with their "deeply held beliefs," placing LGBTQ+ and other marginalized clients at risk of exclusion from care (Movement Advancement Project, 2024).

This moment has far-reaching implications for our profession. These policy shifts affect how we train counselors, who enter the profession, and how our ethical codes and competencies are interpreted and upheld. As a field founded on advocacy and justice, we must not waver. We are called to remain steadfast in our commitment to equity, cultural humility, and social responsibility.

Counselor educators must engage in resistance by continuing to train students in culturally responsive, justice-oriented ways, even as external pressures push back. That means uplifting marginalized voices in the classroom, challenging White supremacy, patriarchy, and heteronormativity in our materials and methods, and grounding our teaching in the competencies that define ethical counseling practice.

Our clients, especially those from marginalized communities, are watching and waiting. Many are more fearful and hopeless than ever. They seek brave, affirming spaces, and research continues to show that clinical outcomes improve when clients see a counselor who shares or deeply respects their identity. Cultural humility isn't optional; it's the standard.

Regardless of your personal background, your job is to listen, affirm, and validate, especially when your clients' lived experiences are different from your own. Advocacy carries risk. Speaking out can cost us opportunities, jobs, leadership roles, or access to influential spaces. That's why those of us who choose to resist must do so strategically and sustainably. Find your niche. Set your boundaries. Practice radical self-care. Don't give away your knowledge—or your pain—for free.

To the counselors who are tired but committed: Know your worth, protect your voice, and continue the work. Our communities need us. Our profession needs us. And we need each other.

---

The counseling profession doesn't just respond to social change. It's shaped by social change. As we navigate the economic and policy shifts ahead, we can't lose sight of our ethical mandate: to care for those most affected by injustice. Dr. Ford's call to action reminds us that the most important trends aren't always visible on spreadsheets. They show up in classrooms, in clinical spaces, and in every decision we make about who we serve and how we serve them.

## References

Acker, G. M. (2012). Burnout among mental health care providers. *Journal of Social Work, 12*(5), 475–490. https://doi.org/10.1177/1468017310392418

Al-Massalkhi, R., & Ajonbadi, H. A. (2024). Pushing beyond limits: Has gig work exacerbated precarious and psychological contracts in China? In O. D. Adekoya, C. Mordi, & H. A. Ajonbadi (Eds.), *HRM, Artificial Intelligence and the Future of Work: Insights from the Global South* (pp. 61–80). Palgrave Macmillan Cham.

American College of Obstetricians and Gynecologists. (2023). ACOG publications June 2023. *Obstetrics and Gynecology, 141*(6). https://http://doi.org/10.1097/AOG.0000000000005175

American Council on Education. (2023). The American college president: 2023 edition. https://www.acenet.edu/Documents/American-College-President-2023-Exec-Summary.pdf

Andersson, G., Titov, N., Dear, B. F., Rozental, A., & Carlbring, P. (2019). Internet-delivered psychological treatments: From innovation to implementation. *World Psychiatry, 18*(1), 20–28. https://doi.org/10.1002/wps.20610

Baral, S. P., & Raghuvamshi, G. (2022). Mental health awareness and the generation gap. *Indian Journal of Psychiatry, 64*(Suppl. 3), S636. https://doi.org/10.4103/0019-5545.341859

Barnett, M. L., Ray, K. N., Souza, J., & Mehrotra, A. (2018). Trends in telemedicine use in a large commercially insured population, 2005–2017. *JAMA, 320*(20), 2147–2149. https://doi.org/10.1001/jama.2018.12354

Békés, V., & Aafjes-van Doorn, K. (2020). Psychotherapists' attitudes toward online therapy during the COVID-19 pandemic. *Journal of Psychotherapy Integration, 30*(2), 238–247. https://doi.org/10.1037/int0000214

Berg, J., Hoskovec, J., Hashmi, S. S., McCarthy Veach, P., Ownby, A., & Singletary, C. N. (2018). Relieving the bottleneck: An investigation of barriers to the expansion of supervision networks at genetic counseling training programs. *Journal of Genetic Counseling, 27*(1), 241–251. https://doi.org/10.1007/s10897-017-0142-3

BetterHelp. (2025). *BetterHelp* [Online counseling platform]. BetterHelp. Retrieved October 28, 2025, from https://www.betterhelp.com/

Bryant, J. & Appleby, C. (2025). These states' anti-DEI legislation may impact higher education. *BestColleges*. Retrieved

October 31, 2025, from https://www.bestcolleges.com/news/anti-dei-legislation-tracker/

Cantor, J., McBain, R. K., Kofner, A., Hanson, R., Stein, B. D., & Yu, H. (2022). Telehealth adoption by mental health and substance use disorder treatment facilities during the COVID-19 pandemic. *Psychiatric Services, 73*(4), 411–417. https://doi.org/10.1176/appi.ps.202100191

Centers for Medicare & Medicaid Services. (n.d.). *The Mental Health Parity and Addiction Equity Act (MHPAEA)*. CMS. https://www.cms.gov/marketplace/private-health-insurance/mental-health-parity-addiction-equity

ChangeLab Solutions. (2024, April 8). Addressing children's behavioral health workforce shortages through state licensure systems. *ChangeLab Solutions*. https://www.changelabsolutions.org/sites/default/files/2024-04/Addressing-Behavioral-Health-Workforce-Shortages-State-Licensure_FINAL_20240408A.pdf

Coaston, S. C., & Cook, E. P. (2017). Burnout in counselor education: The role of cynicism and fit in predicting turnover intention. *Journal of Counselor Preparation and Supervision, 10*(1), 8. https://research.library.kutztown.edu/jcps/vol10/iss1/8

Corrales Compagnucci, M., Fenwick, M., Haapio, H., Minssen, T., & Vermeulen, E. P. M. (2021). Technology-driven disruption of healthcare and "UI layer" privacy-by-design. In M. Corrales Compagnucci, M. L. Wilson, M. Fenwick, N. Forgó, & T. Bärnighausen (Eds.), *AI in eHealth: Human Autonomy, Data Governance and Privacy in Healthcare* (pp. 19–67). Cambridge University Press.

Crusto, M. F. (2023). A plea for affirmative action. *Harvard Law Review, 136*(3). https://harvardlawreview.org/forum/vol-136/a-plea-for-affirmative-action/

Denecke, K., Abd-Alrazaq, A., Househ, M. (2021). Artificial Intelligence for Chatbots in Mental Health: Opportunities and Challenges. In M. Househ, E. Borycki, & A. Kushniruk (Eds.), *Multiple Perspectives on Artificial Intelligence in Healthcare: Opportunities and Challenges*. Springer Cham. https://doi.org/10.1007/978-3-030-67303-1_10

Di Filippo, L., Doga, M., Frara, S., & Giustina, A. (2022). Hypocalcemia in COVID-19: Prevalence, clinical significance and therapeutic implications. *Reviews in Endocrine and Metabolic Disorders, 23*(2), 299–308. https://doi.org/10.1007/s11154-021-09655-z

Gelatt, J. (2024). Explainer: Immigrants and the U.S. economy. *Migration Policy Institute*. https://www.migrationpolicy.org/sites/default/files/publications/mpi-immigrants-us-economy-explainer-2024_final.pdf

Gibson, D. M., Dollarhide, C. T., & Moss, J. M. (2010). Professional identity development: A grounded theory of transformational tasks of new counselors. *Counselor Education and Supervision, 50*(1), 21–38. https://doi.org/10.1002/j.1556-6978.2010.tb00106.x

Goodnight, J. R. M., Ragsdale, K. A., Rauch, S. A. M., & Rothbaum, B. O. (2019). Psychotherapy for PTSD: An evidence-based guide to a theranostic approach to treatment. *Progress in Neuro-Psychopharmacology and Biological Psychiatry, 88*, 418–426. https://doi.org/10.1016/j.pnpbp.2018.05.006

Hendrikse, C., & Limniou, M. (2024). The use of Instagram and TikTok in relation to problematic use and well-being. *Journal of Technology in Behavioral Science, 9*, 846–857. https://doi.org/10.1007/s41347-024-00399-6

Human Rights Campaign. (2024). *2024 state equality index*. Human Rights Campaign. https://www.hrc.org/resources/state-equality-index

Ibarra, H. (1999). Provisional selves: Experimenting with image and identity in professional adaptation. *Administrative Science Quarterly, 44*(4), 764–791. https://doi.org/10.2307/2667055

Kaplan, D. M., Tarvydas, V. M., & Gladding, S. T. (2014). 20/20: A vision for the future of counseling: The New Consensus Definition of counseling. *Journal of Counseling and Development, 92*(3), 366–372. https://doi.org/10.1002/j.1556-6676.2014.00164.x

Kim, J., & Kim, M. (2022). Rise of social media influencers as a new marketing channel: Focusing on the roles of psychological well-being and perceived social responsibility among consumers. *International Journal of Environmental Research and Public Health, 19*(4), 2362. https://doi.org/10.3390/ijerph19042362

Lorenzo-Luaces, L., Dierckman, C., & Adams, S. (2023). Attitudes and (mis)information about cognitive behavioral therapy on TikTok: An analysis of video content. *Journal of Medical Internet Research, 25*, Article e45571. https://doi.org/10.2196/45571

MacNeill, A. L., Doucet, S., & Luke, A. (2024). Effectiveness of a mental health chatbot for people with chronic diseases: Randomized controlled trial. *JMIR Formative Research, 8*, Article e50025. https://doi.org/10.2196/50025

Marcelle, E. T., Nolting, L., Hinshaw, S. P., & Aguilera, A. (2019). Effectiveness of a multimodal digital psychotherapy platform for adult depression: A naturalistic feasibility study. *JMIR mHealth and uHealth, 7*(1), Article e10948. https://doi.org/10.2196/10948

Merriam, S. B., & Tisdell, E. J. (2016). *Qualitative research: A guide to design and implementation* (4th ed.). Jossey-Bass. https://opac.marmot.org/ExternalEContent/.b4910259x/

Moh, Y. S., & Sperandio, K. R. (2022). The need to consider requiring trauma training in entry-level academic training programs in clinical mental health counseling. *Journal of Mental Health Counseling, 44*(1), 18–31. https://doi.org/10.17744/mehc.44.1.03

Morris, D. B., & Chen, J. A. (2023). A social cognitive perspective of educators' moral agency. *Theory Into Practice, 62*(3), 306–317. https://doi.org/10.1080/00405841.2023.2226556

Movement Advancement Project & CenterLink. (2024). *2024 LGBTQ community center survey report.* Movement Advancement Project. https://www.mapresearch.org/file/2024-LGBTQ-Community-Centers-Report.pdf

Moylan, K., & Doherty, K. (2025). Expert and interdisciplinary analysis of AI-driven chatbots for mental health support: Mixed methods study. *Journal of Medical Internet Research, 27*, Article e67114. https://doi.org/10.2196/67114

National Conference of State Legislatures. (2024). *Behavioral health workforce shortages and state resource systems.* National Conference of State Legislatures. https://www.ncsl.org/labor-and-employment/behavioral-health-workforce-shortages-and-state-resource-systems

Nguyen, V. C., Birnbaum, M., & De Choudhury, M. (2023). Understanding and mitigating mental health misinformation on video-sharing platforms. *ArXiv preprint arXiv:2304.07417*. https://doi.org/10.48550/arXiv.2304.07417

Panchal, N., Saunders, H., Rudowitz, R., & Cox, C. (2023). *The implications of COVID-19 for mental health and substance use.* Kaiser Family Foundation. https://www.kff.org/mental-health/the-implications-of-covid-19-for-mental-health-and-substance-use/

Pierce, B. S., Perrin, P. B., & McDonald, S. D. (2020). Demographic, organizational, and clinical practice predictors of U.S. psychologists' use of telepsychology. *Professional Psychology: Research and Practice, 51*(2), 184–193. https://doi.org/10.1037/pro0000267

Reese, R. F., Young, J. S., & Hutchinson, G. A. (2013). Preparing counselors-in-training for private practice: A course in clinical entrepreneurship. *The Professional Counselor, 3*(1), 23–33. https://tpcjournal.nbcc.org/preparing-counselors-in-training-for-private-practice-a-course-in-clinical-entrepreneurship/

Schweiger, W. K., Henderson, D. A., McCaskill, K., Clawson, T. W., & Collins, D. R. (Eds.) (2012). *Counselor preparation: Programs, faculty, trends* (13th ed.). Routledge.

Snow, W. H., Lamar, M. R., Hinkle, J. S., & Speciale, M. (2018). Current practices in online counselor education. *The Professional Counselor, 8*(2), 131–145.

Southern Poverty Law Center. (2025). *The year in hate and extremism 2024* [Report]. Southern Poverty Law Center. https://www.splcenter.org/resources/reports/year-hate-extremism-2024/

Talkspace. (n.d.). *Talkspace* [Online therapy platform]. Talkspace. Retrieved October 28, 2025, from https://www.talkspace.com/

VandeVusse, A., Mueller, J., Haas, M., Osias, P., & Tchou, T. A. (2024, November). *Publicly supported family planning clinics in 2022–2023: Trends in service delivery practices and protocols.* Guttmacher Institute. https://www.guttmacher.org/report/publicly-supported-family-planning-clinics-2022-2023

Wysa. (2025). *Wysa: Mental Wellbeing AI* (Version 9.8.0) [Mobile app]. Touhckin. Apple App Store. https://apps.apple.com/us/app/wysa-mental-wellbeing-ai/id1166585565

Yonatan-Leus, R., & Brukner, H. (2025). Comparing perceived empathy and intervention strategies of an AI chatbot and human psychotherapists in online mental health support. *Counselling and Psychotherapy Research, 25*(1), Article e12832. https://doi.org/10.1002/capr.12832

# 3

# Our Earning Potential

For most counselors fresh out of graduate school—before licensure, before specialization, and before you feel like you know what you're doing—the average starting salary hovers around $50,000 a year (U.S. Bureau of Labor Statistics [BLS], 2025). In some settings, it's even lower. Nonprofits and community mental health agencies often post starting salaries in the $42,000–$48,000 range, even for full-time, master's-level positions. These numbers can sting, especially considering hefty tuition fees, student loans, unpaid internships, and the mandatory supervision hours that entry-level counselors often end up paying for out of pocket. Here's a breakdown of what entry-level salaries tend to look like across common counseling work settings.

- **Community mental health agencies and nonprofits ($45,000–$52,000):** These jobs are stable. They often come with free supervision, consistent referrals, and a predictable schedule. The trade-offs for these roles are high caseloads, extensive documentation, and little flexibility.
- **School counseling ($55,000–$60,000):** Public school counselors' salaries depend on district budgets and state funding. These roles usually offer strong benefits, retirement packages, and summer breaks or reduced summer workloads.

- **Hospitals and integrated health-care settings ($55,000–$65,000):** These positions offer strong interprofessional learning and upward mobility post-licensure. Many counselors working in integrated care benefit from medical benefits and continuing education stipends.
- **Group or 1099 contractor private practice (compensation highly variable):** This one is a wildcard. Some early-career counselors in group practice settings earn around $35–$45 per session. If you're seeing 15 to 20 clients per week, you're fully booked, have minimal no-shows, and negotiate a fair split, that might translate to $45,000–$60,000 annually after expenses. It's possible, but it takes strategy.

The obvious, but often overlooked, factor is location. If you're working in high-cost states like California, New York, or Massachusetts, average counselor salaries often exceed $70,000 (BLS, 2024; National Compensation Survey, 2024). However, those dollars don't stretch as far when rent payments eat half your paycheck. In rural regions, like parts of the South, Midwest, or Mountain West, you might top out around $45,000–$55,000, even with the same education and credentials. Cost of living balances some of that out, but your lifestyle options may still feel tight.

The range is wide, and the entry point for counselors may feel discouraging, but that's not where your story ends. The real point of this chapter is to show you that you do not have to stay where you start forever. You can earn more. You can specialize. You can learn to position yourself wisely in the market. You can build something that honors both your calling and your financial future.

## Salary Evolution

Starting salaries may feel underwhelming, but they're just that—a start. According to recent national data, the average counselor earns about $60,510 per year, though this varies widely by specialization and experience level. For example, substance abuse and behavioral disorder counselors average around $53,490, while school and career counselors earn closer to $64,200, and marriage and family counselors make about $63,300 annually. With experience, advanced credentials, and full licensure, many counselors move into higher-paying roles in private practice or supervision, often earning $70,000 or more over time as their expertise deepens (Bouchrika, 2025). It's not just about time served. Salary growth is about value added—both real and perceived.

The more experienced you become, the more efficient, grounded, and precise your work gets. You learn to articulate your niche, communicate your value, and set fees that reflect your training and expertise. This is especially true in private practice. If you've held your rates steady for years, you may be undercutting your own growth. Reviewing your fee structure annually is good business. Ask yourself three questions.

1. Have my expenses increased?
2. Have I added certifications or continuing education units?
3. Am I turning away ideal clients or building a waitlist?

If you answered yes to any of these questions, it may be time to raise your rates. Standard practice is to give clients 30 days' notice and explain your reasoning clearly, whether it is due to rising operational costs, advanced training, or increased demand. Some counselors grandfather long-term clients into older rates, while others raise fees across the board. Do what fits your practice. A well-run, fairly compensated practice leads to better presence, better boundaries, and better care. That's the definition of doing good work for a long time.

# Factors Influencing Income

## The Influence of Education and Licensure on Counselor Income

In this field, your degree and license carry significant weight. Most counselors enter the profession with a master's degree, but the decisions you make after graduation can open (or close) doors regarding income.

### Master's-Level, Pre-Licensure

If you have a master's degree but no license, expect entry-level pay—usually somewhere between $44,000 and $52,000, depending on where you are and who you're working with (BLS, 2024). These jobs often include supervision and steady referrals, but have limited autonomy.

### Licensed (LPC, LMFT, LCSW)

Becoming a licensed professional counselor (LPC) is a game-changer. For example, in Texas, LPCs average about $75,000 a year, with many earning closer to $90,000 as they gain experience (Texas Workforce Commission, 2024). Licensure gives you more clinical freedom and job options, and the ability to directly bill clients.

### Supervisory Credentials (LPC-S, LMFT-S, LCSW-S)

If you go a step further and become a board-approved licensed professional counselor supervisor (LPC-S), you can add another income stream. Many supervisors charge $75–$150 per supervision hour, depending on location and experience (National Board for Certified Counselors [NBCC], 2023). It's not passive income, but it is a way to give back and grow your earnings.

### Doctorate (PhD, PsyD, EdD)

Earning a doctoral degree in counseling or counselor education opens the door to a variety of opportunities in teaching, supervision, research, and leadership. Many professionals use it to deepen their clinical expertise, while others transition into academia or train future counselors. According to recent data, individuals with a Ph.D. in Counselor Education and Counseling Psychology earn an average salary of about $62,000 per year, with the potential for significantly higher earnings depending on role, experience, and setting (Payscale, n.d.).

### Specializations and Certifications

Specializing in areas like trauma, couples' work, or addiction expands your ability to help clients and makes you more marketable. For example, marriage and family counselors working in government roles earn, on average, around $69,000 (BLS, 2024). If you prove to be good at your niche, you can often set higher fees in private practice.

### Pricing and Community Fit

It is tempting to raise rates just because you earned a new credential, but that only works if clients feel the value. Pricing must fit your market and population. Charging above the norm without delivering something unique can backfire. Keep your fees honest, clear, and in sync with your experience and the service you're offering.

The bottom line is that more letters next to your name *can* mean more money, but only if you use them well. Degrees and licenses open doors, but it's your responsibility to walk through them and build something sustainable.

## *How Geographic Location Influences Counselor Income*

Where you live affects how much you earn and how far that money actually goes. Counselor salaries can swing by $20,000 or more depending

# Our Earning Potential

on the state and city in which you practice, and whether you're in an urban or rural ZIP code (BLS, 2024).

Urban areas pay more, especially in high-demand cities like San Francisco, Boston, or New York. For example, in California, the average salary for LPCs is more than $76,000, with many earning $90,000+ (BLS, 2024). However, don't be fooled by the paycheck alone—those dollars don't stretch as far when high housing and health care costs are taken into consideration.

Rural counselors usually earn less, often between $50,000 and $60,000, but they benefit from lower costs of living and less competition. Some even qualify for federal loan repayment programs through the National Health Service Corps (NHSC), especially if they are practicing in mental health shortage areas (Health Resources & Services Administration [HRSA] & NHSC 2021).

State licensure standards also matter. States such as New Jersey and Massachusetts require more training hours but also tend to pay higher salaries and offer stronger insurance reimbursements (BLS, 2024). In contrast, states with lighter requirements often have lower starting pay and less favorable reimbursement structures.

If you are planning to move, check license portability. Some states have reciprocity or endorsement agreements, while others will have you jumping through hoops in order to practice. The Counseling Compact, an interstate agreement that allows counselors to practice across member states, has made portability easier, but it is still not universal (DeDiego et al., 2023). That reality affects not just your income, but also how long you are sidelined waiting to get back to work.

You must not only chase the highest salary, but you also chase value. A $70,000 job in Colorado might give you more freedom and breathing room than an $85,000 job in Los Angeles. Consider housing, insurance, taxes, and your lifestyle needs. Money does not mean much if it disappears before you can feel it.

## The Role of Business Skills and Marketing Confidence in Counselor Income

Your clinical skills matter, but they alone do not determine success. Counselors who know how to position themselves, communicate clearly, and build a strong professional presence tend to grow faster, keep clients longer, and ride out the ups and downs of this field with more stability (Malley & Deklewa, 2013). Those counselors have usually defined who they help and how, made it easy for people to find them, and don't cringe when someone asks, "What do you do?"

That's not because they're better counselors. It's because they've learned to show up—and not just in session. They've put in the work to clarify their identity, carve out a niche, and share it with the people who need to hear it. As a result, they do not waste time trying to serve everyone. They attract clients who are already halfway in the door (Norcross & Wampold, 2011).

On the other hand, many great counselors are stuck in financial stress because they fear visibility. Within the counseling field, there's a common misconception that self-promotion and marketing are wrong, and that making good money demands exploiting someone's pain. That idea was not created out of nowhere (Rees & Wood, 2024). Counselors are trained to be humble and selfless. Somewhere along the way, many of us internalized that we're only supposed to serve, not sell. But the truth is that if people can't find you, they can't work with you. Counselors who embrace marketing by clarifying their niche and professional identity are more likely to attract their ideal clients (Stargell & Headley, 2023). Research also shows that counselors with a strong professional identity experience lower rates of burnout and higher satisfaction (Gibson et al., 2010; Corey et al., 2023).

Here are a few starting points for a good marketing strategy.

- **Update your website bio:** Make sure it sounds like you and reflects the work you actually do.
- **Pick one platform:** Choose from Instagram, LinkedIn, or Psychology Today, and post once a week. Regularly sharing a thought or a resource reminds people that you exist.
- **Reach out to a local provider:** Introduce yourself to a doctor, pastor, or another counselor. Offer to swap referrals or just connect.

Marketing done well doesn't feel like marketing. It feels like *honesty*. It's you saying, "Here's how I help. Here's what I believe. If that sounds like what you need, I'd love to work with you." When you lead with clarity and compassion, you set the tone for the counseling relationship before the first session even begins.

Over time, these small acts shift how you see yourself. They build your confidence, and they start to rewrite that old narrative that says you're not supposed to take up space.

The goal of marketing is to make your work sustainable. You can build a business that reflects your values, serves your community, and supports your life. Marketing isn't the opposite of helping—it's how you get help to the people who need it.

## The Power of Reputation

In this field, your reputation is your currency. Credentials matter. Marketing matters. But what often matters more, especially long-term, is how people experience you, both in and out of session. Your reputation is the story others tell when you're not in the room. It gets written through every interaction, every referral, and every ethical decision you make.

Word-of-mouth referrals remain the most powerful way to grow a counseling practice (Daltry et al., 2023). Most clients don't find their counselor through a flashy ad. A friend, doctor, or another counselor—someone they already trust—usually recommends them (Bohart & Tallman, 2022). If people find you trustworthy, skilled, and consistent, they will recommend you to others. Establishing these traits requires being a decent person, colleague, collaborator, and counselor; one who is clear, responsive, and respectful. Being liked matters because when likability meets clinical excellence, it becomes a business advantage.

Opportunities to speak, teach, supervise, consult, and write tend to gravitate toward counselors with a reputation for integrity and professionalism. If you are known in your community for your good work, you won't need to chase extracurricular activities. These roles will start showing up in inboxes and conversations because someone thought of you when the opportunity popped up (Moorhead et al., 2023; Skovholt & Trotter-Mathison, 2016).

To achieve this reputation and notoriety, you must show up. Go to conferences. Join a peer consultation group. Mentor a graduate student. Collaborate with other providers in your area. These networking tasks build relationships and stature. Over time, people come to know your name, your work, and how it feels to be in your orbit. As Moorhead et al., 2023 found, professional identity is shaped by these kinds of relational experiences. That identity affects not just your growth but your income.

Integrity is a long game. You won't always see the payoff right away. You might watch others cut corners or market louder and wonder if you should play the same game. People who build with quiet consistency, strong boundaries, and good energy tend to stay in the field longer (Cottone & Tarvydas, 2021). Their referrals increase. Their name carries weight. Their income grows—not just because of what they charge, but because of who they've become.

This is a people-first profession. And in a people-first profession, who you are *is* the brand. When you're known for doing good work—and for being good to work with—doors open. You don't have to force them. You just have to keep showing up.

## Specializations and Their Financial Impact

*Specializing with Purpose*

In this field, specialization can be both meaningful and strategic. The right focus can help you do work that matters *and* carve out a financially sustainable path. However, it only works when it's intentional—when it's more than just a string of letters behind your name, and instead a real alignment between what you care about and what your community needs. As of 2025, there are a few areas where demand is high and growing.

- **Trauma-informed counseling:** The need for trauma work continues to rise, especially post-COVID-19 and amid rising awareness of racial, systemic, and generational trauma. Counselors trained in approaches like eye-movement desensitization and reprocessing (EMDR), somatic counseling, or trauma-focused cognitive behavior therapy (CBT) are often booked months out (Courtois & Ford, 2016). These modalities require advanced training and the ability to hold heavy stories with skill and care.
- **Substance use and addiction counseling:** The opioid epidemic hasn't gone anywhere. Addiction is touching every corner of our communities. According to the Bureau of Labor Statistics, employment in this specialty is expected to grow 17% from 2024 to 2034 (BLS, 2024). If you can pair this with trauma training, all the better. The two often go hand in hand.
- **Child and adolescent counseling:** Kids and teenagers are struggling, and the systems in place to support them are too. If you are trained in play counseling, behavioral interventions, or working with neurodiverse youth, you are likely in high demand. Counselors who specialize in early intervention can literally shift life trajectories (Kazdin, 2018). School referrals, pediatricians, and parents are constantly looking for child-focused clinicians, often because they see the first signs of trouble long before a crisis emerges. Teachers may refer a student when their academic performance suddenly drops, or their behavior escalates in the classroom (American School

Counselor Association [ASCA], 2025). Pediatricians frequently notice when anxiety, sleep, or eating patterns begin to interfere with health (American Academy of Pediatrics [AAP], n.d.). Parents themselves often reach out when relationships at home become strained, when their child withdraws socially, or when everyday routines feel like a battle (Centers for Disease Control and Prevention [CDC], 2023).

- **Couples and family counseling:** Relationships are under stress from technology, economic strain, parenting challenges, and more. Counselors who can navigate conflict, attachment dynamics, and intergenerational trauma are essential. They're often able to charge higher fees, especially if working with multiple family members or offering intensives (Lebow & Snyder, 2022).

However, it will not serve you or your communities to chase certifications just to collect them. Each one costs time, money, and bandwidth. Without a plan for how it fits into your practice, you risk burning out without seeing a return. Instead, pick one or two areas where passion and need intersect and build from there. Let your niche grow organically as your experience deepens.

Your specialization should reflect both what lights you up and what serves your community. That combination constitutes the real value of a specialization. When your value is clear, your marketing is easier, your referrals multiply, and your income grows.

## When You Are Known for Something, You Earn More

Specializing isn't just about clinical depth—it's a business move. When clients know exactly what you do and trust that you're good at it, they're more willing to pay for it. Because they're seen as the go-to person for a specific need, niche counselors—whether trained in EMDR, dialectical behavior therapy (DBT), the Gottman Method, or play counseling—often command higher rates and get more referrals (Malley & Deklewa, 2013; BLS, 2024).

When you focus your training and messaging around a niche, your marketing becomes clearer. You waste less energy trying to reach everyone. Instead, your website, referrals, and elevator pitch all point in the same direction. People know what clients to send you—and they do (Moorhead et al., 2023).

Of course, specialization usually comes with costs—training fees, supervision hours, and time. But it also unlocks doors. Counselors certified in EMDR, for example, can work with complex trauma populations and often charge more per session. DBT-trained clinicians run groups. Gottman-trained couples counselors offer intensives. These credentials are tools that expand your reach and build income without burning out (Institute for Creative Mindfulness, n.d.).

## Scaling Your Niche

Specializing doesn't mean locking yourself into one aspect of counseling forever. Done right, a niche lets you build sideways, not just by stacking more clients, but by layering different roles. Here's how it works:

- A trauma counselor starts seeing clients weekly.
- They add an EMDR intensive option (three sessions in a week).
- They train other counselors, offer supervision, or consult with clinics on trauma-informed care.

Each new income stream draws from the same core specialty. You're not reinventing yourself—you're scaling what you already know. According to Colbun 2013, counselors with clear specialties were significantly more likely to diversify their income through teaching, consultation, and curriculum development. Those roles often pay better and offer more flexibility (Colburn, 2013).

This model also protects against burnout and instability. If your caseload dips, your workshop income keeps things steady. If you need a break from counseling, you can pivot to writing or teaching. You're still helping people, but on your terms. This only works if your foundation is solid. You can't fake expertise. Clients, colleagues, and referral sources can tell the difference. So yes, invest in good training, get supervision, and track your outcomes. Build your niche on a sturdy foundation.

The most successful specialists aren't always loud or flashy. They're steady. They listen to what their communities need. They pick a specialty, go deep, and then let that depth open doors.

Sometimes, it starts small. Maybe you start with one workshop, or one email list, or one direct message from a counselor who wants to learn from you. You don't have to launch an empire overnight, but if you do the work and stay consistent, your niche can carry you, and you can build something that lasts.

## Expertise That Pays (and Lasts)

At some point in your career, you will realize that making a living in this field is not just about clinical skill. It is about learning how to position yourself, how to talk about what you do, and how to build a life that can sustain the weight of this work.

Specialization can open doors if it aligns with who you are and what your clients need. Reputation can carry you if you protect it with integrity and consistency. And visibility doesn't have to feel wrong—it can just feel clear. You don't need to do everything. You just need to do *your* thing and do it well. Let your work speak for you. When opportunities show up—whether it's a new client, a speaking gig, or a chance to lead—say yes like someone who earned it because you did.

# References

American Academy of Pediatrics. (n.d.). Mental health initiatives. *AAP*. Retrieved October 28, 2025, from https://www.aap.org/en/patient-care/mental-health-initiatives/?srsltid=AfmBOopM73PokOxBzroeesFQeyMhvIohzYlWmeJAKjAbxqR-ZWRLJGl8

American School Counselor Association. (2025). *The role of the school counselor*. ASCA. https://www.schoolcounselor.org/getmedia/ee8b2e1b-d021-4575-982c-c84402cb2cd2/Role-Statement.pdf

Bohart, A. C., & Tallman, K. (2022). Client expertise: The active client in psychotherapy. In J. N. Fuertes (Ed.), *The other side of psychotherapy: Understanding clients' experiences and contributions in treatment* (pp. 13–43). American Psychological Association. https://doi.org/10.1037/0000303-002

Bouchrika, I. (2025, December 11). 2026 Counseling salaries: How much does a counselor make? *Research.com*. Retrieved December 16, 2025, from https://research.com/careers/counseling-salaries-how-much-does-a-counselor-make

Centers for Disease Control and Prevention (CDC). (2023). Youth mental health data portal. https://www.cdc.gov/media/releases/2024/p0806-youth-mental-health.html

Colburn, A. A. (2013). Endless possibilities: Diversifying service options in private practice. *Journal of Mental Health Counseling, 35*(3), 198–210. https://doi.org/10.17744/mehc.35.3.8870230745378517

Corey, G., Muratori, M., Austin, J. T., II, & Austin, J. A. (2023). *Counselor self-care* (2nd ed.). American Counseling Association.

Cottone, R., & Tarvydas, V. M. (2021). *Ethics and decision-making in counseling and psychotherapy* (5th ed., M. Hartley, Ed.). Springer Publishing Company.

Courtois, C. A., & Ford, J. D. (Eds.). (2016). *Treatment of complex traumatic stress disorders in adults: Scientific foundations and therapeutic models* (2nd ed.). Guilford Press.

Daltry, R. M., Mehr, K. E., & Keenan, L. (2023). Student-athletes and counseling services: Recommendations for identifying and developing referral sources. *Journal of College Student Psychotherapy, 37*(2), 196–207. https://doi.org/10.1080/87568225.2021.1957338

DeDiego, A., Maurya, R. K., Rujimora, J., Simineo, L., & Searls, G. (2023). Counseling and the interstate compact: Navigating ethical practice across state lines. *The Professional Counselor, 13*(3), 177–192. https://doi.org/10.15241/ad.13.3.177

Gibson, D. M., Dollarhide, C. T., & Moss, J. M. (2010). Professional identity development: A grounded theory of transformational tasks of counselors. *Counselor Education and Supervision, 50*(1), 21–38. https://doi.org/10.1002/j.1556-6978.2010.tb00106.x

Health Resources & Services Administration, and National Health Service Corps. (2021). *Loan repayment*. HRSA. Retrieved October 28, 2025, from https://nhsc.hrsa.gov/loan-repayment

Institute for Creative Mindfulness. (n.d.). *EMDR therapy training*. Institute for Creative Mindfulness. Retrieved October 28, 2025, from https://www.instituteforcreativemindfulness.com/emdr-therapy-training/

Kazdin, A. E. (2018). *Innovations in psychosocial interventions and their delivery: Leveraging cutting-edge science to improve the world's mental health*. Oxford University Press. https://doi.org/10.1093/med-psych/9780190463281.001.0001

Lebow, J. L., & Snyder, D. K. (Eds.). (2022). *Clinical handbook of couple therapy* (6th ed.). Guilford Publications.

Malley, P. B., & Deklewa, E. P. (2013). *Legal and ethical dimensions for mental health professionals*. Taylor & Francis.

Moorhead, H. J. H., Duncan, K., & Fernandez, M. S. (2023). The critical need for professional advocacy: A call to the counseling profession to value professional counselor identity. *Journal of Counselor Leadership and Advocacy, 10*(1), 3–17. https://doi.org/10.1080/2326716X.2023.2178985

National Board for Certified Counselors (NBCC). (2023). *Approved clinical supervisor credential requirements*. Center for Credentialing and Education (CCE). https://www.cce-global.org/credentialing/acs/requirements

Norcross, J. C., & Wampold, B. E. (2011). Evidence-based therapy relationships: Research conclusions and clinical practices. *Psychotherapy, 48*(1), 98–102. https://doi.org/10.1037/a0022161

Payscale. (n.d.). *Doctor of Philosophy (PhD), Counselor Education & Counseling Psychology salary*. Payscale.com. https://www.payscale.com/research/US/Degree=Doctor_of_Philosophy_(PhD),_Counselor_Education_&_Counseling_Psychology/Salary

Rees, S. D., & Wood, S. A. (2024). Marketing your practice. In S. Rees, *A therapist's guide to private practice: Building a values-based business* (pp. 65–81). Routledge.

Skovholt, T. M., & Trotter-Mathison, M. (2016). *The resilient practitioner: Burnout and compassion fatigue prevention and self-care strategies for the helping professions*. Routledge.

Stargell, N. A., & Headley, J. A. (2023). From envisioning to actualization: Marketing yourself in the 21st century. In B. T. Erford (Ed.), *Practicum and internship experiences in counseling* (pp. 268–286). Routledge.

Texas Workforce Commission. (2024). Mental health counselors: Texas labor market information. *MyTexasFuture*. https://www.mytexasfuture.org/career-explorer/mental-health-counselors/

U.S. Bureau of Labor Statistics. (2024). *National Compensation Survey: Wages and benefits*. https://www.bls.gov/ocs/home.htm

U.S. Bureau of Labor Statistics. (2025). *Occupational Outlook Handbook*. Office of Employment and Unemployment Statistics, U.S. BLS. Retrieved October 16, 2025, from https://www.bls.gov/ooh/home.htm

# 4

# Getting Out of the Hole

Counselors talk a lot about congruence and incongruence. Financial incongruence—preaching self-care while drowning in student debt, charging too little because you feel bad, or staying at a job that's not sustainable—can chip away at that integrity.

This chapter isn't a budgeting tutorial or a lecture on compound interest. It's about making sense of the financial hole: how we get into it, why we stay stuck, and how we start climbing out. We discuss the real cost of becoming a counselor, including the expected fees like tuition and the costs of continuing education units (CEUs), and the unexpected ones, including relocation costs, unpaid hours, and lost income due to delayed licensure. We detail how to start building a financial foundation that supports the life you want, rather than keeping you stuck in the one you can't afford to risk leaving.

The truth is that money doesn't make you a better counselor, but being financially unstable can make it difficult to be a good one. Financial wellness is part of ethical practice (Lawson & Myers, 2011). It is crucial to sustain a good practice. Let's take a deep breath and look at the numbers—without shame, without panic, and without pretending it's not part of the job.

## What Does "Getting Out of the Hole" Mean to You?

Before you make a plan, you need a goal. What does financial health look like for you? For some counselors, "getting out of the hole" means being completely debt-free. For others, it means taking two guilt-free vacations a year. For many, it's as simple as not feeling anxious when rent is due. There's no universal benchmark. What matters is that your financial goals are based on your needs, not those of your peers, your professors, or someone else's highlight reel on social media. When you define what financial peace means for you, your decisions become easier to make. You stop chasing other people's metrics and start building something that fits.

## The Cost of Becoming a Counselor

We're shaped by a culture that frames financial conversations as a distraction from the work, like being mission-driven and money-aware can't exist in the same space, but they do. Money shapes the decisions we make every day: what jobs we take, which trainings we delay, and how many hours we overwork to keep up.

We (Jude and Julius) have felt it ourselves. We've taken jobs that didn't pay enough because we just felt like we "should." We've skipped the CEUs we needed because they weren't in the budget. We've justified stress as a rite of passage while quietly losing sleep over money. At the same time, we've told our clients to set boundaries, prioritize their wellness, and build balanced lives.

That gap between what counselors know and how they live adds up. If we want to build careers that last, we must start being honest about what this profession actually costs—not just in tuition, but in time, lost wages, delayed licensure, and the emotional toll of staying silent. We can't keep pretending financial stress is just a personal issue. It's also a professional one, and if we don't address it directly, it will continue to erode the very thing we're trained to protect: our presence.

Financial stress shows up in the room. Counselors carrying that weight are more vulnerable to burnout, blurred boundaries, and diminished presence (Lawson & Myers, 2011). It also compromises our ability to do the work well. Still, many of us undercharge, overextend, and absorb guilt when our fees don't match our needs. We make professional decisions based on fear instead of strategy. Over time, that pattern pushes good clinicians out of the field (Wardle & Mayorga, 2016).

Getting out of the hole is about more than debt. It's also about building a sustainable foundation for a life and career that works. That starts with being honest: becoming and staying a counselor costs money. If we ignore that truth, we risk making decisions that keep us stuck. This chapter walks through the costs of tuition, supervision, and licensure gaps and how those costs shape your clinical choices. It's a guide for designing your career with the same clarity and care you bring into the counseling room. Whether you're deep in debt or just getting started, this chapter helps you build something that lasts.

When we meet with undergraduate students or second-career professionals considering counseling, one of the biggest barriers they bring up isn't licensure, clinical work, or imposter syndrome—it's the cost. They look at the numbers and imagine themselves climbing into a hole of debt from which they may never emerge. Before they ever sit in a classroom or a counseling room, they feel the weight. Financial concerns are one of the most frequently cited obstacles to entering the mental health workforce, especially for students from underrepresented backgrounds or those pursuing counseling as a second career (Deenanath, 2017).

Becoming a counselor is often framed as a calling, but we rarely discuss how expensive answering that call is. Most students expect graduate school to cost something. What might catch people off guard is how deep that cost runs and how long its impact lingers. The meter starts the moment you enroll. Tuition ranges widely, from $30,000 to $70,000 a year (Hanson, 2024), depending on the institution. Private universities land on the higher end. That is just the beginning. Textbooks can cost students hundreds of dollars per semester. Then come the university fees, often disguised under vague names like "technology" or "student services." Some programs also charge liability insurance, clinical placement fees, or graduation processing fees.

Don't forget practicum and internships. These experiences are essential, but unpaid. Expect to log 10 to 20 hours a week at a clinical site, often while still in classes or working another job. That time costs money, too—whether in lost wages, missed job opportunities, or added stress. Olson-Garriott et al. (2015) found that the average counselor-in-training sacrifices over $10,000 in lost income during their clinical training year alone.

## In-Person Versus Online CACREP Programs: Different Models, Different Costs

Online Council for Accreditation of Counseling and Related Educational Programs (CACREP)-accredited counseling programs have expanded rapidly since the mid-2010s through the pandemic years (2020–22) (Kelly, 2025). Their rise is no surprise; they offer flexibility that opens doors for working adults, caregivers, and students in rural communities. For many, online education is the only feasible option, but there are trade-offs—especially when it comes to clinical readiness, connection, and cost (Kupczynski et al., 2018).

Online programs often charge higher tuition fees per credit hour, despite the perception that they are more affordable. For students balancing full-time work or family responsibilities, degree completion tends to take longer, which spreads tuition payments over more semesters and delays entry into full-time clinical work. On paper, it looks like a win. In practice, it can be a financial strain that lasts longer than expected.

Clinical placements introduce another layer of challenge. In-person programs tend to have established relationships with local agencies, with faculty playing a direct role in securing sites and supervising clinical hours. Online students, by contrast, are frequently left to coordinate their own placements, sometimes in communities with limited access to qualified supervisors. Many end up paying out of pocket for supervision or struggling to find consistent sites—issues that can delay graduation or undercut the quality of the clinical experience (Nelson, 2015).

As someone who has worked closely with students across settings, I (Jude) have yet to meet a graduate from an online counseling program who walked away feeling deeply connected to their faculty, meaningfully supported through supervision, or fully confident in their clinical skills. When students transfer from an online program to our in-person program, they often describe the shift as shocking. "Not even on the same planet," one of them said. Many of these students had no idea what they were missing until they stepped into a more engaged, face-to-face learning environment.

That's not a critique of all online programs—some are doing it right. Research has shown that online counselor education can work, especially when programs are intentionally designed to offer real-time (synchronous) interaction, well-supported placements, and robust supervision systems (Snow & Coker, 2020). If you're choosing an online program for cost and convenience, it's worth asking: What's the trade-off? Are you sacrificing mentorship, supervision, support, and clinical readiness for the sake of flexibility? For some students, the answer is yes—and the impact is felt long after graduation.

### Unaccredited and Predatory Programs: A Hidden Trap

There's also another serious risk that doesn't get talked about enough: unaccredited or predatory counseling programs, especially in the for-profit sector. These programs often advertise aggressively, make big promises, and then disappear—leaving students with massive debt, no license eligibility, and no path forward (U.S. Senate Health, Education, Labor, and Pensions Committee [HELP], 2010). The collapse of Corinthian Colleges and Argosy University is just two examples of where students were left in limbo, unable to transfer credits or qualify for licensure (Deming et al., 2013).

Unaccredited programs can drain your money, time, and emotional energy without providing what you need to be a counselor. Students in these programs often discover too late that they are not eligible for licensure in their state or that they have been misled about job prospects. These are not rare cases. They are systemic patterns in underregulated corners of higher education (Deming et al., 2013).

So, what should future counselors look for? Start with accreditation—CACREP or equivalent—and then dig deeper. Does the program offer synchronous instruction? Are faculty involved in clinical placement? What's the licensure pass rate? How connected do current students feel to their professors and supervisors? Don't stop at tuition cost; look at what you're receiving from your investment. What matters is structure, mentorship, supervision, and how well a program prepares you for the real world. Once you graduate, you won't just be managing debt—you will be managing people's lives.

## The Intersections of Race, Gender, and Class in Access to Education

Not everyone pays the same price to become a counselor. Students of color, first-generation students, and those from lower-income backgrounds often carry heavier debt burdens because their financial safety nets are smaller compared to White students with heftier financial backgrounds. Without access to generational wealth or family support, many students rely solely on loans, side jobs, or credit to make it through graduate school (Hill et al., 2007; Shepard, 2021). This financial pressure stacks on top of academic demands and can influence course loads and internship decisions.

The costs aren't just financial. Navigating academic spaces in which you're one of the only Black or Brown students can be emotionally heavy. The cumulative impact of microaggressions, cultural isolation, and subtle forms of exclusion adds up—especially in predominantly White counseling programs (Henfield et al., 2011; Williams et al., 2014). It's a psychological tax that doesn't show up on a billing statement but still affects how students perform in class, at practicum sites, and eventually with clients.

Gender plays a role, too. Women in counseling programs often juggle caregiving responsibilities or are funneled into lower-paying niches of the profession. Research has shown that women in helping professions are more likely to experience financial insecurity, in part due to wage disparities and the added pressure of unpaid domestic labor (Adediran, 2017). These dynamics compound when race and socioeconomic status intersect.

The field has made gains in access. More students from historically underrepresented groups are entering counseling programs than ever before. This is a crucial step, but access isn't the same as equity. Getting into a program is one thing. Getting through, and being supported while doing it, is another. When students graduate without a strong financial footing or adequate professional support, their options are limited, and they risk experiencing burnout before they've even found their rhythm. For many, the question is "What will graduate school cost me—emotionally, financially, relationally?" Those are the kinds of questions this chapter is here to help answer.

## Hidden Costs: Relocation, Supervision Gaps, and Licensing Delays

Most people budget for tuition. The expenses that come after they enroll—or after they graduate—are the ones that catch people off guard. Some counseling programs require relocation, which means the cost of housing, moving, and leaving behind your community and support system. Others require travel for in-person intensives or residencies. These costs—gas, flights, hotels, food—aren't always listed in admissions materials, but they can add up fast. For students already working with tight margins, it can be the difference between staying on track and pausing their degree.

Then comes the licensing phase. After graduation, you still need to complete your supervision hours before becoming fully licensed. Ideally, you'd get supervision through your job, but some employers don't offer that, so you end up paying out of pocket. Additionally, licensing boards move slowly. Background checks get delayed. Applications sit in review. Exam scheduling gets pushed back. While all that plays out, you're in limbo—not fully licensed, not fully employable, and not fully earning compensation for the job you're trained to do. This delay affects not only income but confidence, momentum, and long-term planning (Rossi, 2024).

These structural barriers disproportionately affect those who have already stretched themselves to get into the profession in the first place. If they're not anticipated and planned for, they can derail even the most committed early-career counselors. Planning for tuition is essential—but it's not enough. To build a sustainable career, you also have to budget for what comes next.

## The Reality of Educational Debt

For many counselors, student loan debt is the most persistent financial pressure they face. It doesn't just affect your budget—it shapes your job decisions, your sense of freedom, and how you plan your life after graduation. If you're carrying debt, the goal, other than paying it off, should be to manage it in a way that supports your career, rather than limits it.

### Start with the Basics: Know What You Owe

Before making any decisions, you need a clear understanding of your loans. Are they federal or private? Subsidized or unsubsidized? Are they all in one place, or split across multiple providers? Federal loans often come with flexible repayment options and potential forgiveness programs. Private loans may carry higher interest rates, stricter repayment terms, and fewer borrower protections. If you haven't already, download your loan summary. This is your starting point. Knowing your interest rates, loan types, and servicers helps you create a plan.

### Repayment Strategies That Fit Your Life

If you have federal loans, there are several income-based repayment (IDR) options that can lower your monthly payments (Federal Student Aid, U.S. Department of Education, n.d.). Pay As You Earn (PAYE), Saving on a Valuable Education (SAVE), Income-Based Repayment (IBR), and Income-Contingent Repayment (ICR) plans cap your payments based on income and family size. These plans are especially useful in the early stages of your career when your income may not match your education level yet.

If you work full-time for a nonprofit, school, or government agency, you may be eligible for Public Service Loan Forgiveness (PSLF). After 120 qualifying payments (10 years if you stay in an eligible job and plan), the remainder of your federal loans can be forgiven (U.S. Department of Education, n.d.). Eligibility requires that you stay current with documentation, like the Employment Certification Form, every year. These programs can save you money and give you breathing room so you can grow your career without being cornered by your debt.

## When (and When Not) to Refinance

Refinancing your loans might make sense if you have private loans with high interest rates, a strong credit profile, and/or you're not planning to pursue PSLF or any federal loan-forgiveness program. However, refinancing federal loans with a private lender comes at a cost: You lose access to federal protections, including income-driven plans and PSLF. That trade-off might not be worth it, especially if your income is still growing or unpredictable (Poplaski et al., 2019). Always run the numbers and talk to a financial advisor who understands your work context before refinancing.

## Debt and Mental Health: Naming the Weight

Student loan debt can weigh heavily on your mental health. Research has shown that graduate-level debt is significantly correlated with higher levels of anxiety and perceived stress in helping professionals (Sinha et al., 2024). We (Jude and Julius) have both carried balances that shaped our daily decisions. We've talked to students and colleagues who have avoided looking at their statements for months out of fear or shame.

The emotional impact is substantial, but debt isn't a character flaw. It's a structural issue baked into how higher education is financed. You are not behind. You're navigating a broken system with integrity. What matters is that you remain active and aware in your debt management process. Here are five simple steps to take.

1. **Get the full picture:** Log in and look at your total loan balance, interest rates, and monthly payments.
2. **Explore IDR plans:** Use the Loan Simulator at studentaid.gov to compare repayment options.
3. **Plan monthly check-ins:** Set aside 30 minutes each month to review and adjust your repayment strategy.
4. **Certify for PSLF:** If eligible, submit your Employment Certification Form annually.
5. **Talk to someone:** A financial advisor or counselor can help clarify your options, especially if your debt feels overwhelming.

Getting out of the hole doesn't necessitate being debt-free. Sometimes, it means building a life where your loans don't control your every decision.

## Licensure and Professional Development Expenses

Once you graduate and start chipping away at your student loans, it may feel like you have crossed the last big hurdle. Unfortunately, the financial demands do not end with graduation; they simply shift. The next wave comes quietly, and most new counselors do not see it coming. After earning your degree, you still need to apply for a provisional license, secure supervised clinical hours, pass your licensing exam, and apply for full licensure. Each of these steps carries a cost: application fees, supervision fees, exam fees, and continuing education expenses. Licensure and professional growth are not optional; they are required. Unfortunately, most of us enter this phase completely unprepared for what it will cost.

Here is a brief overview of the steps (and accompanying fees) that you can expect to face after graduating from a CACREP-accredited master's program.

1. **Apply for an associate or provisional license:** Most states require this before you can begin postgraduate practice (often $100–$200).
2. **Secure clinical supervision:** States typically mandate between 2,000 and 3,000 hours of supervised experience. Supervisors charge anywhere from $75 to $150 per hour, which can add thousands of dollars over the supervision period.
3. **Pass the licensing exam(s):** Depending on your license, you may need to take the National Counselor Examination (NCE), National

Clinical Mental Health Counseling Examination (NCMHCE) or the Association of Marital and Family Counseling Regulatory Boards (AMFTRB) exam for LMFTs. These tests cost around $275–$400 each.
4. **Submit your application for full licensure:** This includes paperwork, documentation of hours, and verification of exam scores, with state application fees usually running $100–$250.
5. **Maintain continuing education:** Once licensed, most states require ongoing CEUs to renew your license. This adds several hundred dollars per renewal cycle, often every two years.

## The Cost of Licensure

Before you can legally practice, you need a license. Earning that license comes with its own set of fees. Depending on your state, you might spend between $500 and $1,000 just to submit the paperwork (American Counseling Association, n.d.). These expenses usually hit before your first counseling paycheck. You're trying to launch your career while paying for the right to start.

## Supervision Isn't Always Free—and It Adds Up Fast

Most states require between 2,000 and 4,000 hours of supervised postgraduate experience before full licensure. Your job may provide supervision for free, but many new counselors have to secure supervision on their own, and it's not cheap. Weekly supervision can cost anywhere from $75 to $150 per session. At $100 a week over two years, that's more than $10,000—before you're even fully licensed (Dainty, 2021). This doesn't account for transportation, scheduling challenges, or the stress of juggling full-time work with weekly one-on-one meetings.

To add to that, supervision isn't reliable across the board. We've heard from counselors who cycled through multiple supervisors trying to find someone affordable, ethical, and clinically aligned. Others have delayed licensure altogether because they couldn't afford to continue. These common stories speak to a larger issue in how we structure access to full professional standing. Licensure is a milestone, but it's also a paywall. Unless you plan for these costs early, it can feel like you're taking one step forward and two steps back.

## The Continuing Education Hustle

Getting licensed doesn't mean you're done learning—or spending. Most states require between 20 and 40 CEUs every renewal cycle, often with specific requirements in areas like ethics, suicide prevention, cultural competence, or trauma-informed care.

Some employers cover the cost of CEUs, but many don't. While there are free or low-cost options out there, the trainings that actually sharpen your clinical edge—the ones that shape your identity and expand your scope—usually aren't cheap. For example, EMDR training costs around $1,500 (EMDR International Association [EMDRIA], n.d.). Gottman Level I costs around $500 (Gottman Institute, n.d.). There's also play counseling, trauma certification, and eating disorder work, to name a few. Those fees can stack up quickly, but if you want to move toward specialization or private practice, this is the path.

We encourage counselors to treat CEUs as a professional investment, rather than a nuisance or an afterthought. Your clinical competence is part of what you offer, and keeping it sharp is an ethical responsibility (Lawson & Myers, 2011). You owe it to your clients and to yourself to stay current. That doesn't mean participating in every training that pops into your inbox. It means being strategic.

- Plan for CEU costs ahead of time.
- Budget for them annually, as you would for taxes or rent.
- Negotiate training stipends when considering job offers.
- If you're in private practice, build a small margin into your session fees to cover continuing education.

The best counselors are the ones who keep growing. The ones who can afford to grow are usually the ones who planned for it.

## Financial Planning Strategies

No matter how good you are in the counseling room, if you're financially disorganized outside of it, burnout will find you. We (Jude and Julius) learned this the hard way. We've worked full caseloads, taught courses, and supervised students, and still felt financially overwhelmed. We weren't planning like business owners. That must change. Building a financial system that supports you and your work can be as simple as following these steps.

## Know Your Numbers

Start with the facts. You need clarity about your budgetary needs before you can make any financial plans.

- **Personal budget:** What does it cost to live each month? Rent or mortgage, groceries, car, insurance, loans, childcare, utilities—list it all.
- **Professional budget:** What does it cost to do your job? Include liability insurance, CEUs, supervision, electronic health record (EHR) platforms, taxes, software, and anything else your practice depends on.

Combine these two budgets. Once you have your monthly number, you can start setting session fees and making career decisions that are based on reality.

## Set Fees That Reflect the Cost of Becoming You

Your session fees should reflect what it costs to become and stay a counselor, and should take into account your community's demographics, your licensure and status, and your reputation. Those considerations ensure you charge a fee that feels fair while also meeting your breakeven point. When you understand your breakeven point, you can start answering key questions:

- Which jobs are worth it?
- How many clients do I need per week?
- Can I afford to specialize or take Fridays off?
- Which certifications will pay off—and which are just expensive distractions?

Let your numbers shape your strategy. Let your values shape the delivery.

## Build Financial Buffers (Because Life Happens)

Counseling work is unpredictable. Clients cancel. Holidays slow down referrals. Summers and Decembers can feel quiet. That's why a buffer is essential. Saving one to two months of expenses in a separate account creates breathing room. A bad week becomes a bump, not a crisis. You can stay grounded and make decisions without panicking. Planning can assuage your peace of mind.

## Separate Your Business and Personal Money

If you're running a practice—even part-time—you need to separate your business and personal money. Open a business checking account. Use it for everything related to counseling work. This single habit will help you track income and expenses accurately, make tax season easier, and give your practice the structure it deserves.

## Use a System That Works for You

There's no one-size-fits-all method for budgeting, but ignoring your money altogether isn't an option. Some people use the Profit First method (Michalowicz, 2017), which divides income into separate categories like profit, taxes, and salary. Others use apps like You Need A Budget (n.d.), Intuit (Credit Karma, 2025), or even a shared spreadsheet. The right system is the one you actually use. The goal is to check in regularly and use data to guide your choices.

## Start With the End in Mind

Financial planning covers what's due next month and helps long-term by enabling you to build the life and career you want. Features of your practice that might seem insurmountable, like offering sliding scale payment options, can be possible if you plan for them. Or, if you have a longer-term goal like retiring early, taking biannual sabbaticals, or starting a group practice, financial planning can help ensure the feasibility of those benchmarks.

Reverse-engineering your income goals—planning your finances starting with the end in mind—makes long-term aspirations tenable. Ask yourself questions like, "If you want to earn $80,000 and take eight weeks off per year, how many clients do you need to see?"; "What's your minimum fee?"; and "What expenses can you cut, and which ones are non-negotiable?" Instead of making your work overly rigid and structured, planning can multiply your options. It gives you agency, and it makes sure you can keep showing up for your clients without burning out or selling yourself short.

## Aligning Money and Mission

Of course, the goal of financial planning isn't just to make money—it's to give you the freedom to make decisions that reflect who you are and how you work. The sweet spot is when your financial life is aligned with your clinical values. If you believe in boundaries, does your budget reflect that? If you teach clients to ask for what they need, are you charging what you need? If you believe in healing over time, does your business model allow for rest, sabbaticals, or scaling back when needed? Financial alignment is a form of clinical integrity. It reinforces the message you give your clients: it's okay to have needs—and it's okay to meet them.

## Financial Integrity Makes You a Better Counselor

There's a clear link between financial strain and clinical performance. Counselors under financial stress are more likely to experience burnout, lose focus in session, and struggle with emotional availability and ethical decision-making (Lawson & Myers, 2011). That's not just bad for you; it affects your clients as well. When you have clarity and sustainability in your financial life, you're able to be more grounded, more present, and more effective in the room. You're building a career that lasts—not just emotionally, but economically. You don't need to be rich, but you do need to be resourced. That starts with being honest—with yourself, your work, and what you need to do this job well.

## Financial Values and Identity Work

At some point, every counselor has to look up from the numbers—tuition, debt, fees, budgets—and ask a more personal question: "What does money mean to me?" No matter how good your financial plan is, it won't stick if it's built on beliefs that aren't fully yours. Your relationship with money started long before graduate school and long before your first paycheck. It's shaped by the stories you absorbed about worth, security, success, and survival at home, in your culture, and in this profession.

We (Jude and Julius) both grew up in working-class households where money was earned through sacrifice and often held tightly once it arrived. The messages were quiet but powerful:

- Don't ask for too much.
- Be grateful for what you get.
- Talking about money is tacky.
- People who want more are short-sighted.

Those ideas still echo. If we're not intentional in our financial decision-making, they start running the show—quietly steering decisions about fees, job choices, and career paths.

Perhaps you are beholden to the ideas that, in this field, earning a profit makes you less caring, or that helping necessitates sacrifice, or that ambition isn't compatible with integrity. Maybe you grew up in an environment in which money was tied to conflict or silence, leading you to avoid monetary discussions entirely. Whatever the message, it matters. Unspoken beliefs shape behavior. That's where financial planning breaks down—not because we didn't try hard enough, but because we never examined the story underneath. Naming those messages gives you the power to rewrite them and to stop letting fear, shame, or inherited guilt dictate your choices. Financial identity work isn't separate from your growth as a counselor. It's part of it.

## References

Adediran, I. A. (2017). Counseling as an effective tool for empowering women against the global economic crisis and political challenges. *Nigerian Journal of Clinical and Counselling Psychology,* 40–57. https://www.academia.edu/124440658/Counselling_As_An_Effective_Tool_For_Empowering_Women_Against_Global_Economic_Crisis_And_Political_Challenges

American Counseling Association. (n.d.). *Licensure requirements.* ACA. Retrieved October 31, 2025, from https://www.counseling.org/knowledge-center/licensure-requirements

Committee on Health, Education, Labor, and Pensions, United States Senate. (2012). *For-profit higher education: The failure to safeguard the federal investment and ensure student success* (Vol. 1). U.S. Government Printing Office. https://www.govinfo.gov/content/pkg/CPRT-112SPRT74931/pdf/CPRT-112SPRT74931.pdf

Credit Karma. (2025). *Intuit Credit Karma* (Version 25.44) [Mobile App]. Credit Karma. *Apple App Store.* https://apps.apple.com/us/app/intuit-credit-karma/id519817714

Dainty, M. (2021). *Understanding the quality and cost of professional counselor supervision: A qualitative descriptive study* [Unpublished doctoral dissertation]. Grand Canyon University. https://www.researchgate.net/publication/357575385_Understanding_the_Quality_and_Cost_of_Professional_Counselor_Supervision_A_Qualitative_Descriptive_Study

Deenanath, V. (2017). *Financial concerns and financial stress: Factors influencing first-generation college students' success* [Doctoral dissertation, University of Minnesota]. University Digital Conservancy. https://hdl.handle.net/11299/211745

Deming, D., Goldin, C., & Katz, L. (2013). For-profit colleges. *The Future of Children, 23*(1), 137–163.

EMDR International Association. (n.d.). *EMDR basic training.* EMDRIA. Retrieved October 31, 2025, from https://www.emdria.org/emdr-training/

Federal Student Aid & U.S. Department of Education. (n.d.). *Income-driven repayment plans.* Federal Student Aid. Retrieved October 31, 2025, from https://studentaid.gov/manage-loans/repayment/plans/income-driven

Gottman Institute. (n.d.). *Gottman Method Couples Therapy – Level 1*. The Gottman Institute. Retrieved October 31, 2025, from https://www.gottman.com/professionals/

Hanson, M. (2024). *Average cost of a master's degree*. Education Data Initiative. Retrieved October 31, 2025, from https://educationdata.org/average-cost-of-a-masters-degree

Henfield, M. S., Owens, D., & Witherspoon, S. (2011). African American students in counselor education programs: Perceptions of their experiences. *Counselor Education and Supervision, 50*(4), 226–242. https://doi.org/10.1002/j.1556-6978.2011.tb00121.x

Hill, C. E., Sullivan, C., Knox, S., & Schlosser, L. Z. (2007). Becoming psychotherapists: Experiences of novice trainees in a beginning graduate class. *Psychotherapy: Theory, Research, Practice, Training, 44*(4), 434–449. https://doi.org/10.1037/0033-3204.44.4.434

Kelly, J. (2025). *The counseling supervisory bond: Creating relationships through distance supervision* [Unpublished doctoral dissertation]. Capella University.

Kupczynski, L., Garza, K., & Mundy, M. A. (2018). Counselor self-efficacy: The effects of online preparatory counseling programs. *Journal of Educational Psychology, 12*(1), 1–7.

Lawson, G., & Myers, J. E. (2011). Wellness, professional quality of life, and career-sustaining behaviors: What keeps us well? *Journal of Counseling and Development, 89*(2), 163–171. https://doi.org/10.1002/j.1556-6678.2011.tb00074.x

Michalowicz, M. (2017). *Profit first: Transform your business from a cash-eating monster to a money-making machine*. Portfolio.

Nelson, L. M. (2015). *Off and practicing: Online counseling learners experience as they transition from online coursework into internship fieldwork* (Publication No. 3671937) [Doctoral dissertation, Capella University]. ProQuest Dissertations and Theses Global.

Olson-Garriott, A. N., Garriott, P. O., Rigali-Oiler, M., & Chao, R. C.-L. (2015). Counseling psychology trainees' experiences with debt stress: A mixed methods examination. *Journal of Counseling Psychology, 62*(2), 202–215. https://doi.org/10.1037/cou0000051

Poplaski, S., Kemnitz, R., & Robb, C. A. (2019). Investing in education: Impact of student financial stress on self-reported health. *Journal of Student Financial Aid, 48*(2), Article 3. https://doi.org/10.55504/0884-9153.1611

Rossi, M. (2024). Breaking barriers: Cross-state licensing reform for licensed professional counselors. *Minnesota Journal of Law, Science and Technology, 25*(2), Article 5, 195–220. https://scholarship.law.umn.edu/mjlst/vol25/iss2/5

Shepard, D. (2021). *Addressing social class in counselor education curriculum* [Doctoral dissertation, University of Tennessee, Knoxville]. Tennessee Research and Creative Exchange. https://trace.tennessee.edu/utk_graddiss/7046/

Sinha, G. R., Viswanathan, M., & Larrison, C. R. (2024). Student loan debt and mental health: A comprehensive review of scholarly literature from 1900 to 2019. *Journal of Evidence-Based Social Work, 21*(3), 363–393. https://doi.org/10.1080/26408066.2023.2299019

Snow, W. H., & Coker, J. K. (2020). Distance counselor education: Past, present, future. *The Professional Counselor, 10*(1), 40–56. https://doi.org/10.15241/whs.10.1.40

U.S. Department of Education. (n.d.). Public Service Loan Forgiveness (PSLF). Federal Student Aid. Retrieved October 31, 2025, from https://studentaid.gov/manage-loans/forgiveness-cancellation/public-service

Wardle, E. A., & Mayorga, M. G. (2016). Burnout among the counseling profession: A survey of future professional counselors. *Journal of Educational Psychology, 10*(1), 9–15. https://files.eric.ed.gov/fulltext/EJ1131850.pdf

Williams, J. M., Greenleaf, A. T., Albert, T., & Barnes, E. F. (2014). Promoting educational resilience among African American students at risk of school failure: The role of school counselors. *Journal of School Counseling, 12*(9), n9. https://files.eric.ed.gov/fulltext/EJ1034726.pdf

You Need A Budget. (n.d.). *You need a budget* [Budgeting platform]. Retrieved October 31, 2025, from https://www.youneedabudget.com/

# 5

# Professional and Legal Considerations

This may not be the chapter you were most excited to read. Legal forms? Liability coverage? State board rules and tax codes? Yawn, right?

Trust us: This chapter could save your career. Utilizing the tools in these pages will protect all the hours you spent in school, all the sacrifices you made to get through supervision, and all the effort you put into showing up for your clients, day after day. If we ignore the business side of counseling, especially the legal and ethical foundations on which it rests, we risk building something beautiful on shaky ground.

Counselors spend years learning how to help others, but too many of us overlook the legal and ethical ground on which counseling is built (Remley & Herlihy, 2021). If that ground isn't solid, it won't matter how good you are in the room. You will always be one misstep away from risk. I (Jude) remember renting my first office. I had a logo, business cards, and a fake plant, but I didn't have an LLC or insurance. If something had gone wrong, I would have been exposed. My situation wasn't unique. We all know someone who is "winging it" without realizing how vulnerable that makes them.

This applies to more than just private practice. Whether you work in an agency, supervise, administer workshops, or see clients over Zoom, there are rules. Neglecting to learn those rules won't save you from their consequences (American Counseling Association [ACA], 2014). We cover business structures, licensure, the Health Insurance Portability and Accountability Act (HIPAA), taxes, ethics, and determining when to hire help. Good counseling can't happen when you're constantly looking over your shoulder. Let's build something solid.

## Why This Matters

Protecting your work can be easy to overlook when you're buried in paperwork and trying to help people. No matter where you practice—at an agency, school, private practice, or a supervision gig—you're not solely a clinician. You're also a businessperson. That business side shows up in your documentation, licensure status, consent forms, and policies. Whether we like it or not, business savvy makes this work sustainable.

Most of us weren't trained for this. Graduate school taught us how to build rapport and track affect—not how to read a lease, document a telehealth consent form, or identify a risk to a licensing board. That means we often learn the hard way when something goes wrong. The cost of reactive learning is more than financial. It's also emotional, reputational, and avoidable (Remley & Herlihy, 2021). In agencies, mistakes can cost your job or funding. In group practice, one misstep can affect the entire team.. Even in university settings, ethical or legal misalignment can compromise both clients and careers.

Don't think of legal and ethical systems as red tape—think of them as the skeleton of your practice. When we ignore them, we're not just risking lawsuits—we're risking the ability to keep doing this work. Burnout is more than emotional fatigue. Sometimes, it's the stress of avoidable administrative chaos: surprise audits, unclear policies, or that nagging feeling that you missed something important. It's hard to be present in the counseling room when the back end of your practice feels held together with duct tape.

For example, a couple of years into working at an agency, I (Jude) remember walking into the office one morning to catch up on paperwork before my first client. I was in a good place. My caseload was full, I had a waitlist, and I felt confident in my clinical work. Then I saw him—a man in a sharp suit holding a folder stamped "Confidential." He flashed an FBI badge, and my heart dropped. He explained that he was following up about a former client who was applying for security clearance and that he had a signed release form to speak with me and review my records. He was polite, even kind, but having an FBI agent ask to see your notes puts you on edge.

As we talked, it hit me how much weight our words carry. In that moment, my clinical opinion could shape the course of someone's career. When he left, I sat there thinking about how loose my safety net really was. I had followed all the ethical protocols, but the encounter exposed some cracks in the clinic's systems. We realized how long it was taking us to complete notes and how inconsistent some of our documentation had become. Within weeks, we upgraded our online platform, added structured templates for treatment goals, and reworked our note-writing policies. That experience changed how I thought about the "business" side of counseling—not as red tape, but as the backbone that holds up the work we do. Ethical systems and clinic policies make it possible for our work to stand up under pressure.

This chapter provides clarity and guidance on the underlying administrative, legal, and ethical aspects of your counseling practice. How do you stay legally protected? What does good documentation really look like? When do you bring in a certified public accountant (CPA) or lawyer? How do you manage dual roles or out-of-state clients? When you know the rules, you can stop looking over your shoulder—and stay focused on what matters most.

## Business Structure and Liability

Choosing a business structure might not feel urgent, but it's one of the first and most important decisions you need to make if you're earning money outside of agency work. Whether you're starting a private practice, supervising, consulting, or doing contract work, how you structure your business affects your taxes, liability, and long-term protection (Bartolucci, 2017).

Let's break down your options.

- **Sole proprietorship:** This is the easiest structure to establish. All you need is a name and a bank account, but the downside is that it offers no legal separation between you and your business. That means if you're sued, your personal assets (home, savings, income) are on the line.
- **LLC (Limited Liability Company):** This is the most popular option for solo counselors. It separates your personal and business liabilities and still allows for pass-through taxation (IRS, 2024). It's simple, flexible, and protective.
- **Professional corporations or S corporations:** Some states (like California) don't allow counselors to form LLCs, so counselors set

up professional corporations or elect S corp status for tax benefits (Bartolucci, 2017). But rules vary by state, so it's important to always check.

Even if you're joining a group practice, you need to know if you're a W-2 employee or a 1099 contractor. That simple difference affects your taxes, liability, and insurance coverage (Beidas et al., 2016). Don't assume you're off the hook if you are in agency practice. If you earn income outside your full-time job—say, from supervision, speaking, or weekend clients—you need a separate legal entity. Otherwise, you're exposed.

I (Jude) learned this the hard way. I took on a side supervision contract without a formal business setup. Once money exchanged hands, I realized I had zero protection. That experience pushed me to form an LLC, secure liability insurance, and take the business side of counseling seriously. One of the biggest mistakes counselors make is saying, "It's just one client," or "It's just a quick workshop." Even one gig without a formal business setup can lead to a tax headache, a boundary issue, or a legal mess. By the time you realize you need structure, you might already have fallen behind.

Fortunately, setting up a business today is more accessible than ever. There are CPAs, attorneys, and platforms built for mental health professionals. At a minimum, you need an LLC or S corp, an employer identification number, a business bank account, and liability insurance. Your business structure creates clear boundaries for your time, money, and risk. It's not just about legality. It's about sustainability.

## Licensure and Scope of Practice

Licensure defines your legal boundaries, protects your clients, and anchors your professional identity. It evolves, varies by state, and changes with laws, trends, and technology. Every state has its own licensing board, renewal process, and continuing education requirements. What counts in Texas may not count in California. There's no universal rulebook—especially if you're licensed in more than one state or thinking about relocating (ACA, n.d.).

The rise of telehealth, while advantageous in many ways, complicates the licensure process. Since the COVID-19 pandemic, many counselors have been seeing clients virtually, including across state lines. However, most states require you to be licensed in the state where the client is physically located during the session (the Counseling Compact [n.d.] is changing that, but it is not yet universal) (APA Services, 2020). Good intentions—wanting to treat patients regardless of where they physically are—are part of the job, but they don't protect you from licensing violations. I (Jude) once supervised a counselor who unknowingly provided services to a client who had moved out of state. It felt harmless because they had an existing relationship, but the counselor wasn't licensed in the new state, and that alone made it a violation.

Where you work also matters. In agencies, you often have oversight—clinical directors, audits, and team consults. Your scope may also be shaped by funders, policies, or accreditation standards. You might be fully licensed and still not permitted to do certain work because of the setting. In private or group practice, you're on your own. No one tracks your continuing education units (CEUs), reminds you about jurisprudence exams, or flags when you've drifted out of scope. That autonomy can feel freeing, but it also means you're 100% responsible for staying in bounds.

Unintentional violations are common and costly. Licensing boards don't offer much grace for ignorance. Practicing outside your scope or offering services without proper training can lead to license suspension, fines, or worse (Kaplan et al., 2017). The *ACA Code of Ethics* (2014) makes it clear: Counselors must stay within their competence and seek supervision or training when expanding into new areas. That's not gatekeeping—that's protecting people. Whether you are a brand-new counselor or you have decades of experience, do your due diligence to keep your license clean. Know your laws and take this part of the job as seriously as you take your clinical work. Your clients, your career, and your peace of mind depend on it.

## Insurance and Risk Management

There's a quiet confidence that comes from knowing you are covered—not just clinically, but legally and financially. In counseling, that kind of protection doesn't come automatically. It must be built. Whether you're in private practice, an agency, a school, or juggling side work, insurance is a non-negotiable part of staying professionally safe.

### *The Essentials*

At a minimum, every counselor should have professional liability insurance. This covers legal defense and damages if a client accuses you of harm, even if the claim is unfounded (Walfish & Barnett, 2009). If you see clients in a physical space, you should also consider general liability insurance. It protects you if someone slips, falls, or claims injury on your premises (Zur, 2023).

With the rise of electronic health record (EHR) systems and telehealth, cyber liability insurance is increasingly important. It helps cover costs tied to data breaches, privacy violations, and recovery if protected health information (PHI) is compromised (APA Services, 2020). If you lease space, employ others, or have valuable equipment, consider a business owner's policy (BOP). It combines multiple coverages—including business interruption insurance—into one policy (Walfish & Barnett, 2009).

### Not All Coverage Is Equal

Don't assume you're covered just because you work for an agency or group. Some employers have limited policies that don't extend to off-the-clock work, supervision, or side gigs. If you're an independent contractor (1099), you almost always need your own policy. If you're a W-2 employee, you should double-check what's included. When something goes wrong, liability doesn't care about your job title—it cares whose name is on the chart.

### The Cost of Being Underinsured

Just one complaint can lead to thousands in legal fees. It also brings emotional stress, doubt, and the risk of losing money if you're not protected (Knapp & Fingerhut, 2024). Insurance doesn't prevent problems, but it ensures you won't face them alone.

### It's an Ethical Issue, Too

The *ACA Code of Ethics* (2014) reminds us that competent care includes being prepared for risk. Insurance isn't just smart—it's part of practicing responsibly. Take a moment. Check your policies. Ask questions. Get covered. Hope isn't a reliable safety plan, and your peace of mind is worth protecting.

## Confidentiality, Consent, and HIPAA

Protecting client privacy isn't just ethical—it's the law. Whether you're in private practice, an agency, or part of a group setting, you have a legal and professional responsibility to safeguard client information.

Professional and Legal Considerations

## What You Must Do

Confidentiality starts with securing PHI. That means locking up paper files, encrypting digital records, and being mindful of every phone call, email, and virtual session (Office for Civil Rights, 2024). These responsibilities fall under HIPAA, the federal law that sets the standard for protecting client health information. Before you release any client information, you need a signed release form—period. That form should clearly state what is being shared, with whom, and why. In counseling, this might include sharing treatment updates with a client's primary care physician, collaborating with a psychiatrist about medication management, or coordinating care with a school counselor, probation officer, or family member at the client's request. Sometimes, information is released to insurance companies for billing, or to attorneys or courts when a client provides written consent. Whatever the situation, the guiding principle is the same: Release only what is necessary, only to those specified, and only for the purpose the client has approved (Szalados, 2021). HIPAA compliance isn't a one-time task—it's an ongoing process. Everyone on your team, from administrative staff to interns, should be regularly trained and retrained. Breaches, even accidental ones, can lead to serious penalties and loss of trust among clients (Szalados, 2021).

**Consent, Documentation, and Legal Protection**

Informed consent is more than just a form. It's an ongoing dialogue between you and your client. It should cover the counseling process; the risks, benefits, and limits of confidentiality; and how client data is handled. Revisit it when plans change or new disclosures arise (Corey et al., 2023). Release of information (ROI) forms are separate and specific. There should be no blanket consents. Each ROI form should name the specific person or organization receiving information, describe exactly what will be shared, and state why it is being shared. Clients should have the right to approve or decline each request individually rather than sign one broad consent that covers everything. Fill out each form carefully, store them securely, and remember that thorough documentation is your best legal defense. If something goes wrong, your notes should clearly show that you acted ethically and within your scope (Knapp & Fingerhut, 2024).

**Group and Agency Compliance**

In larger settings, HIPAA compliance is a shared responsibility. Everyone, from clinicians to administrative staff and tech support, needs to know how to protect PHI. Policies, procedures, and regular training should cover everything from breach protocols to proper documentation (Person Centered Tech, n.d.). Compliance protects your license, your clients, and your reputation.

## Telehealth and Cross-State Work

The world of counseling has changed, and one of the biggest shifts has been the rise of telehealth. Whether you conduct Zoom sessions with clients across town or across the country, the flexibility and reach of virtual care are reshaping our profession. However, with that flexibility comes a tangled web of legal and ethical responsibilities, especially when our clients aren't sitting in the same state—or even the same time zone—as we are.

### *The Legal Landscape of Cross-State Practice*

Counselors must be licensed in the state in which the client is physically located during the session, not where the counselor is located. This rule catches many by surprise, especially when long-term clients move or travel (Barnett et al., 2014). What feels like a simple continuation of care can quickly become unlicensed—and therefore illegal—practice.

The Counseling Compact, launched in 2021, is addressing this challenge. It allows eligible Licensed Professional Counselors (LPCs) in participating states to legally provide services across state lines without needing a license in each one (National Center for Interstate Compacts, 2023). This is a game-changer for border-state providers and telehealth specialists. Unfortunately, the Compact is not yet universal, even though it is making good progress. As of 2025, the Counseling Compact is live for licensees in Minnesota and Arizona. The District of Columbia and 37 states passed Counseling Compact legislation and are actively "completing the steps needed to begin issuing and receiving privileges under the Counseling Compact" (Counseling Compact, n.d.). To be eligible for Compact privileges, counselors must hold an active, unencumbered license in their home state, have completed a CACREP-accredited master's program or the equivalent, and have no disciplinary actions on record. These are the baseline requirements established by the Compact itself. However, each participating state may include its own administrative steps, such as background checks, application fees, or state-specific jurisprudence exams, before granting the authority to practice across state lines. Even with the Compact, it is not a blanket pass. If your state is not a member, or if your client is in a non-Compact state, you still need to be licensed where they are. Practicing across state lines without authorization can result in board complaints, license suspension, or civil penalties (Blundell et al., 2022).

## Informed Consent and Crisis Planning in Telehealth

Telehealth requires a different kind of informed consent. It should cover more than just confidentiality and fees—it must explain technology risks, limits of encryption, what happens if the call drops, and who to contact in a crisis (Reamer, 2021). If you're not updating your forms to reflect this, you're not fully covered.

Crisis management becomes trickier in telehealth settings. In person, you know your client's location. Online, unless you ask them, you don't. Counselors should confirm the client's physical location at the start of each session, document it, and follow the appropriate ethical protocol should that client's location prevent counseling from continuing. You should also collect emergency contacts and keep a list of local crisis resources on hand. These proactive steps may just end up being your liability shields.

## Staying Informed and Compliant

Telehealth laws are not static. They shift as state policies evolve, especially as more states join the Counseling Compact. That means counselors must take ownership of staying informed. One way is by regularly checking in with your state's licensing board and signing up for newsletters or alerts. Organizations like ACA and the National Board for Certified Counselors (NBCC) provide regular updates and resources to help you keep your practice compliant. You can also bookmark the Counseling Compact's official website, which includes a real-time map of participating states, updates on legislation, and implementation timelines. If you're a telehealth provider—even part-time—you should be checking that site a few times a year.

# Tax Responsibilities and Financial Compliance

Navigating the financial side of counseling can feel overwhelming, especially when transitioning from agency work to private practice. Understanding tax responsibilities is crucial for maintaining a sustainable and legally compliant practice.

## Quarterly Tax Payments

If you're self-employed—as a sole proprietor, LLC, or S corp—you are required to pay estimated taxes quarterly. These payments include both income tax and self-employment tax, which covers Social Security and Medicare contributions. The Internal Revenue Service mandates these payments if you expect to owe at least $1,000 in taxes for the year (IRS, 2024). Due dates are April 15, June 15, September 15, and January 15 (of the following year).

Missing a payment can result in penalties and interest charges. You can estimate your payments using IRS Form 1040-ES or work with accounting software designed for small businesses. Counselors are strongly advised to set calendar reminders and track income monthly using platforms like QuickBooks or Wave (Legge, 2014).

## Deductible Expenses

Deductions help reduce your taxable income and are a key part of financial efficiency. Common deductions for mental health professionals include:

- Office rent and utilities;
- Professional liability and cyber insurance;
- Continuing education and license renewal fees;
- Marketing and website expenses;
- Telehealth and EHR software; and
- Accounting and legal services.

Keeping detailed records and receipts is essential. A common practice is to scan or photograph receipts at the point of purchase and upload them directly into a secure cloud-based system to prevent data loss or documentation gaps (Gresham, 2017).

## Bookkeeping and Financial Awareness

Bookkeeping provides real-time visibility into your financial health and is foundational for accurate tax reporting. At a minimum, a sound bookkeeping system should record income and expenses, reconcile monthly bank and credit card statements, generate profit and loss statements, and maintain records of deductible business expenses.

Counselors should avoid mixing personal and business finances. Maintaining a dedicated business bank account improves clarity and reduces errors, particularly during tax preparation or audits (Ovharhe & Chukwuemeka, 2023).

## When to Hire a CPA

As your practice grows, hiring a CPA can provide both financial clarity and risk mitigation. A CPA can assist with tax planning and an estimated payment strategy, ensuring federal and state compliance, identifying overlooked deductions, and preparing and filing quarterly and annual returns.

It is recommended that counselors work with CPAs who specialize in health care or small business services. These professionals are more familiar with the specific nuances of mental health practices and can offer tailored advice that general tax professionals may not be equipped to provide (Libby, 2017; Gresham, 2017).

I (Jude) hired a CPA when my private practice started to grow. There was more of everything—more clients, more supervisees, and more moving parts. Even with all of that growth, it was the increased liability that kept me up at night. Supervisees operate with some degree of independence, and I wanted someone who could help me think through how my personal and professional finances were structured to make sure I wasn't overlooking anything.

After talking with other counselors and small business owners in my area, I connected with a local CPA. From the very first meeting, I felt taken care of. She was supportive, practical, and—importantly—honest with me. I had big plans for the practice, and while some of them were solid, others just weren't feasible or carried tax risks I hadn't even considered. That outside perspective helped me dream smarter, not just bigger.

If you're wondering when to bring in a CPA, my advice is to do so as soon as you can afford one. I could have done the taxes myself, but having a professional took a whole category of stress off my plate. Even if you think you can't afford one, call anyway. I used to assume CPAs were only for people with major money, but that's not true. They're people like us—coaches, parents, PTA members—who understand the ins and outs of small businesses and want to help you get it right.

## Core Documents Every Counselor Needs

Let's start with the non-negotiable documents that every practicing counselor should have in place before seeing a single client.

- **Informed consent:** This is the foundation of your relationship with each client. It outlines the scope of services, the risks and benefits of counseling, the limits of confidentiality, and other vital information. Beyond being a legal requirement, it's an opportunity to foster trust through transparency (APA Services, 2020).
- **HIPAA privacy notice:** Required for all HIPAA-covered entities, this document informs clients of how their PHI is used and shared. It should reflect how you actually run your practice, especially if you use digital platforms or cloud storage.
- **Good faith estimate (GFE):** Mandated by the No Surprises Act, this document informs uninsured or self-paying clients of their expected charges (Centers for Medicare and Medicaid Services, n.d.). It's a key part of financial transparency and helps avoid misunderstandings around billing.
- **Cancellation and no-show policies:** These protect your time and energy. Having a clear, upfront policy on how cancellations are handled—and what fees apply—can prevent conflicts down the line.
- **ROI forms:** These authorize you to share client information with specified parties and are a critical tool for staying within ethical and legal boundaries.
- **Supervision agreements:** If you supervise interns or provisionally licensed counselors, this contract should outline expectations, responsibilities, and boundaries for both parties.

When thoughtfully written and revisited as needed, these documents support both ethical practice and peace of mind. They're not just paperwork—they're proactive protection.

## Understanding Contracts: Watch for These Red Flags

Let's talk about contracts, especially if you're joining a group practice, consulting for an agency, or even just picking up side work. Too many counselors have landed in exploitative situations simply because they didn't know what to look for. Here are key contract clauses you need to read very carefully.

### Non-Compete Clauses

These restrict where—and sometimes when—you're allowed to practice after leaving a job. Some prevent you from seeing clients within a specific radius or timeframe, even if those clients followed you. While the Federal Trade Commission and some states are starting to push back against overly restrictive non-competes, they're still enforceable in many areas (Goldstein & Schmid, 2024). Always check your state laws, and don't assume it's "just standard."

**Minimum Employment Periods**

Some contracts require you to stay at a job for a set amount of time, often 12 months. If you leave before the set amount of time ends, you may have to repay costs like onboarding, credentialing, or training. This can make changing jobs expensive or difficult if life circumstances shift. If there's no flexibility written into the clause, that's a red flag.

**Client Ownership**

Make sure you understand who "owns" the client relationship. If you leave the practice, can you keep seeing your clients? Some contracts prohibit it altogether. Others require you to buy out the client list or impose restrictions that make the transition difficult. In private practice, this can affect both your income and continuity of care.

**Pay and Collection Policies**

This is where many counselors get blindsided. Make sure you know how you're paid (i.e., flat fee versus percentage of each session), whether percentages are based on billed or collected revenue, who handles billing and collections, and what happens if a client doesn't pay.

These terms affect your take-home pay, financial stability, and overall job satisfaction (Purtle et al., 2023). Contracts that leave you responsible for unpaid client fees without giving you control over billing are especially risky.

Even if the contract looks simple or comes from someone you trust, hire a health care attorney to review it. It might cost a few hundred dollars, but it could save you thousands, not to mention time, stress, and legal trouble later.

# Compliance and Audits

No one gets into this field because they love documentation audits. A documentation audit is a formal review of your clinical records to make sure your notes, treatment plans, and billing align with ethical, legal, and insurance standards. These audits can come from licensing boards, insurance panels, or internal agency supervisors, and they are designed to confirm that your documentation accurately reflects the care you provide. Compliance is one of those behind-the-scenes responsibilities that can make or break your career. Whether you are in private practice, an agency, or a group setting, it is not enough to be a good counselor. You also have to be organized, ethical, and ready because audits do not give you a warning (Remley & Herlihy, 2021; Walfish & Barnett, 2009).

## What Triggers an Audit?

In both private and agency settings, there are a few common red flags that can trigger an audit.

- **Inconsistent documentation:** Missing or vague progress notes, outdated treatment plans, or disorganized charts are major triggers. If your documentation doesn't support the clinical services you billed for, you are vulnerable (Wheeler & Bertram, 2019).
- **Billing discrepancies:** This includes overbilling, underbilling, or using incorrect billing codes, especially for insurance-based practices or Medicaid-funded programs. Even honest mistakes can raise red flags (Sampson, 2016).
- **Client complaints:** One disgruntled client can initiate an investigation. If their experience doesn't align with your paperwork, you may find yourself on the defensive regardless of your clinical intent (Knapp & Fingerhut, 2024).

Audits can come from multiple sources: state boards, insurance companies, licensing agencies, or accreditation bodies. When they show up, they don't just skim the surface—they comb through your records, systems, and communications (Corey et al., 2023).

## Building an "Audit-Ready" Practice

The best way to survive an audit is to always be ready for one. Don't live in fear. Instead, build solid systems now so you're not scrambling later (Wheeler & Bertram, 2019; Corey et al., 2023).

### Use a Reliable EHR System

Make sure it timestamps your notes, prompts for treatment plan updates, and stores ROIs and consent forms securely. A compliant EHR system not only improves workflow but also meets HIPAA privacy and security requirements (Reamer, 2021).

### Back Up Your Files

Even if you're using a cloud-based system, it's smart to have secure local backups and a written data recovery plan. This is essential for minimizing data loss and ensuring continuity of care during tech failures or cyber threats (APA Services, 2020; Zur, 2023).

### Document Consultations

Any time you consult with a peer, supervisor, or legal professional, jot it down in a progress note or designated log. This shows that you took thoughtful, ethical steps in complex situations and helps support your decisions during review (Knapp & VandeCreek, 2012).

### Review Your Billing Codes Regularly

If you use insurance, make sure the services billed match the services documented. Mismatches—even accidental ones—can trigger audits or accusations of fraud (Weltman, 2020; Wheeler & Bertram, 2019). If you outsource billing, meet quarterly with your biller to confirm accuracy and resolve discrepancies.

### Update Client Records Routinely

Don't wait for a crisis to update informed consent forms, emergency contact information, or treatment plans. Routine maintenance of clinical records is a core component of both risk management and ethical practice (Corey et al., 2023; Remley & Herlihy, 2021).

## *Staying on Top of Compliance*

Personally, I (Jude) like to schedule what I call "Admin Days" about once a month. It's a day I set aside specifically to update forms, review caseload documentation, check on billing, and read through any updates from my board or professional associations. Twice a year, I "audit myself." I pretend I'm the licensing board, and I randomly select 2–3 files. If something feels incomplete or out of alignment, I fix it. Checklists are also lifesavers. I use checklists for new client onboarding, documentation procedures, and end-of-service file closures. When things get busy—and they always do—those checklists keep me from dropping the ball.

Compliance is about being prepared. When you take the time to build systems that work, you don't have to fear the email that says, "We're reviewing your files." You can keep your focus where it belongs—on your clients.

## Protect the Work So You Can Keep Doing the Work

You didn't choose this field to become a tax expert, legal scholar, or compliance officer. You chose it because you care about people. If you're going to build a career that lasts—one that gives you the freedom to keep showing up for clients year after year—you have to protect what you've built.

Professional and legal considerations may not be what drew you to counseling, but they are what allow you to keep doing it. Setting up the right business structure, staying within your legal scope, securing insurance, documenting wisely, and knowing when to call in help are stewardship. It's the behind-the-scenes discipline that makes the front-of-the-room work possible.

The good news is that you don't have to be perfect; you just have to be proactive. Surround yourself with the right professionals, stay curious about your obligations, and treat your business like something worth protecting. You and your clients deserve that.

The counselors who last in this field aren't just clinically sharp. They're also organized, protected, and prepared. So, breathe deep. Take it one step at a time. Revisit the checklists, review your contracts, and schedule your admin days. When your foundation is solid, you're freer to focus on what matters most: the people you're here to help. Let this chapter serve as a reminder that protecting your practice is part of protecting your purpose.

# References

American Counseling Association. (2014). *ACA Code of Ethics*. ACA. https://www.counseling.org/docs/default-source/default-document-library/ethics/2014-aca-code-of-ethics.pdf

American Counseling Association. (n.d.). *Licensure requirements*. ACA. Retrieved October 28, 2025, from https://www.counseling.org/resources/licensure-requirements

APA Services. (2020). *Telepsychology best practice 101 series: Legal and ethical telepractice guidelines*. American Psychological Association. https://apa.content.online/catalog/product.xhtml?eid=15132&eid=1921

Barnett, J. E., Zimmerman, J., & Walfish, S. (2014). *The ethics of private practice: A practical guide for mental health clinicians*. Oxford University Press.

Bartolucci, A. D. (2017). *Business basics for private practice: A guide for mental health professionals*. Routledge.

Beidas, R. S., Stewart, R. E., Benjamin Wolk, C., Adams, D. R., Marcus, S. C., Evans, A. C., Jr., Jackson, K., Neimark, G., Hurford, M. O., Erny, J., Rubin, R., Hadley, T. R., Barg, F. K., & Mandell, D. S. (2016). Independent contractors in public mental health clinics: Implications for use of evidence-based practices. *Psychiatric Services, 67*(7), 710–717. https://doi.org/10.1176/appi.ps.201500234

Blundell, P., Oakley, L., & Kinmond, K. (2022). Who are we protecting? Exploring counsellors' understanding and experience of boundaries. *European Journal of Qualitative Research in Psychotherapy, 12*, 13–28.

Centers for Medicare and Medicaid Services. (n.d.). *No surprises: What's a good faith estimate?* Centers for Medicare and Medicaid Services. Retrieved October 28, 2025, from https://www.cms.gov/files/document/nosurpriseactfactsheet-whats-good-faith-estimate508c.pdf

Corey, G., Muratori, M., Austin, J. T., II, & Austin, J. A. (2023). *Counselor self-care* (2nd ed.). American Counseling Association.

Counseling Compact. (n.d.). *Compact map*. Retrieved October 28, 2025, from https://counselingcompact.gov/map/

Goldstein, M. S., & Schmid, B. L. (2024, July 11). The Federal Trade Commission's attempt to ban U.S. non-compete agreements. *Reuters*. https://www.reuters.com/legal/legalindustry/

federal-trade-commissions-attempt-ban-us-non-compete-agreements-why-what-next-2024-07-11/

Gresham, M. (2017). Financial planning for the private practitioner. In S. Walfish, J. E. Barnett, & J. Zimmerman (Eds.), *Handbook of private practice: Keys to success for mental health practitioners* (pp. 206-221). Oxford University Press. https://doi.org/10.1093/med:psych/9780190272166.003.0018

Internal Revenue Service (IRS). (2024). *Small business and self-employed tax center.* IRS. https://www.irs.gov/businesses/small-businesses-self-employed

Kaplan, D. M., Francis, P. C., Hermann, M. A., Baca, J. V., Goodnough, G. E., Hodges, S., Spurgeon, S. L., & Wade, M. E. (2017). New concepts in the 2014 *ACA Code of Ethics. Journal of Counseling and Development, 95*(1), 110–120. https://doi.org/10.1002/jcad.12122

Knapp, S. J., & Fingerhut, R. (2024). *Practical ethics for psychologists: A positive approach* (4th ed.). American Psychological Association. https://doi.org/10.1037/0000375-000

Knapp, S. J., & VandeCreek, L. D. (2012). *Practical ethics for psychologists: A positive approach* (2nd ed.). American Psychological Association. https://doi.org/10.2307/j.ctv1chrr1z

Legge, D. (2014). Financial planning can yield higher returns for your private practice. *The Advocate, 37*(10), 26+. https://link.gale.com/apps/doc/A427008056/AONE?u=txshracd2593&sid=googleScholar&xid=5c106469

Libby, D. (2017). The role of a certified public accountant in planning, structuring, and running a private practice. In S. Walfish, J. E. Barnett, & J. Zimmerman (Eds.), *Handbook of private practice: Keys to success for mental health practitioners* (pp. 191–198). Oxford University Press. https://doi.org/10.1093/med:psych/9780190272166.003.0016

National Center for Interstate Compacts. (2023). *The Counseling Compact 2022 annual report.* Council of State Governments. https://counselingcompact.gov/wp-content/uploads/2025/02/annual-report-2022-counseling-compact.pdf

Office for Civil Rights. (2024). *Health information privacy.* U.S. Department of Health and Human Services (HHS). https://www.hhs.gov/hipaa

Ovharhe, O. H., & Chukwuemeka, S. P. (2023). Sustainable development goals: Therapeutic entrepreneurship and mental health conditions.

*British Journal of Multidisciplinary and Advanced Studies, 4*(1), 81–119. https://doi.org/10.37745/bjmas.2022.0107

Person Centered Tech. (n.d.). *Group practice optimization and HIPAA compliance system.* Person Centered Tech. Retrieved October 31, 2025, from https://personcenteredtech.com/start-here-for-group-practices/

Purtle, J., Wynecoop, M., Crane, M. E., & Stadnick, N. A. (2023). Earmarked taxes for mental health services in the United States: A local and state legal mapping study. *The Milbank Quarterly, 101*(2), 457–485. https://doi.org/10.1111/1468-0009.12643

Reamer, F. G. (2021). *Ethics and risk management in online and distance social work.* Cognella.

Remley, T. P., & Herlihy, B. (2021). *Ethical, legal, and professional issues in counseling* (6th ed.). Pearson.

Sampson, A. (2016). Risk management in practice. In M. J. Murphy & L. Hecker (Eds.), *Ethics and professional issues in couple and family therapy* (2nd ed., pp. 151–172). Routledge.

Szalados, J. E. (2021). Medical records and confidentiality: Evolving liability issues inherent in the electronic health record, HIPAA, and cybersecurity. In J. E. Szalados (Ed.), *The medical-legal aspects of acute care medicine: A resource for clinicians, administrators, and risk managers* (pp. 315–342). Springer International Publishing. https://doi.org/10.1007/978-3-030-68570-6_13

Walfish, S., & Barnett, J. E. (2009). *Financial success in mental health practice: Essential tools and strategies for practitioners.* American Psychological Association. https://doi.org/10.1037/11851-000

Wheeler, A. M., & Bertram, B. (2019). *The counselor and the law: A guide to legal and ethical practice.* American Counseling Association.

Zur, O. (2023). *Risk management: Toward ethical risk management practices.* Zur Institute. https://www.zurinstitute.com/courses/risk-management-ethical-practices/overview/

# 6

# Traditional Business

There's something quietly thrilling about opening the door to your own practice for the first time. There's no agency overhead or clinical director waving another form in your face. It's just you, your work, and the clients you're called to serve. For a lot of counselors, private practice is the dream. But here's the catch: it's not the *only* dream—and it shouldn't be the only one we discuss.

Too often, "business" in counseling gets reduced to solo practice. You graduate, get licensed, open an office, and hope your Psychology Today profile does the trick. That's just one version of a much bigger story. Some of the most respected, impactful, and well-paid counselors we know have never built a website or posted a single reel. They're thriving in government agencies, hospitals, schools, universities, nonprofits, and community clinics. Yes, some go on to start their own practice. Others don't, and they're not any less successful because of it.

This chapter gives you the full picture before you commit to one narrow path. It seeks to reclaim the word "traditional" and expand it to include all the solid, time-tested roles that have supported counselors and clients for decades. This chapter equips those of you who do want to run your own practice with the foundational tools to build something sustainable.

Wherever you are in your journey—just starting, years into agency work, or dreaming of your own office—we hope this chapter helps you breathe a little deeper. You have more options than you think, and every one of them is valid.

## The Myth of the "Only Way"

Private practice is not the only path to a good life in counseling. We love private practice. We've built our careers around it. We teach it and celebrate it, but somewhere along the way, it seems to have been put on a pedestal. It's pitched as the ultimate goal, the true sign that you've "made it" as a counselor. That mindset is misleading, and honestly, it's exhausting. It pushes new graduates into solo business ownership before they're ready and feeds a subtle shame for anyone who chooses a more traditional role. That needs to stop.

There are many ways to build a meaningful, financially stable, and mission-driven counseling career. Government jobs, agency work, school and college counseling positions, and hospital roles are all necessary and offer features private practice can't: predictable income, steady benefits, built-in referrals, and, in many cases, a stronger sense of community. These jobs are the cornerstones of the profession.

You can be an incredible counselor without ever needing a website, a logo, or a Psychology Today profile. Some of the most clinically gifted counselors we know have never directly billed a client. They show up every day in jails, schools, VA hospitals, and residential facilities to do the kind of work that keeps society afloat (Substance Abuse and Mental Health Services Administration [SAMHSA], 2024).

Not everyone is wired to be an entrepreneur. It's a preference. Some counselors crave structure, a team, and the chance to focus purely on the clinical without the burden of marketing, scheduling, and taxes. Some need the stability of a regular paycheck and health insurance. Some want mentorship, supervision, or the chance to work within a system to change it from the inside. All of that is good. All of that counts.

Before we dive into the ins and outs of private practice, take a breath. If you want to work a government job with benefits and clock out at 5 p.m., do it. If you want to join a nonprofit that aligns with your values, go for it. If you want to stay in higher education or become the go-to trauma counselor for a school district, the field needs you. Success in counseling isn't one-size-fits-all. The sooner we release that myth, the freer we become.

# Traditional Counseling Careers That Pay the Bills

In American society, entrepreneurial hustle gets all the praise. Everywhere you turn, someone is urging you to start your own thing, build a brand, and "scale" your practice. We want to recenter something important: You can have a stable, fulfilling, and financially sustainable career in counseling without ever being your own boss. Many of the most seasoned and impactful counselors we know work within already established systems—agencies, schools, hospitals, and government organizations. These roles come with structure, benefits, and built-in caseloads. They often offer clinical supervision, growth opportunities, and community impact that's hard to replicate in private practice.

## Community Mental Health and Nonprofits

Community mental health agencies and nonprofit organizations are critical hubs of care for underserved populations. These roles often place you at the intersection of mental health and social justice. Counselors in these settings typically work with clients navigating housing instability, trauma, severe mental illness, or substance use, all while collaborating with wraparound services like case management, housing support, and legal aid.

The pay is often modest compared to private practice, but the training and supervision opportunities are unmatched. Many agencies provide structured pathways to licensure, with built-in supervision and regular case consultations (Craig & Sprang, 2010). You work with diverse populations and clinical presentations that deepen your skills quickly. Burnout, driven by productivity demands, complex caseloads, and limited resources (Morse et al., 2012), is a documented concern. However, many clinicians report that these positions offer meaning and purpose that outweigh their challenges (Troup et al., 2022).

### Getting Started

Start with your internship or practicum. Many community agencies rely on interns and develop a "grow-from-within" hiring model. Show up consistently, get to know the team, and ask thoughtful questions. In other words, work hard to get your foot in the door.

Lean into generalist experience. These organizations often seek counselors who are flexible, coachable, and comfortable with a wide variety of clinical presentations. Demonstrating that you're open to training and growth goes a long way (Barnett et al., 2007).

Look for nonprofit job boards and networks. Beyond the usual sites (i.e., Indeed, LinkedIn), try platforms like Idealist.org, the National Council for Mental Wellbeing, and your state's mental health department website. These agencies don't always advertise on the big commercial boards.

Become familiar with Medicaid systems. Many community-based programs are funded through Medicaid or grant-based contracts. Garnering even a basic understanding of documentation, coding, and outcome tracking will set you apart.

Demonstrate that you are both ethical and efficient. Productivity expectations exist, so agencies are drawn to clinicians who can balance relational depth with time-sensitive documentation and scheduling. If you've worked in fast-paced roles before, even outside counseling, highlight that experience.

Above all, lead with your "why." These settings are full of people who care deeply about justice, equity, and healing. If that's you, say so. Let your mission be part of your application.

## *School Counseling*

School counselors serve on the front lines of student development. Their work spans mental health support, academic planning, crisis intervention, career readiness, and social-emotional development. It's a role that shapes lives, and sometimes saves them. With public retirement systems, health insurance, union protections, and predictable hours, school counseling offers a unique blend of purpose and stability. Summers off? Maybe. Steady work with built-in impact? Almost always. But let's be clear: This isn't private practice in a school building.

Too many counselors enter school systems with unrealistic expectations. We've seen students picture their future roles as blends of play counseling, college advising, and classroom push-ins. While some of that may be true in well-funded schools, the reality can look very different. Most school counselors carry large student caseloads, face high expectations for testing and documentation, and find themselves navigating unclear job descriptions (Lambie & Williamson, 2004). Depending on the district, you might coordinate 504 plans. These plans provide legally required accommodations for students with disabilities under Section 504 of the Rehabilitation Act of 1973. You may also manage disciplinary cases or supervise lunch duty (Goodman-Scott & Boulden, 2020).

Despite these challenges, school counselors report high levels of career satisfaction, especially when they can focus on relational work with students (Gündüz, 2012). The ability to journey with students through critical developmental stages, as far-reaching as middle school identity crises to post-high school planning, is a deep privilege.

**Getting Started**

Earn a state-approved school counseling degree. Most states require a master's degree in counseling or a closely related field with a concentration in school counseling, plus coursework in areas like educational law, developmental theory, and multicultural counseling.

Get certified and licensed for schools. Requirements vary by state, but you will often need to pass an exam like the Praxis School Guidance and Counseling test or meet specific coursework and internship hours (American School Counselor Association, n.d.). Some states also require teacher certification even if you don't plan to teach.

Complete a school-based internship. Your internship or practicum should be in an actual K–12 school and supervised by a certified school counselor. Many districts hire directly from their intern pool, so treat this like a semester-long job interview.

Get fluent in educational lingo. Understand how key systems like the Family Educational Rights and Privacy Act (FERPA), Response to Intervention (RTI), Multi-Tiered Systems of Support (MTSS), Individualized Education Programs (IEPs), and Section 504 plans (504s) operate within school settings. These are not just acronyms. They shape how support is delivered, how students are protected, and how counselors collaborate across teams. School counselors are expected to be team players who can bridge conversations with teachers, administrators, and families.

Clarify the culture of your district. One school counseling job may be heavy on scheduling and standardized testing. Another might be deeply trauma-informed with a robust wellness curriculum. Ask about role expectations during the interview process.

Even with its stressors, school counseling is a field that allows you to embed yourself in a community, build multiyear relationships with students, and witness growth over time. If you're drawn to systemic impact and structured environments, this is one of the most rewarding tracks in the profession.

## *Government and Veterans Affairs Jobs*

If you're looking for job security, strong benefits, and a clear clinical structure, government and VA positions are worth serious consideration.

These roles offer some of the most stable and well-compensated positions in the counseling field, often with union protection, robust benefits packages, and a mission-focused environment.

Counselors in these positions might work in crisis response units, rehabilitation centers, outpatient mental health clinics, veterans' hospitals, or family support programs. The work can range from post-traumatic stress disorder (PTSD) and trauma recovery to substance use interventions, case management, and integrated health care delivery. These settings often emphasize team-based models, wherein you are part of a multidisciplinary group that includes psychiatrists, social workers, medical providers, and peer support specialists (Cully et al., 2008).

The beauty of these roles is that you don't need to brand yourself. You don't have to network to fill your caseload or worry about billing platforms. You can focus on deep, long-term, and structured care while your paycheck shows up predictably on the 1st and the 15th. With federal holidays, defined retirement systems, and upward mobility options, it's a career track that lets you grow with both purpose and stability (Zivin et al., 2022). Of course, there are trade-offs. Government systems can be slow-moving. Policy changes take time. Paperwork can be dense. For many, the benefits outweigh the bureaucracy.

**Getting Started**

Get credentialed appropriately. For most federal and state jobs, a master's degree in counseling or a related field from a Council for Accreditation of Counseling and Related Educational Programs-accredited (CACREP) program is preferred. Licensure as a licensed professional counselor (LPC) or equivalent is often required, and many VA roles prioritize candidates with licensure plus supervision experience.

Use the federal job portal. Most VA and federal mental health positions are posted on USAJOBS.gov. This site can be intimidating, so take time to understand federal resume formatting and include relevant keywords like "mental health counselor," "case manager," and "behavioral health specialist."

Highlight trauma-informed and veteran-specific training. If you've completed training in areas like PTSD treatment, suicide prevention, eye-movement desensitization and reprocessing (EMDR), or military culture, make sure to spotlight that. These experiences stand out in VA applications and show readiness for high-need roles.

Get federal internship or practicum experience if possible. Some VA systems offer training opportunities to graduate students. These internships can lead to job offers after graduation and help you understand the VA's documentation and delivery systems.

Consider rural or underserved placements. These positions often have fewer applicants and may come with loan repayment options through the National Health Service Corps or VA-specific incentives (Spoont et al., 2015).

Government work isn't just a fallback. For many counselors, it's the ideal long-term home. You can serve with integrity, grow with structure, and focus on impact without the business pressure. Sometimes, a predictable paycheck, a pension plan, and a team that has your back are exactly what you need to thrive.

## *University and College Counseling Centers*

If you love developmental work and appreciate academic rhythms, university counseling centers (UCCs) might feel like home. These positions let you work with emerging adults navigating identity formation, grief, relational chaos, academic pressure, family expectations, and, sometimes, existential collapse. The work is meaningful, and the setting is often vibrant.

UCC jobs typically align with the academic calendar, offer professional development funding, and emphasize short-term, evidence-based modalities like cognitive behavioral therapy (CBT), acceptance and commitment therapy (ACT), or brief psychodynamic therapy (Sharkin, 2012). These centers are generally embedded in the student affairs ecosystem, meaning you will collaborate with residence life, academic support, and Title IX offices, especially when addressing trauma or crisis care.

UCCs aren't immune to pressure. Demand is high. Many centers are understaffed, and counselors face increasing caseloads, administrative expectations, and short-session models that sometimes clash with client needs. Even so, research has shown that clinicians in UCCs often report high job satisfaction, citing team collaboration, institutional mission, and ongoing learning opportunities as key motivators (Gallagher, 2014).

**Getting Started**

Get campus-based experience. If you're in graduate school, push to complete your internship at a UCC. These sites often give hiring preference to former trainees who already understand the setting's pace and expectations.

Emphasize your work with young adults. In your resume and interviews, highlight experience with developmental issues typical to this age group, such as identity confusion, academic anxiety, relational trauma, and life transitions.

Build clinical range. UCCs value counselors who are both flexible and grounded. Training in suicide prevention, group counseling, substance use, and trauma care—especially related to sexual assault or marginalized identity stress—will help you stand out.

Expect short-term, high-acuity care. Some centers cap sessions (e.g., 6–12 per academic year). Others operate on a "stepped care" model. Understand these structures and be ready to explain how your clinical style aligns with them.

Fit the culture, not just the credentials. We've both worked in UCCs. Like anywhere, the culture of the team matters. Some clinics thrive on transparency, collegiality, and shared values. Others don't. If you're interviewing, ask yourself what it might be like to share clinical space with the team. Are they growth-oriented? Do they reflect the diversity of the student body? Do they seem emotionally available, or emotionally exhausted?

UCCs aren't the fantasy of long-term counseling with sleepy undergrads. They're fast-paced, deep-feeling, high-impact environments. If you're someone who thrives on growth, loves collaboration, and values the energy of campus life, this might be your lane.

## *Hospitals and Integrated Care Systems*

If you're a team player who thrives in high-paced environments, hospitals, and integrated care settings might be your sweet spot. These roles embed counselors within interdisciplinary treatment teams—working shoulder-to-shoulder with physicians, nurses, social workers, case managers, and physical health providers to treat the whole person, not just the symptoms. You're not just an add-on. You're an integral part of care delivery.

Integrated behavioral health is designed to bridge the gap between mental and physical health, especially for patients who may never make it to a standalone counseling office. You will often work with clients experiencing chronic illness, acute pain, medical trauma, or comorbid mental health and substance use concerns (Blount, 2003). That necessitates quick assessments, solution-focused interventions, and seamless referrals to external care when needed.

These positions are typically salaried and come with strong benefits like health insurance, retirement contributions, paid training, and CME/CEU stipends. You will also gain experience in documentation systems, interdisciplinary care planning, and outcome-based service delivery. These skills translate into nearly every other setting in the counseling field.

## When Private Practice Still Calls You

This path calls to counselors for many reasons. The freedom to set your schedule, choose your clients, and design a work life that aligns with your values is powerful. For some, it is less about money and more about reclaiming time. For others, it is about creating a space where your therapeutic identity does not get diluted by red tape or misaligned agency priorities. When done well, private practice can be a deeply creative, liberating way to live out your calling (Schwab, 2016).

However, private practice is not an escape hatch. It is a business. Like any business, it comes with risks. It asks you to juggle roles: counselor, scheduler, marketer, biller, bookkeeper, and compliance officer. It asks you to withstand the slow build and to show up before you're full, before the calls come in, and, maybe, before you fully believe in yourself. That can be disorienting.

The trade-offs of private practice are considerable. You will trade a salary for the potential of profit, but that comes with uncertainty and volatility, especially in the first stages. You will trade a team for autonomy, but that can also mean isolation. You will trade structured systems for freedom, but you will have to build those systems yourself. And if you are not careful, you will go from hating your 9-5 to being crushed by your 24/7.

Many counselors step into private practice after they've done time in structured settings such as community agencies, schools, and clinics. There, they honed their clinical voice, deepened their skills, and saw what they loved (and did not love) about different populations. That experience is a gift. It can give you a foundation on which to build and a clear sense of what kind of practice fits your life and your values.

Studies have shown that counselors with prior agency or institutional experience report greater satisfaction and clinical confidence when transitioning into private practice, compared to those who jump in at once post-licensure (Landon et al., 2021). The slower path is not a sign of hesitation. It is a sign of intentionality. If private practice is calling you, listen. But also check in with yourself: Do you know who you want to serve and why? Do you have a plan for the business side of counseling? Do you have the emotional bandwidth to hold risk right now? Do you know who to call when you hit a wall?

If your answers are yes—or even "I'm getting there"—then you are in a good place to begin. Private practice is not the right move for everyone, but for the right person at the right time, it is a beautiful, brave next step.

I (Jude) never wanted to go into private practice. My private practice had to sneak up and find me. I'm a "1st and 15th" type of person. I like a paycheck that shows up on time without me needing to chase it down. I didn't want to know how QuickBooks worked, and I didn't think about quarterly taxes or how much liability insurance costs when you add interns. I just wanted to show up, sit down, help people in my community, and then slink out the back door to live my life.

For a while, that worked. My primary job was teaching and training counselors. Clinical work was never my main hustle. It was how I kept my edges sharp, how I stayed grounded in the realities my students were preparing for. Agency work or a group practice made sense. Someone else ran the show, and I got to be the designated hitter. Do the work, then go home.

Even low-maintenance setups come with trade-offs. Red tape accompanied the comfort of group practice. The longer I stayed, the more I noticed the service slowly shifting into compliance. I was spending more time explaining documentation procedures than actually documenting. I started to feel the drag. My caseload picked up. The onboarding process for new clients felt clunky. Something that used to be simple—sitting with people and doing the work—started to feel off. I found myself asking questions: "Why do we do it this way?" "What's the reason behind this form?" "Is this policy about care or about covering liability?"

Slowly, my identity started to shift. The guy who always wanted to stay in his lane—who proudly avoided the business side—started thinking, "If not me, then who?" If the frustration is getting louder, maybe it's because it's time to take more ownership. I didn't leap into private practice. I drifted into it, nudged by a string of small irritations and bigger realizations. The old system stopped fitting, and that's okay. It had its time.

If you're there, sitting in a job that's mostly good but starting to feel cramped, don't ignore that feeling. It might not mean you need to quit tomorrow or open an office next month. It might just mean it's time to get curious and ask what kind of practice would actually work for you. You get to define what freedom looks like, and if you're anything like me, you might find that the path you were avoiding is actually the one you've been building all along.

## Setting Up a Counseling Practice

There are a lot of books about how to start and run a private practice. Counselors today have access to more practical, business-savvy resources than ever before. If you're hungry to go deeper, here are a few standout titles from the last few years that can complement what you will find in this chapter:

- *The Profitable Private Practice: How to Start, Run, and Grow Your Therapy Business* by Melissa DaSilva (2019) – A clear, systems-driven roadmap for building a scalable, financially stable practice. Think structure, delegation, and sustainability.
- *The Purposeful and Profitable Therapist's Guide on Diversifying Income* by Dr. Anita M. Robinson (2024) – A must-read if you want to earn ethically beyond the counseling hour. Great for counselors exploring workshops, consulting, or online courses.
- *The Graduate Course You Never Had: How to Develop, Manage, and Market a Flourishing Mental Health Practice* (2nd ed.) by Dr. Larry Waldman (2021) – A short, straight-to-the-point book filled with practical tips that grad school forgot to teach you.
- *Building Your Counseling Empire: From Start to Success* by Laura Blair (2023) – A newer, approachable read that encourages counselors to dream bigger without losing their clinical integrity.

**Legal Structures and Tax Status**

Choosing the right legal structure for your business matters more than most clinicians realize. A sole proprietorship might be the easiest way to get started, but it offers little protection. An LLC (Limited Liability Company) gives you more legal and financial security, separating your personal assets from your business. For some practices that grow in scale or complexity, an S corporation election—made through the IRS—can offer major tax advantages. The key here is simple: Don't make this decision in isolation. Talk with a CPA or small business attorney who understands mental health practices. You don't want to backtrack later because of a filing mistake or missed tax benefit.

Here's a quick breakdown of common business structures:

| Structure | Liability Protection | Tax Treatment | Best for |
|---|---|---|---|
| Sole proprietorship | None (personal assets at risk) | Income is taxed as personal income | Counselors testing the waters or moonlighting |
| LLC | Yes | Pass-through (protests taxed once) | Solo practitioners seeking protection and simplicity |
| S corp (via LLC) | Yes | Salary taxed and profits taxed as dividends | Growing practices wanting to save on self-employment taxes |
| C corp | Yes | Double taxation (corporate and personal) | Larger businesses with employees and complex structures |

You don't need to have everything perfect on day one—but establishing separation early helps you build credibility with clients, protects your personal assets, and keeps tax season from becoming a nightmare.

**Start-Up Costs and Budgeting**

It's possible to start a counseling practice with minimal investment, but "minimal" doesn't mean "zero." Typical start-up costs can include liability insurance, website creation, telehealth platform fees, electronic health record (EHR) systems, basic office furniture (if you're going in-person), and initial marketing expenses. These are the foundational investments that help you open ethically, legally, and professionally (Carney & Granato, 2000).

One of the best things you can do early on is create a lean 6–12-month budget. Map out your personal financial needs (like rent, student loans, health insurance) and your practice's operating costs (monthly software fees, supervision, marketing). Then ask yourself:

- How many clients do I need to see each week to break even?
- How many to pay myself well?
- How many to take time off without financial stress?

Thinking this way doesn't make you cold or money-driven—it makes you steady. It helps you build something that lasts. In a profession built on being fully present, financial stability is a gift you give both yourself and your clients (Danco, 1982).

## Business Permits and Zoning

Many cities and counties require businesses to register locally, even if you're operating solo from home. This might include a home occupation permit or business license. Check your local zoning laws, especially if clients will be coming to your house. The last thing you want is a legal notice about violating a residential zone policy.

## Malpractice and Liability Insurance

As soon as you're operating independently, you need liability insurance. This is non-negotiable. Providers like CPH & Associates (n.d.) or HPSO (n.d.) offer policies specifically designed for counselors. Make sure your policy includes both general liability (in case someone slips and falls in your office) and professional liability (in case a client has a grievance or formal complaint). You will also want to check whether your policy is occurrence-based or claims-made. Occurrence-based policies provide lifetime coverage for incidents that occurred while the policy was active—even if the claim is filed later. Claims-made policies only cover incidents that are reported while the policy is active. Know what you're buying.

### Other Essential Insurances

If you're renting a space, you may be required to carry business property insurance. If you're providing telehealth, look into cyber liability insurance, which protects you in the event of a data breach. If you hire anyone, even a part-time assistant, you may be required by law to carry workers' compensation insurance.

## Contracts and Informed Consent

Written policies protect everyone, including you, your clients, and your business. At minimum, have a signed informed consent form that outlines confidentiality, fees, cancellation policy, risks, and benefits of counseling, and emergency procedures. Many counselors also include a Good Faith Estimate in compliance with the No Surprises Act (Centers for Medicare & Medicaid Services, 2022). You can create your own documents, adapt professional templates, or work with an attorney to draft a custom set. Just make sure they're legally sound and clinically clear. Strong paperwork isn't just risk management—it's professional integrity (Zur, n.d.).

### Serving Diverse Communities

A welcoming environment also means considering access and representation. Are your materials available in multiple languages? Is your website screen reader-friendly? Do you offer evening or weekend hours for clients who can't take time off work? Representation matters. Whether it's the art on your wall or the people in your network, clients notice when they're reflected and when they're not (Sue et al., 2015). Designing with inclusion in mind is part of the clinical work.

# Building Your Brand: Marketing Strategies for Counselors

## What Is a Brand for a Counselor?

Your brand isn't just your logo or your color scheme. It's the emotional tone you set across every client touchpoint, from your Psychology Today profile to the signature on your email. A strong brand reflects who you are, how you work, and who you're best equipped to serve. It's not about being loud—it's about being clear. A clear brand attracts the right clients and repels the ones who need something different. That's a good thing.

## Website, Directories, and SEO

You don't need a $5,000 website to have a powerful online presence. What you do need is a clean, mobile-responsive site that explains who you are, what you offer, how to book, and how to contact you. If your audience is local, make sure your site is customized for local search terms (e.g., "anxiety counseling Lafayette, Louisiana") and utilize search engine optimization (SEO). List your practice on key directories like Psychology Today, Therapy Den, or Inclusive Therapists. These platforms are often where clients start their search, and good profiles convert.

## Business Is a Healing Practice

You can be both a healer and a business owner. You can think strategically and act compassionately. You can charge ethically and still rest freely. Building a counseling business isn't separate from the work—it is the work. It's the container that allows your presence to thrive. With the right tools, structure, and vision, it can hold you just as well as you hold others.

*Traditional Business*

You've read about choosing a location, designing your space, and setting up your systems. Most private practices don't start with a grand opening and a full caseload. They start in the margins. They start after hours. They start in the mind of someone who has more passion than time. What follows is a glimpse into that beginning—from vision to grind. Arkitia Pegram-Crawley, LPC, is the owner of Moving Forward Counseling & Consulting, LLC, in Virginia. Arkitia's story reminds us that starting a traditional practice is rarely neat, but always meaningful.

## Voices from the Field

### ARKITIA PEGRAM-CRAWLEY, LPC

In January 2019, I completed my residency hours in Virginia. It was finally time to study for the licensure exam, which I scheduled for April. Truthfully, I gave myself plenty of space to procrastinate, avoid, and—let's be honest—freak out. I dabbled in practice tests, but it wasn't until mid-March that I had a wake-up call. I could not afford to take this exam more than once. That moment shifted everything. I created a focused 30-day study plan and passed the exam on my first attempt.

At the time, I was balancing my roles as a full-time counselor, wife, and mother to a three-year-old. Although I was grateful, I recognized a growing need for more flexibility and financial options. The idea of private practice emerged, but so did a wave of anxiety. I turned to my clinical supervisor, expecting that she would invite me to work under her. To my surprise, she said, "No. You're going to start your own practice."

Initially, that idea terrified me, but she reminded me of my strengths, including my experience managing operations and working for Fortune 100 and 500 companies. She promised to help me lay the groundwork for success. With that reassurance, I began to believe that maybe I could really do this.

### *Laying the Groundwork with Intention*

By May 2019, I was fully immersed in research and preparation. I named my practice Moving Forward Counseling & Consulting, LLC, to reflect my mission of helping clients transition from surviving to thriving. One of the best pieces of advice I received early on was to learn every aspect of my business from billing, marketing, and credentialing to insurance navigation and compliance. That knowledge allowed me to keep overhead low and maintain continuity, even if circumstances changed. Here are a few ways that I started small and intentionally.

- I subleased space from an existing group practice.
- I worked evenings and Saturdays while maintaining my university counseling job.
- I reinvested all part-time income back into the business.
- I furnished my office with secondhand items.
- I hired an accountant to establish financial stability.

These early decisions helped me grow slowly, wisely, and sustainably.

## Pivoting With Purpose: Creative Diversification

Less than a year into private practice, the COVID-19 pandemic reshaped everything. Like many counselors, I transitioned to telehealth. Unexpectedly, this expanded my reach across all of Virginia, and my caseload grew rapidly.

At that point, I began to diversify my services beyond the traditional private practice model in the following ways.

- I hosted workshops focused on mental health, trauma, and coping skills.
- I spoke on podcasts to share insights and increase visibility.
- I provided support for individuals coping with pandemic-related stress.
- I partnered with churches to challenge mental health stigma and address church-related trauma.
- I collaborated with predominantly White institutions to advocate for culturally responsive care for BIPOC students.

These experiences allowed me to expand my professional reach and align my work more closely with my values and the communities I care about.

## Designing a Values-Driven Business Model

Three months into the pandemic, I felt a divine push to pursue full-time entrepreneurship. My husband and I sat down to map out a business plan that would provide balance, financial stability, and time for our family. Here are ways I crafted a model that was financially sound and emotionally sustainable.

- I calculated all monthly expenses, including rent, insurance, and health benefits.
- I determined my reimbursement rate and how much to pay myself per session.
- I built in a cushion for sick time, vacation, and personal wellness.
- I set firm boundaries: four workdays per week and no weekends.

That clarity gave me both professional and personal freedom.

## Sustaining Growth Through Structure and Self-Awareness

I quickly learned that a healthy practice requires being a healthy business owner. I had to accept that I could not be everything to everyone. Identifying my ideal clients—those ready, willing, and open to doing the work—was critical in helping me avoid burnout and stay aligned with my purpose.

Here are a few sustainable habits I developed over time.

- I capped my client load at six to eight sessions per day.
- I established seasonal schedule resets in the fall and spring.
- I adopted a three-day work week during spring and summer (Tuesday through Thursday).
- I prioritized early morning sessions to align with my energy and meet client needs.

These habits created space for family, faith, volunteerism, and self-care—all core values in my life.

## Living the Mission: Faith, Legacy, and Community

Faith has been the foundation of every step I've taken, guiding everything from my business name to daily operations. By 2024, Moving Forward Counseling & Consulting had grown into a six-figure business. This success allowed me to give back in meaningful ways. I was able to start offering sliding scale and pro bono sessions to clients in need. I expanded into community-based services and support. I began mentoring and supervising two resident contractors who were preparing to open their own practices.

Now, I can focus this next chapter of my work on legacy: building generational wealth, mentoring future business owners, and normalizing entrepreneurship in mental health, especially among underrepresented professionals.

### Key Takeaways for Nontraditional Practice Success

- **Start with what you have:** Sublease a space, use secondhand furniture, and reinvest your early income.
- **Learn every aspect of your business:** From billing to branding, understanding the operations empowers you to lead confidently.
- **Use telehealth to scale and serve:** It's flexible, cost-effective, and accessible for clients.
- **Diversify your offerings:** Workshops, trainings, speaking engagements, and podcasts all create income and impact.
- **Partner with your community:** Collaborate with churches, schools, and cultural institutions.
- **Build around your values:** Flexibility isn't optional—it's vital for longevity.
- **Mentor others:** Pour into the next generation of counselors.
- **Stay anchored in your purpose:** Let your "why" lead every business decision.

## Walking in Purpose, Building With Intention

Launching a private practice is creating a life rooted in clarity, courage, and calling. You do not need a big office or a large staff to begin. What you need is vision, intentionality, and a willingness to grow through each season.

When you understand every layer of your business, from billing to branding, you position yourself to lead with resilience and grace. Expanding your reach through telehealth, diversifying income through creative outlets, and engaging your community allow your work to stretch far beyond the counseling room.

Whether you're working with churches to dismantle stigma, mentoring new clinicians, or supporting BIPOC students in majority institutions, you are building something that heals. Something that lasts. Let your business reflect your faith, your values, and your vision. When fear inevitably shows up, come back to your "why." You are not just building a business; you are moving lives forward.

This is what it looks like to build a practice before it feels like one. The dreams are valid. The exhaustion is often paralyzing. The learning curve is steep, but so is the sense of ownership that comes with doing it your way. As we shift into the next chapter on nontraditional businesses and side hustles, keep Arkitia's story in mind. Every big idea—every program, product, or passive income stream—begins with someone dreaming between clients, between classes, or between dinner and bedtime.

Arkitia's story demonstrates what it takes to start a practice from scratch: hope, vision, and a steep learning curve. But what happens when that vision expands into a clinic with staff, structure, and financial responsibility? In this reflection, Dr. Gregory C. Lemich, PhD, LPC, and owner and Clinical Director of the Lemich Clinic for Military Mental Health in Norfolk, Virginia, shares how he built a thriving, purpose-driven practice from the ground up. His story is a blueprint for growing a traditional clinic with clarity, compassion, and serious business chops.

## Voices from the Field

### DR. GREGORY C. LEMICH, PHD, LPC

Over the years, I've watched many clinics become more business-centric by minimizing salaries, increasing workloads, and stripping away benefits like private offices. You could blame COVID-19 recovery, inflation, stagnant insurance rates, or shifting legislation. Regardless of the cause, the result is the same: Counselor burnout is rising, and so is the strain on our communities. Waitlists are growing, but the deeper crisis isn't demand—it's building sustainable models that support quality care.

How do we build a clinic that works? It starts with knowing who you are and why that matters. A quick scroll through Psychology Today will show you an endless stream of counselors who are "compassionate," "empathetic," and "specialize in anxiety and depression." That doesn't make you stand out. Clients aren't just looking for warmth, and employees aren't just looking for a job. They're looking for a cause worth joining.

That's why ego has no place in clinic ownership. Strong clinics are built on vision, not personality. I founded the Lemich Clinic for Military Mental Health because my vision matched a local need. We're located four miles from a Navy base that serves 82,000 sailors, and no other clinic in the area has a focused mission to serve the military community. Our staff is made up of veterans and military spouses. Our core focus is reducing military suicide. That focus is what draws in both clients and clinicians. They aren't working for me. They're working for the cause.

When it comes to hiring, I've learned that it takes a group of good employees to build a great clinic, but it only takes one bad hire to wreck it. I evaluate every person as both a clinician and an employee. On the clinician side, I believe most people can grow with feedback, self-reflection, and a willingness to put in the work. I'm happy to invest in someone still learning the craft if they're open to development.

Considering someone as a future *employee* is often more complicated. A clinical misdiagnosis might slow down a client's progress, but poor employee behavior can sink the ship. Sloppy notes can lead to audits or insurance clawbacks. Intentional mistakes become insurance fraud. Poor suicide risk documentation can lead to lawsuits. A bad clinician can cost both the clinic and the client time, but they can usually learn and become better. A bad employee, on the other hand, can cost your license, your money, and your clinic's reputation.

My advice is to hire people you believe will be good employees. Then, you can train them to be great clinicians. Once you have a team that believes in the mission, you must support both aspects of their professional role: the clinician and the employee.

The clinician's side is empathetic, dedicated, and wants to help. They love the work. They thrive on connection. Support that side through regular training, peer feedback, and freeing them from unnecessary administrative work. Let clinicians be clinicians.

The employee side is the part that needs paid time off, a 401(k), and a room that's not too hot or cold. This is the side that gets tired, anxious, and overwhelmed. If your employees are showing up to talk clients down from a crisis and then having panic attacks in the breakroom over scheduling issues, you have a support issue. Be kind. Be patient. Give your employees the same unconditional positive regard you give your clients.

That dual-support model works. I launched the Lemich Clinic in 2022 with one intern and a single rented room. Two years later, we are 20 employees strong with a 3,000-square-foot building and over $1 million in annual revenue—without debt, and with only a $30 monthly advertising budget.

We're still growing, and we're still grounded in what matters: the mission, the people, and the community we serve.

---

Arkitia reminded us how personal the journey of starting a practice can be. Dr. Lemich shows us how that vision becomes a business—and how not to lose yourself or your values in the process. A thriving practice isn't built on charisma or hustle alone. It's built on clarity, consistency, and a willingness to care for your team just as fiercely as you care for your clients.

## References

American School Counselor Association. (n.d.). *State/territory certification.* American School Counselor Association. Retrieved October 31, 2025, from https://www.schoolcounselor.org/About-School-Counseling/State-Requirements-Programs

Barnett, J. E., Baker, E. K., Elman, N. S., & Schoener, G. R. (2007). In pursuit of wellness: The self-care imperative. *Professional Psychology: Research and Practice, 38*(6), 603–612. https://doi.org/10.1037/0735-7028.38.6.603

Blair, L. (2023). *Building your counseling empire: From start to success.* Therapist Toolkit Publishing.

Blount, A. (2003). Integrated primary care: Organizing the evidence. *Families, Systems, and Health, 21*(2), 121–134. https://doi.org/10.1037/1091-7527.21.2.121

Carney, J. S., & Granato, L. A. (2000). The business of counseling: Planning and establishing a private practice. *Counseling and Human Development, 32*(5).

Centers for Medicare & Medicaid Services. (2022, January 3). *No surprises: Understand your rights against surprise medical bills* [Fact sheet]. CMS Newsroom. https://www.cms.gov/newsroom/fact-sheets/no-surprises-understand-your-rights-against-surprise-medical-bills

Craig, C. D., & Sprang, G. (2010). Compassion satisfaction, compassion fatigue, and burnout in a national sample of trauma treatment therapists. *Anxiety, Stress, and Coping, 23*(3), 319–339. https://doi.org/10.1080/10615800903085818

CPH & Associates. (n.d.). *Professional liability insurance.* CPH & Associates. Retrieved October 31, 2025, from https://www.cphins.com

Cully, J. A., Tolpin, L., Henderson, L., Jimenez, D., Kunik, M. E., & Petersen, L. A. (2008). Psychotherapy in the Veterans Health Administration: Missed opportunities? *Psychological Services, 5*(4), 320–331. https://doi.org/10.1037/a0013719

Danco, J. C. (1982). The ethics of fee practices: An analysis of presuppositions and accountability. *Journal of Psychology and Theology, 10*(1), 13–21.

DaSilva, M. (2019). *The profitable private practice: How to start, run, and grow your therapy business.* CreateSpace Independent Publishing Platform.

Gallagher, R. P. (2014). *National Survey of College Counseling Centers 2014*. International Association of Counseling Services. https://d-scholarship.pitt.edu/28178/1/survey_2014.pdf

Goodman-Scott, E., & Boulden, R. (2020). School counselors' experiences with the Section 504 process: "I want to be a strong team member... [not] a case manager." *Professional School Counseling, 23*(1), 1–10. https://doi.org/10.1177/2156759X20919378

Gündüz, B. (2012). Self-efficacy and burnout in professional school counselors. *Educational Sciences: Theory and Practice, 12*(3), 1761–1767. https://files.eric.ed.gov/fulltext/EJ1000895.pdf

Healthcare Providers Service Organization (HPSO). (n.d.). *Professional liability insurance*. Retrieved October 31, 2025, from https://www.hpso.com

Lambie, G. W., & Williamson, L. L. (2004). The challenge to change from guidance counseling to professional school counseling: A historical proposition. *Professional School Counseling, 8*(2), 124–131. https://www.jstor.org/stable/42732614

Landon, T. J., Levine, A., Brinck, E. A., Soldner, J. L., & Schultz, J. C. (2021). The role of the supervisor in counselor professional development. *Journal of Rehabilitation Administration, 42*(1), 53–70.

Morse, G., Salyers, M. P., Rollins, A. L., Monroe-DeVita, M., & Pfahler, C. (2012). Burnout in mental health services: A review of the problem and its remediation. *Administration and Policy in Mental Health and Mental Health Services Research, 39*(5), 341–352. https://doi.org/10.1007/s10488-011-0352-1

Robinson, A. M. (2024). *The purposeful and profitable therapist's guide on diversifying income*. Legacy Wellness Group.

Schwab, E. F. (2016). Surviving and thriving your first year in private practice. *Seminars in Hearing, 37*(4), 293–300. https://doi.org/10.1055/s-0036-1594001

Sharkin, B. S. (2012). *Being a college counselor on today's campus: Roles, contributions, and special challenges*. Routledge.

Substance Abuse and Mental Health Services Administration. (2024). *Behavioral health workforce*. SAMHSA. https://www.samhsa.gov/workforce

Sue, D. W., Rasheed, M. N., & Rasheed, J. M. (2015). *Multicultural social work practice: A competency-based approach to diversity and social justice* (2nd ed.). Wiley.

Troup, J., Lever Taylor, B., Sheridan Rains, L., Broeckelmann, E., Russell, J., Jeynes, T., Cooper, C., Steare, T., Dedat, Z., McNicholas, S., Oram, S., Dale, O., & Johnson, S. (2022). Clinician perspectives on what constitutes good practice in community services for people with complex emotional needs: A qualitative thematic meta-synthesis. *PLOS ONE, 17*(5), Article e0267787. https://doi.org/10.1371/journal.pone.0267787

Waldman, L. (2021). *The graduate course you never had: How to develop, manage, and market a flourishing mental health practice* (2nd ed.). Outskirts Press.

Zivin, K., Chang, M.-U. M., Van, T., Osatuke, K., Boden, M., Sripada, R. K., Abraham, K. M., Pfeiffer, P. N., & Kim, H. M. (2022). Relationships between work-environment characteristics and behavioral health provider burnout in the Veterans Health Administration. *Health Services Research, 57 Suppl 1*(Suppl 1), 83–94. https://doi.org/10.1111/1475-6773.13964

Zur, O. (n.d.). *Introduction to informed consent in psychotherapy, counseling, and assessment*. Dr. Ofer Zur. Retrieved November 3, 2025, from https://drzur.com/informed-consent/

# 7

# Nontraditional Business and Side Hustles in Counseling

If you've made it this far, you've already walked the foundational paths of building a traditional counseling career. You've experienced the office setup, the credential grind, the budget lines, and the steady rhythm of clinical work. That's the straight path, and it's solid, but not every counselor thrives on straight paths.

This chapter is definitely nontraditional. If the last chapter was the well-lit path paved with receipts and state forms, this one is the alley around the back with the handwritten sign that says, "Open for business. Knock twice." It's the creative, scrappy, build-it-yourself side of counseling. The one that asks, "What else can I do with what I know?" This isn't about doing less counseling. It's about imagining more ways to do good work.

We aim to help counselors think outside the box, not just for the sake of income, but for the sake of sustainability, personal growth, and professional impact. Readers will be introduced to practical, ethical, and creative ways to diversify their income through online counseling platforms, public speaking, content creation, group work, and other clinical-adjacent services. These options not only create new revenue streams but also allow counselors to leverage their knowledge and experience new ways to stay energized and professionally fulfilled.

Each section includes practical insights, guiding questions, and real-life examples to inspire counselors to imagine new possibilities for their work. While this chapter is not a call to abandon traditional counseling, it is an invitation to expand how we understand our role, our skill set, and the ways we can contribute to the world without burning out in the process.

## Why Counselors Need Side Hustles

Having a side hustle does not mean a counselor is greedy or distracted. It means they are resourceful and prioritizing longevity in a field that is both beautiful and emotionally taxing. Most importantly, it means they are building a career that supports them financially and holistically (Taylor, 2025).

There are a couple of reasons side hustles have historically been frowned upon in counseling. First, there is a deeply rooted belief that helping professionals should not focus on making money. The image of the "selfless therapist" continues to be reinforced in graduate programs, supervision, and even pop culture (Rees, 2024). Second, there are legitimate concerns around ethics, dual relationships, and crossing boundaries. Somewhere along the way, the assumption that all side work is risky or exploitative took hold. That's simply not true. Like anything else in our field, it is not just about what we do—it is about how we do it (American Counseling Association [ACA], 2014).

In reality, pursuing side hustles can be one of the most ethical, empowering, and sustainable decisions a counselor makes. Counselors are often underpaid, overworked, and expected to absorb everyone else's pain while figuring out how to manage their own student loans, family obligations, and professional growth (Yang & Hayes, 2020). A side hustle can provide supplemental income and offer creative outlets, professional expansion, and long-term career security. It can even protect your clinical work by giving you other ways to stay engaged and make money that do not require you to carry an unsustainable caseload (Taylor, 2025).

Side hustles can create freedom to grow and experiment, take pressure off your primary job, and grant a little more breathing room. We've seen counselors who take on a single workshop or write one continuing education unit (CEU) course and suddenly find themselves reenergized by their work. It's not just about the paycheck—it's about ownership (Taylor, 2025).

Diversifying your income also diversifies your professional identity. When counselors see themselves also as teachers, creators, coaches, authors, speakers, or consultants, they begin to develop new skills, find new passions, and connect with broader audiences. This opens doors to new opportunities, but it also strengthens your work in the counseling room. The confidence and creativity you build outside of clinical work can deepen your presence inside it (Mellin et al., 2011).

Of course, every side hustle must be approached with intention and care. One of the first questions counselors should ask is, "How do I know if this is within my scope?" There is no one-size-fits-all answer. A good rule of thumb is to ask yourself the following:

- Does this activity align with my training and experience?
- Could this be misinterpreted as counseling by a client or the public?
- Have I reviewed my licensure board's ethical guidelines, and would I feel comfortable defending this activity in front of said board?
- Am I being transparent with clients and separating this work clearly from clinical services?

If the answer to those questions leans toward yes, you are likely within your professional boundaries. And if you are unsure, consult with colleagues, supervisors, or legal/ethical experts. Good businesspeople do not avoid risk; they mitigate it.

Counselors who pursue side hustles are expanding their impact, protecting their well-being, and creating models of success that others can follow. In a profession that desperately needs longevity, that is something we should be celebrating, rather than side-eyeing.

## The Future of Online Counseling as a Side Hustle

The rise of online counseling didn't just change how we deliver care—it changed the counseling profession itself. What started as a crisis adaptation during the COVID-19 pandemic has become a permanent fixture of modern practice. Telehealth has grown from an experiment on the edges of clinical work to one of the most accessible, flexible, and scalable platforms for counselors to earn income, expand reach, and explore nontraditional business models (Robledo Yamamoto et al., 2021).

This shift has opened new doors for clients and for counselors looking to diversify their income. Digital work makes private practice more accessible for those without office space, allows for creative clinical-adjacent services, and lowers the barrier of entry for new professionals. For many counselors, telehealth offers counselors freedom to choose hours, environment, clients, and revenue models.

It's important to remember that ethical practice still applies, even if you never meet your client in person. Before starting an online side hustle, take time to clarify your goals, know your scope, and ensure your new venture still reflects the same professional values that brought you to this work in the first place. There are two main avenues for counselors interested in building income through online services. You can join a third-party platform (e.g., BetterHelp, 2025; Talkspace, n.d.). This is the easier route, and its lower revenue reflects that. Alternatively, you can build your own digital brand. This requires more upfront work, but it gives you more control and higher revenue in the long run

Each path comes with trade-offs, and both require a clear understanding of licensure, informed consent, client safety protocols, and confidentiality in digital settings (Luxton et al., 2024). For those who approach it with care and creativity, telehealth can be a new frontier for building a sustainable, flexible counseling career.

### *Third-Party Platforms: Convenience at a Cost*

Companies like BetterHelp (2025), Talkspace (n.d.), Thriveworks (n.d.), Cerebral (n.d.), and Amwell (n.d.) have exploded in popularity. These platforms advertise heavily, remove the burden of marketing, and connect clients to counselors quickly. From a side hustle perspective, they seem ideal: Sign up, create a profile, and start receiving client referrals without the stress of managing a full business.

While some counselors appreciate the convenience and steady referrals, others find that the compensation is far below standard rates—sometimes as low as $30 per session (Mendes-Santos et al., 2022). There are also serious concerns about autonomy, data privacy, client continuity, and how counseling is marketed to the public. Here are a few major drawbacks of using large-scale counseling platforms.

- **Low pay rates:** Many providers report earning significantly less per session than they would in private practice, often without benefits or protections (Jo et al., 2023).
- **High client volume pressure:** Counselors are often encouraged to take on more clients than is clinically sustainable, leading to rushed sessions and burnout (Barnett & Sheen, 2023).

- **Lack of clinical oversight:** Some platforms offer little to no clinical supervision or case consultation, increasing risk for newer professionals (Jo et al., 2023).
- **Unclear ethical lines:** Some services have been criticized for advertising "messaging counseling" or pushing counselors to practice in ways that may not align with their state laws or ethical standards (Johnston & Slye, 2025).

That said, platforms like BetterHelp can be a decent fit for clinicians who want supplemental income without taking on the full weight of building a private practice. The key is knowing the risks, setting clear boundaries, and ensuring your work still meets your ethical and professional standards.

## Building Your Own Telehealth Brand

Building your own telehealth brand offers much more control and income potential in the long term. Many counselors are launching or expanding their own fully digital private practices, either as a full-time shift or as a side business that complements their day job. Counselors who succeed at this model often start small. They identify a niche (e.g., working with new moms, attention-deficit/hyperactivity disorder [ADHD] coaching, religious trauma recovery). They set up a platform that complies with the Health Insurance Portability and Accountability Act (HIPAA), such as TherapyNotes (n.d.), or Zoom for Healthcare (n.d.). They invest in basic branding, including a website, email marketing tools, and a social media presence. They clearly articulate how their services are different from those on big counseling apps.

Research has suggested that digital counseling, when done well, is not only effective but also preferred by some clients due to the convenience, reduced travel time, and increased accessibility (Passmore & Fillery-Travis, 2011). For counselors, online work can also offer more flexible hours, the ability to work from home, and access to underserved populations in rural or high-demand areas. Counselors can build income through online services in the following ways:

- Offering individual telehealth sessions through their own website or electronic health record (EHR) system.
- Hosting virtual group counseling or psychoeducational groups.
- Providing online coaching services (distinct from counseling) for clients across state lines.

- Creating on-demand digital products (e.g., webinars, courses, or guided workbooks).
- Implementing subscription models offering access to exclusive content, community, or support forums.

### Legal and Ethical Considerations

Whether joining a platform or going solo, counselors must stay vigilant about licensure, informed consent, and confidentiality. Nearly all states require that the client be physically located in a state where the counselor is licensed, even for virtual work (Counseling Compact, n.d.). Counselors should also ensure their consent forms clearly explain the risks of digital communication and describe how emergencies will be handled. Some professionals choose to offer coaching in areas where they have expertise but do not provide counseling, especially when serving clients outside of their licensed state. While this is legally possible in many cases, it requires clear branding, separate documentation, and a strong understanding of the line between coaching and counseling (Bachkirova & Baker, 2018).

## Speaking, Teaching, and Hosting Workshops

If you have ever stayed late after class to explain a tricky concept, used a whiteboard in session to illustrate a metaphor that made a theory finally click, or told a story in supervision that helped a student breathe easier, then you already have the core skills that it takes to be an influential speaker or workshop leader. The ability to communicate clearly, connect personally, and teach meaningfully is a huge professional asset. It can also be a legitimate income stream.

Speaking, teaching, and leading workshops allow counselors to extend their clinical knowledge into educational and professional development spaces. Whether they are facilitating a community training, delivering a keynote, or teaching a CEU course, counselors can monetize their experience in ways that are not only financially beneficial but deeply fulfilling. These side ventures can also position counselors as leaders in the field and open doors to broader influence and opportunities.

We gave a virtual guest lecture at a university where we explained how counselors can help clients deepen emotional insight through reflections of content, feelings, and processes. We discussed tracking emotions with a feelings wheel, matching reflections to emotional shifts, and following the client's lead with intentional presence. No matter what we said, the students weren't getting it. One thing led to another, and I (Jude) turned my camera to the whiteboard in my office and drew a diagram that framed the therapeutic process. Essentially, the diagram showed how a 60-minute counseling session can be broken up into four 15-minute sections. Within each section, the counselor can spend five minutes reflecting on the client's content, five minutes reflecting on the client's emotions, and five minutes reflecting on the therapeutic process. The counselor should reflect the next deeper feeling. The lecture ended, but the drawing stayed. That same week, I used the drawing in supervision. My supervisee and I looked at the board and started with the most surface-level feeling on the wheel. While watching a recording of her session, we used the diagram on my whiteboard to trace the client's emotional experience, moving from the outer layer of surface feelings to the deeper core emotions. Together, we practiced reflections of both feeling and content, and she began to see how tracking and accurately naming emotions help clients move toward greater awareness and insight.

What started as a spontaneous sketch became a workshop. That diagram, drawn spontaneously to answer a student's question in a lecture, ended up being used in a workshop for hundreds of people. We had always assumed that workshop material had to be flashy or wrapped in some kind of vacuum-cleaner-sales-pitch polish. Turns out, it just needs to be useful.

## *How Do I Start Running My Own Workshops?*

Creating and hosting your own workshops might sound daunting, but it's more accessible than it seems. Most successful workshop leaders begin by focusing on a very specific audience and topic. They don't try to teach everything. Instead, they solve a specific problem or answer a pressing question. Here are a few steps to help you get started.

- **Pick a focused topic:** What concepts or practices do you love to teach? What do people ask you about all the time? What gap do you see in your community or among your colleagues?
- **Choose your audience:** Is this for other counselors? The general public? Parents? Teenagers? Your ideal audience will shape your delivery.
- **Build a simple outline:** Don't overcomplicate it. Start with a problem or a question, provide useful information or steps, and allow space for discussion or practice.

- **Secure a space (physical or virtual):** You can partner with a local agency, host it at your clinic, or use a Zoom account. Some counselors even run workshops in yoga studios, libraries, or coffee shops.
- **Set a price:** Even if it's low at first, charging a fee sets the tone for professionalism and value. Many counselors start with $20–$50 per person for community events and $75–$150 per person for CEU-level trainings (Peeters et al., 2018).

Research on counselor-led community workshops and psychoeducational groups has shown that participants report increased trust in the profession and greater access to services (Yau et al., 2023). In other words, your side hustle could be a service to your community, too.

## How Do I Start Speaking at Conferences?

The path to paid speaking engagements often begins with free speaking. Many counselors present at local, state, and national conferences just to get their name out there and build credibility. Over time, with strong evaluations and clear communication, you can turn that momentum into a paid opportunity. Here are a few tips to build your speaking career.

- **Start where you are:** Submit proposals to local conferences, CE events, or university workshops. Even department brown-bag lunches are good practice.
- **Collect feedback:** Ask organizers or attendees for evaluations, testimonials, or reviews. These build your speaker profile.
- **Create a speaker one-sheet or landing page:** Distribute these sheets or share links at every speaking event. Include your photo, biography, list of topics, and past speaking events. Make it easy for people to book you.
- **Network like it's your job:** Many speaking gigs come from word-of-mouth or referrals. Stay in touch with people who see you speak and follow up with new contacts after conferences.

Once you have a few presentations under your belt, you can start submitting proposals with speaker fees attached. Some conferences do not pay, but many agencies, school districts, and nonprofit organizations do. According to Story (2024), counselor educators and licensed clinicians can earn between $300 and $3,000 per speaking engagement, depending on audience, topic, duration, and setting.

## What Topics Are People Actually Paying to Hear About?

Find the sweet spot where your passion meets public demand. That's your topic lane. People will always pay to learn about things that (1) solve a problem they're struggling with, (2) help them serve others better, or (3) give them personal or professional clarity. While trending topics vary, research on workshop attendance patterns in counseling-related professional spaces has shown high demand in the following areas (Anctil et al., 2012):

- Burnout, self-care, and compassion fatigue
- Trauma-informed care and crisis response
- Multicultural competency and anti-oppressive practice
- Telehealth best practices and digital boundaries
- Ethics updates and clinical documentation
- Creative interventions (e.g., art, play, mindfulness, somatic work)
- Working with youth, families, or special populations (e.g., neurodiverse clients, LGBTQIA+ youth, high-conflict couples)

When in doubt, ask, "What do I wish someone would've taught me earlier in my career?" Someone else likely needs that knowledge, too.

## Once I Book a Speaking Gig, How Do I Perform Well?

Securing the invitation is only the beginning. Delivering a strong presentation can turn a one-time event into repeat business. Here are a few hard-earned tips we've learned from the stage and the classroom.

- **Respect your audience's time:** Start and end on schedule. Keep the pacing tight and the content focused.
- **Tell stories:** Examples from your clinical work (appropriately de-identified) bring abstract concepts to life. In our experience, stories stick more than statistics.
- **Keep it interactive:** Break up lecture-style content with reflection questions, pair-shares, or experiential exercises. Make space for participation.
- **Be picky with the text:** Include only key points in PowerPoint presentations. There is nothing more disappointing than paying good money to sit and listen to an "expert" recite line by line from a presentation for a couple of hours.
- **Don't overstuff the slides:** Use visuals to anchor your points, not to drown them.

- **Land the plane:** Summarize key takeaways at the end. Help participants feel like they learned something valuable and practical.
- **Follow up:** Send a thank-you note to the organizer. Share your contact information with attendees. If the experience goes well, you've just added one more link to your speaker network.

One of the most powerful parts of speaking and teaching is that it reshapes your identity. When you step into the role of educator or trainer, you begin to see your experience and voice as valuable in fresh ways. That confidence rolls into every part of your practice. It also allows you to reach more people, including those who might never come to counseling, but who still need healing, guidance, and tools. In a field where burnout is a tangible risk, speaking and training can be the spark that reminds you why you started in the first place. And, yes, it can pay well, too.

## Writing, Publishing, and Creating Content

Counselors are writers, even if we don't always claim that title. We write progress notes, treatment plans, case conceptualizations, and responses to crises. We translate messy, human experience into language every single day. When counselors wonder whether they have anything worth saying or selling through writing, the answer is almost always yes (Cozolino, 2015).

Writing is one of the most flexible and sustainable ways counselors can generate extra income. The upfront effort can be significant, but the return can last for years. Once a product like a workbook, course, or even a short downloadable guide is created, it can become scalable by generating income long after the initial work is done. It's not tied to a clock or a clinical hour. In a profession where emotional fatigue is a growing risk, creative outlets like writing can also help protect counselors' mental health and reconnect them with meaning in the work (Corey et al., 2023).

### *You're Already Writing*

The beauty of writing is that most counselors are already doing it. The next step is learning how to monetize it. That intake packet you built for your practice might be helpful to other counselors. The journaling prompts you gave to your grief group could be a digital workbook. The way you explain trauma to your clients using metaphors and diagrams is educational content, possibly even a course. Counselors everywhere are earning income from the following products:

- Guest blog posts and magazine articles
- Self-help books and e-books on niche topics
- Counseling worksheets, tools, and psychoeducational resources
- Continuing education manuals and training guides
- Subscription newsletters or member-based communities
- Guided journals or client-facing mental health workbooks

In a national study, nearly half of surveyed clinicians who pursued side hustles reported creating digital content of some kind, including handouts and worksheets that stemmed directly from their clinical work (Tudor Car et al., 2019). In short, the work you're already doing has value beyond the counseling session. It just needs structure and delivery.

## *From Ideas to Income: The Writing Pathway*

How do you move from "I have some good stuff" to earning money from your content? It begins with clarity. Ask yourself who will benefit from your work. You're writing for someone, often a former version of yourself. You're likely writing what you needed to hear when you were struggling with burnout, navigating anxiety, or figuring out your role as a new counselor. You might be writing for a client you wish you could support beyond the session, or a supervisee or colleague who keeps asking the same question. That clarity shapes everything from tone to format to pricing.

Once you have settled on an audience, start small. A great first product is a downloadable guide or a mini workbook. You don't need a 200-page book or a polished course to begin. A five-page PDF that solves a specific problem, like navigating panic attacks in the workplace, or guiding new clients through counseling expectations, can be priced affordably and made available within days. Many counselors sell their resources directly through their websites, or platforms like Etsy (n.d.), Gumroad (n.d.), or Payhip (n.d.), which automate the entire process.

Of course, the content must be original and owned by you. If it was created during agency work or borrowed from training materials, make sure you're not crossing legal or copyright lines. If you built it from scratch, it's ethically and legally yours to share, as long as proper disclaimers (e.g., "not a substitute for counseling") are clearly noted.

Pricing can feel awkward at first, especially when we're used to giving away resources freely, but your time, expertise, and perspective have value. Most clinicians price handouts and worksheets between $5 and $25, while full workbooks or bundles range from $30 to $75 (Therapist Site Toolbox, 2023). Courses, depending on their length and depth, can command anywhere from $99 to $400 or more, especially if they include video content or continuing education hours (TheraPlatform, n.d.). Subscription-based content, such as newsletters or member-only resources, can offer ongoing, predictable income, even if it starts small.

## Can I Really Sell This? What's Allowed and What Works?

You can sell original materials that you've created if you stay transparent, ethical, and intentional. If you've made a worksheet for your clients, and it's your original work, you can turn that into a sellable product. If you've built a PowerPoint for a CEU training, that can be expanded into a course. What you've already created may just need a little polish, formatting, and framing to become a product worth sharing and selling (Lockhart, 2024).

The key is to ensure that customers know you are not selling counseling. The *ACA Code of Ethics* (2014, Standard C.3.a) is clear: Counselors must avoid misleading the public and ensure that all services and materials are accurately represented. Add disclaimers. Be honest in your marketing. Design your materials with the end user in mind. When done right, your writing becomes a connection point that reflects your expertise, voice, and values.

## The Bigger Payoff: Writing That Builds Freedom

Monetized content generates income and builds a professional identity. It shows the world (and reminds you) that you have something to say. It clarifies your voice. It opens doors to speaking gigs, consulting opportunities, and leadership roles. It also works while you rest, making it the definition of passive income. Workbooks that sell while you're out to dinner, courses someone enrolls in while you're asleep, newsletters that connect with someone you've never met, all continuously generate income without adding continuous work to your schedule. Clients come and go, and caseloads shift, but a well-crafted piece of writing can live on long after the session ends, creating income and cementing legacy.

# Private Practice-Adjacent Hustles

A common trap in our profession is the idea that the only way to make money is to sit in a room with one person for 50 minutes at a time. The hour-for-hour model is familiar, predictable, and professionally reinforced, but it's also limited. At some point, you will max out. There are only so many sessions you can take and only so many emotional weights you can carry in a day. Your income is also finite when it's solely tied to how many hours you're awake and available.

That's where private practice-adjacent hustles enter the picture. These are income-generating activities that are directly connected to your clinical expertise, but they don't rely on traditional one-on-one counseling. They still serve people, but they're scalable, creative, and, potentially, more sustainable.

## *How to Earn Passive Income in Counseling*

"Passive income" has become a prominent talking point online, usually in some clickbait-y way. In the counseling world, passive income looks different than what it might in other fields. In our profession, passive income is typically semi-passive in that it requires a heavy lift on the front end—developing a product, planning an intensive, writing a course—but once the initial work is done, you can continue to earn from it without continuous input. Examples of products you can create to start generating passive income include

- An online course or workshop that clients can take before starting counseling with you;
- A recorded parenting class that you sell on your website;
- An assessment package with scoring, recommendations, and a feedback form;
- A retreat model you repeat every few months with minimal changes; and
- CEU content you license to another agency or provider.

This expands your reach, protects your bandwidth, and creates stability when life or caseloads shift. It also gives your clients more ways to engage with your work without adding sessions to your calendar.

## What Services Can Counselors Ethically Sell?

There are many services you can sell if they stay within your scope of competence, are clearly differentiated from clinical treatment, and are marketed honestly. If you're providing a service within your scope that does not function as direct counseling, it can be ethically offered and priced accordingly. Here are examples of services that counselors can sell.

- **Custom coaching packages:** As long as you're not diagnosing or treating clinical conditions, you can offer coaching services focused on wellness, goals, or personal development.
- **Counseling-adjacent groups:** These include drop-in skills groups, mindfulness circles, or post-discharge process groups. These can sometimes fall under group counseling if done under licensure, but they can also be structured as fee-for-service workshops.
- **Consultations:** One-time parent or teacher consultations related to general behavior strategies (not clinical recommendations) or clinical consultations with other counseling professionals can generate income while also benefiting your brand identity.
- **Supervision services:** Many new counselors start positions that don't include supervision, so they have to hire external supervisors.

The *ACA Code of Ethics* (2014, Standard C.7.b) supports innovation and entrepreneurship if counselors maintain transparency, avoid exploitation, and protect client welfare. You are not violating your ethics by monetizing your expertise. You're honoring it and building a more sustainable professional life.

## How Are Counselors Earning Money Through Assessments, Groups, or Intensives?

Assessments, groups, and intensives are some of the most exciting and underutilized ways to earn income while staying aligned with your values. Counselors trained in specific assessments such as the Minnesota Multiphasic Personality Inventory-2 (MMPI-2), the Personality Assessment Inventory (PAI), the Test of Variables of Attention (TOVA), Enneagram, DISC, or custom intake protocols can create powerful, specialized service offerings. For example, you might offer couples premarital assessments with a two-session debrief; career clarity packages with personality profiles, values inventories, and action steps;

or clinical intake bundles that synthesize multiple data points into a well-organized feedback session.

You can ethically charge $250–$800+ for these services, depending on depth, tools used, and reporting needs (Tides Mental Health, 2025). Many clients prefer this one-time deep-dive model when they're not ready for weekly counseling sessions. For licensed counselors using tools that require formal training or interpretation (e.g., the Myers–Briggs Type Indicator [MBTI], PAI, etc.), make sure you follow proper guidelines and include clear limits to scope in your disclaimers.

**Groups That Go Beyond Counseling**

Group work has always been one of the most cost-effective, impactful ways to serve. It's also a smart business move. A one-hour group with eight paying participants at $50 per person earns $400. In the same amount of time, you'd typically earn $125 from an individual session. Group formats that work well include

- Closed groups with a fixed number of sessions (e.g., "Six Weeks of Boundaries");
- Ongoing support circles with drop-in rates;
- Hybrid groups with an online course component and weekly live discussion; and
- Parent or caregiver groups with tools and templates.

The real opportunity here is to take group work and turn it into something bigger: a branded program you can repeat, expand into a workbook, or use to train other counselors to run in their communities.

**Intensives, Retreats, and VIP Days**

Some clients want deep, focused support, and they're willing to pay for it. Intensives offer extended sessions (e.g., three hours, a full day, or a weekend) that help clients move through complex issues more quickly. Counselors are currently offering

- Individual intensives for trauma processing or relationship repair;
- Couples retreats that include structured sessions, worksheets, and meals; and
- One-day VIP experiences for clients flying in for high-value work.

These models often include upfront work, follow-up work, and a custom experience. Prices range from $500 to $3,000+ per person, depending on the time and value provided (Kale Monk et al., 2017). They require careful planning, strong boundaries, and clear contracts, but they can be professionally and financially rewarding. Let's not ignore the power of collaboration. Intensives often work best when counselors partner with coaches, yoga instructors, financial educators, or body-based practitioners to create multidimensional experiences.

Some of these hustles may feel uncomfortable at first. In our experience, the discomfort doesn't come from questions of ethics; it's about permission. Let us say this clearly: You're allowed to build a business that works for you. You can create a business that honors your clients and your capacity, that doesn't collapse if you get sick or take a vacation, and that pays your bills and leaves enough left over to breathe. That security is how you stay in the field and maintain a solid work-life balance. When you start generating a stable income that can withstand busy and slow times, your business stops being a burden and starts becoming a blessing.

## Creative Side Hustles That Work

Not every side hustle has to look like a course or a worksheet. Some of the most successful counseling-adjacent businesses began when a clinician noticed something missing and decided to build it. These ideas weren't always polished or strategic. Many started as passion projects, sparked by frustration, curiosity, or a unique need that no one else was meeting. As counselors move into this space, one of the biggest mindset shifts is realizing that your business doesn't have to fit a mold. There's more room for originality in this profession than we've often been taught (Kidd et al., 2015).

Research has shown that entrepreneurial activity among helping professionals often emerges from perceived service gaps, creative inspiration, or the desire for more flexible work structures, not from traditional business planning models (Kidd et al., 2015). Side hustles born this way are often more authentic, sustainable, and connected to the clinician's values and identity (Skovholt & Trotter-Mathison, 2016). Joe Bennett, a contributor to this chapter, had one such idea for a side hustle. He loved the game *Dungeons & Dragons* (Wizards of the Coast, 2014) and thought it would be a fun and useful tool for younger clients. Now, he runs therapeutic gaming groups for teens. Parents pay $100 per session for role-play-based work that builds confidence, teamwork, and emotional regulation (Here Be Dragons, n.d.).

## Exploring a Unique Business Idea

The first step to executing a unique business idea is to start with what lights you up. What topic could you talk about for an hour with no notes? What have your clients or colleagues repeatedly asked for help with? What intersection of your personal passions and professional skills hasn't been tapped yet? You don't need to know the full path; you just need to follow the idea far enough to test it. Create a pilot, offer a beta version, and ask people you trust for feedback. The more you tinker, the more your idea takes shape, and the less pressure you will feel to get it perfect from the jump. Remember: Just because something hasn't been done yet doesn't mean it shouldn't be done. Innovation in counseling doesn't always come from academia—it often comes from counselors in the trenches, figuring out what really helps people.

## Knowing When a Side Hustle Is Taking Off and When It's Time to Scale Up

There's no universal indication that it's time to scale up your side hustle, but there are many reliable signposts.

- You consistently get referrals, interest, or feedback without having to promote much.
- People ask, "Do you offer this for other groups?" or "Can I share this with someone else?"
- You're starting to feel the limits of time and wondering how to deliver your service in a more sustainable or widespread way.

Scaling doesn't always mean going bigger. Sometimes, it means going deeper by adding structure, automating what you can, or packaging your idea into something that you can sell for independent use.

Counselors are not limited to one way of doing meaningful work. The skills that make you a good counselor—your insight, your creativity, your empathy, and your ability to communicate—can be expressed in far more ways than just the traditional counseling session. When channeled thoughtfully, these same skills can be used to educate, empower, and support people through workshops, courses, groups, written content, and countless other offerings.

When developed ethically and intentionally, side hustles are a natural extension of the counseling profession. They allow you to serve more people, build financial stability, and tap into parts of your identity that may not always find expression in one-on-one clinical work.

For many counselors, these ventures also bring renewed energy and satisfaction, offering a creative outlet that enhances clinical presence.

The truth is, there is no single "right way" to grow your counseling career. The path forward is rarely linear, and it certainly does not need to look like anyone else's. Some of the most impactful, financially successful, and professionally fulfilling ideas in this field came from counselors who allowed themselves to imagine something different. A simple idea sketched in a notebook. A conversation with a colleague that sparked a new offering. A pattern noticed in client work that led to a broader resource. These moments of curiosity and creativity have grown into real, thriving businesses. There is no reason yours cannot do the same.

Your counseling degree is a foundation, not a box. It gives you credibility, insight, and training, but it does not limit your future. We encourage you to pay attention to the ideas that keep tugging at you. Notice the questions people are always asking you. Think about the tools or resources you wish had existed when you were starting.

You don't have to choose between being a compassionate counselor and a confident entrepreneur. The profession needs both. The more counselors permit themselves to think creatively, the more sustainable, inclusive, and innovative this field will become. The only real limit to what you can build in this profession is your imagination.

## Voices from the Field

### JOSEPH BENNETT, LPC-ASSOCIATE

Imagine if you could be anyone else for a little while. Who would you choose to be? Would you want to be brave, powerful, clever, or deeply wise? Would you be someone who laughs at everything, or someone who finally speaks and gets heard? What would it be like to step away from the roles you play every day—counselor, parent, partner, friend—and explore a new identity? These are the kinds of questions that sit at the intersection of tabletop role-playing games (TTRPGs) and counseling.

I'm an LPC-Associate and Founder of Here Be Dragons Counseling in Waco, Texas. I'm also a father, husband, counselor, and—for more hours than I care to admit—a Dungeon Master. In both my personal and professional life, I use TTRPGs, especially *Dungeons & Dragons (D&D)* (Wizards of the Coast, 2014), as a platform for healing, growth, and connection. What began as my primary private practice has since evolved into a consultation and training space where I incorporate TTRPGs with individuals, families, counselor supervision groups, and even organizational teams.

I discovered *D&D* in 2017 after finishing my undergraduate degree. At first, it was just a game and a way to spend time with friends. One night during a campaign, my character, who was searching for his long-lost father, asked a prophetic oracle a question. I felt the emotion well up as I voiced the scene, and suddenly the "game" didn't feel like just a game. I realized my character's journey mirrored my own grief and longing. That moment when I realized the therapeutic power of storytelling, embodiment, and play was a turning point.

When I work with clients using TTRPGs, it all starts with character creation. In *D&D*, players build characters using six ability scores: "Strength, Dexterity, Constitution, Intelligence, Wisdom, and Charisma." I invite clients to rank these traits not as themselves, but as who they want to explore. From there, we collaboratively determine their class (e.g., "barbarian," "bard," "wizard," etc.) and species. I've adapted much of the lore from the original *D&D* content to reflect therapeutic metaphors. Elves, for instance, might be emotionally distant. Dwarves live in cultures of mastery, perfectionism, and legacy. Many species carry themes of intergenerational trauma, colonization, and identity conflict. Clients choose their character's path based on the story they most want, or need, to tell (Wizards of the Coast, 2014).

The last step is developing a backstory. Together, we weave together their characters' family history, cultural identity, pivotal experiences, flaws, and motivations. Then we step back and discuss, asking questions like "What about this character feels like you?", "What feels different?", and "What emotional themes seem familiar?" These insights guide the goals of the group: what roles they'll explore, what behaviors they'll experiment with, and what story arcs we want to pay attention to.

Once the group begins, we play. We role-play. We improvise. It's more than games and dice. I use interventions drawn from sandtray counseling, Gestalt psychology, psychodrama, narrative counseling, internal family systems, and behavioral models to help participants engage with the material on multiple levels. Role-playing in these sessions becomes a process of witnessing, experimenting, and healing.

TTRPGs offer unique clinical benefits (Hartwig et al., 2025). Clients access internal creative resources. They practice social skills and group dynamics. They wrestle with failure through dice rolls and unpredictable turns. For those experiencing depression, anxiety, or isolation, these groups offer a chance to connect, both within the story and outside of it. Because *D&D* is a widely enjoyed hobby, these clients often leave with a newfound interest that expands their social circles.

Beyond counseling, I've found TTRPGs to be powerful tools in counselor supervision and organizational team building. I once ran a game for a group of Jude's supervisees centered around their "shadow selves" (Jung, 1951/2015), aspects of self they struggled to own in the counseling room. The story culminated in a battle where they had to use those very shadow traits to defeat an inventor who was stealing emotions from an entire village. The goal wasn't to win the fight—it was to face the parts of themselves they were avoiding.

More recently, I began running a weekly campaign for the University of Mary Hardin-Baylor counseling faculty. What started as a pilot test for my groups turned into a cherished part of their weekly rhythm. Through shared storytelling, they've found connection, levity, and a way to engage one another beyond the roles of professor, administrator, or colleague.

TTRPGs allow people to connect with imagination, possibility, and one another through play. And play, I believe, is a fundamental part of healing. If more people, especially adults, had access to regular, meaningful play, I believe we'd see less anxiety and depression, and more joy and creative problem-solving in the world.

I'm grateful that one of my hobbies has become one of the most impactful tools in my clinical and professional toolbox. I hope this encourages other counselors to think outside the box—maybe even the dice box—and imagine what healing can look like when we invite people into the story.

---

Joe's story reminds us that nontraditional practices and side hustles do not have to be flashy. What's important is that they reflect you. Whether it's games, writing, teaching, or something no one's thought of yet, there's room in this field for creativity.

# References

American Counseling Association. (2014). *ACA Code of Ethics*. ACA. https://www.counseling.org/docs/default-source/default-document-library/ethics/2014-aca-code-of-ethics.pdf

Amwell. (n.d.). *Amwell: Your partner in care delivery* [Telemedicine company]. Retrieved October 28, 2025, from https://business.amwell.com/

Anctil, T. M., Smith, C., Schenck, P., & Dahir, C. (2012). Professional school counselors' career development practices and continuing education needs. *Career Development Quarterly, 60*(2), 109–121. https://doi.org/10.1002/j.2161-0045.2012.00009.x

Bachkirova, T., & Baker, S. (2018). Revisiting the issue of boundaries between coaching and counselling. In S. Palmer & A. Whybrow (Eds.), *Handbook of coaching psychology: A guide for practitioners* (2nd ed., pp. 487–499). Routledge.

BetterHelp. (2025). *BetterHelp* [Online counseling platform]. BetterHelp. Retrieved October 28, 2025, from https://www.betterhelp.com

Cerebral. (n.d.) *Cerebral: Online mental health care that caters to you* [Telehealth company]. Retrieved October 28, 2025, from https://cerebral.com/

Corey, G., Muratori, M., Austin, J. T., II, & Austin, J. A. (2023). *Counselor self-care* (2nd ed.). American Counseling Association.

Counseling Compact. (n.d.). *Compact map*. Retrieved October 28, 2025, from https://counselingcompact.gov/map/

Cozolino, L. (2015). *Why therapy works: Using our minds to change our brains*. Norton Professional Books.

Etsy. (n.d.). *Sell on Etsy* [E-commerce platform]. Etsy, Inc. Retrieved October 28, 2025, from https://www.etsy.com/sell

Gumroad. (n.d.). *Start selling on Gumroad* [E-commerce platform]. Gumroad. Retrieved October 28, 2025, from https://gumroad.com

Hartwig, E. K., Walker, E., & Stamman, J. (2025). Roll for initiative: Using Dungeons and Dragons in play therapy. *Journal of Creativity in Mental Health, 20*(1), 113–126. https://doi.org/10.1080/15401383.2024.2322521

Here Be Dragons. (n.d.). *Here Be Dragons counseling services*. Retrieved October 29, 2025, from https://www.herebedragonscounseling.com/

Jo, E., Kouaho, W.-J., Schueller, S. M., & Epstein, D. A. (2023). Exploring user perspectives of and ethical experiences with teletherapy apps: Qualitative analysis of user reviews. *JMIR Mental Health, 10,* Article e49684. https://doi.org/10.2196/49684

Johnston, H., & Slye, N. (2025). "Get on board or get off": Nosediving job quality for mental health providers in the age of platform work. *Work, Employment and Society.* Advance online publication. https://doi.org/10.1177/09500170251360175

Jung, C. G. (2015). The shadow. In *Collected works of C. G. Jung: Aion researches into the phenomenology of the self* (Vol. 9, part 3). Routledge. Original work published in 1951.

Kale Monk, J., Oseland, L. M., Nelson Goff, B. S., Ogolsky, B. G., & Summers, K. (2017). Integrative intensive retreats for veteran couples and families: A pilot study assessing change in relationship adjustment, posttraumatic growth, and trauma symptoms. *Journal of Marital and Family Therapy, 43*(3), 448–462. https://doi.org/10.1111/jmft.12230

Kidd, S. A., Kerman, N., Cole, D., Madan, A., Muskat, E., Raja, S., Rallabandi, S., & McKenzie, K. (2015). Social entrepreneurship and mental health intervention: A literature review and scan of expert perspectives. *International Journal of Mental Health and Addiction, 13*(6), 776–787. https://doi.org/10.1007/s11469-015-9575-9

Lockhart, E. N. S. (2024). Silent threats: The unchecked exploitation of client testimonials in online therapy service platforms. *The Family Journal, 33*(3), 433–437. https://doi.org/10.1177/10664807241269466

Luxton, D. D., Nelson, E.-L., & Maheu, M. M. (2024). *A practitioner's guide to telemental health: How to conduct legal, ethical, and evidence-based telepractice* (2nd ed.). American Psychological Association.

Mellin, E. A., Hunt, B., & Nichols, L. M. (2011). Counselor professional identity: Findings and implications for counseling and interprofessional collaboration. *Journal of Counseling and Development, 89*(2), 140–147. https://doi.org/10.1002/j.1556-6678.2011.tb00071.x

Mendes-Santos, C., Nunes, F., Weiderpass, E., Santana, R., & Andersson, G. (2022). Understanding mental health professionals' perspectives and practices regarding the implementation of digital mental health: Qualitative study. *JMIR Formative Research, 6*(4), Article e32558. https://doi.org/10.2196/32558

Passmore, J., & Fillery-Travis, A. (2011). A critical review of executive coaching research: A decade of progress and what's to come.

Coaching: An International Journal of Theory, Research and Practice, 4(2), 70–88. https://doi.org/10.1080/17521882.2011.596484

Payhip. (n.d.). *Payhip: Sell digital downloads, courses, coaching, and more from one simple platform* [E-commerce platform]. Payhip. Retrieved October 28, 2025, from https://payhip.com

Peeters, N., Rijk, K., Soetens, B., Storms, B., & Hermans, K. (2018). A systematic literature review to identify successful elements for financial education and counseling in groups. *Journal of Consumer Affairs, 52*(2), 415–440. https://doi.org/10.1111/joca.12180

Rees, S. D. (2024). Money matters. In S. Rees, *A therapist's guide to private practice: Building a values-based business* (pp. 31–50). Routledge.

Robledo Yamamoto, F., Voida, A., & Voida, S. (2021). From therapy to teletherapy: Relocating mental health services online. *Proceedings of the ACM on Human-Computer Interaction, 5*(CSCW2), 1–30. https://doi.org/10.1145/3479508

Skovholt, T. M., & Trotter-Mathison, M. (2016). *The resilient practitioner: Burnout prevention and self-care strategies for counselors, therapists, teachers, and health professionals* (3rd ed.). Routledge. https://doi.org/10.4324/9781315737447

Story, R., Jr. (2024, November 4). *How much do motivational speakers make?* SpeakerHub. https://speakerhub.com/skillcamp/how-much-do-motivational-speakers-make

Talkspace. (n.d.). *Talkspace* [Online therapy platform]. Talkspace. Retrieved October 28, 2025, from https://www.talkspace.com/

Taylor, D. (2025). *Clinical entrepreneurship and private practice innovation: Curriculum for the graduate-level counseling student* (Publication No. 31770191) [Doctoral dissertation, Regent University]. ProQuest Dissertations and Theses Global.

Therapist Site Toolbox. (2023, March 9). *Breaking free from the hourly rate: How therapists can boost their income with digital products.* Therapist Site Toolbox. https://www.therapistsitetoolbox.com/blog/how-therapists-can-boost-their-income-with-digital-products

TheraPlatform. (n.d.). *Passive income for therapists: Generating revenue through digital products, courses, and tools.* TheraPlatform Blog. Retrieved March 7, 2024, from https://www.theraplatform.com/blog/1546/passive-income-for-therapists

TherapyNotes. (n.d.). *TherapyNotes: The most trusted EHR for behavioral health* [EHR platform]. Retrieved October 29, 2025, from https://www.therapynotes.com/

Thriveworks. (n.d.). *Thriveworks: Therapy and psychiatry covered by insurance* [Online and in-person therapy platform]. Thriveworks. Retrieved October 28, 2025, from https://thriveworks.com/

Tides Mental Health. (2025, July 7). *Average cost of a psychological evaluation in the US: What you need to know.* Tides Mental Health. https://tidesmentalhealth.com/average-cost-of-a-psychological-evaluation-in-the-us/

Tudor Car, L., Soong, A., Kyaw, B. M., Chua, K. L., Low-Beer, N., & Majeed, A. (2019). Health professions digital education on clinical practice guidelines: A systematic review by Digital Health Education Collaboration. *BMC Medicine, 17,* Article 139. https://doi.org/10.1186/s12916-019-1370-1

Wizards of the Coast. (2014). *Dungeons & Dragons Player's Handbook* (5th ed.). Wizards of the Coast.

Yang, Y., & Hayes, J. A. (2020). Causes and consequences of burnout among mental health professionals: A practice-oriented review of recent empirical literature. *Psychotherapy, 57*(3), 426–433. https://doi.org/10.1037/pst0000317

Yau, J. H.-Y., Kanagawa, H. S., Lo, M. W.-S., Wong, S. L.-K., Wong, G. H.-Y., Lum, T., & Liu, T. (2023). Promoting mental health literacy among older adults in the East: An integrative framework. *Innovation in Aging, 7*(Suppl 1), 1171–1172. https://doi.org/10.1093/geroni/igad104.3756

Zoom. (n.d.) *Zoom for healthcare* [telehealth platform]. Retrieved October 29, 2025, from https://www.zoom.com/en/industry/healthcare/

# 8

# Administrative Duties

When most counselors dream about joining the counseling field, they think about deep, transformational sessions, not spreadsheets, scheduling, or note audits. Administrative duties often feel like the "extra" work. They're necessary, but feel somehow separate from the clinical heart of what we do.

Even if it doesn't feel like it, administrative work is clinical work. It's the invisible scaffolding that supports the visible healing. When your finances are organized, your schedule is predictable, and your records are clean, you show up calmer, sharper, and more present for your clients. You make fewer errors. You offer more consistency. Your clients feel that difference, even if they don't know why.

Research has backed this up: Burnout among helping professionals isn't just driven by client load. It's fueled by administrative disorganization and boundary ambiguity (Rupert & Morgan, 2005). When you don't have strong systems, every small task drains mental energy, and that cumulative drainage erodes the quality of your clinical work. Ignoring administrative duties doesn't just cause chaos behind the scenes. It bleeds into client care. Missed appointments, late notes, confusing invoices, inconsistent boundaries—all of these administrative "gaps" create therapeutic micro-ruptures. They send subtle signals that the space isn't fully safe. Reframing administrative systems as acts of protection and professionalism changes everything.

When you create predictable structures for your practice, you're not "selling out" or "getting corporate." You're securing the ground on which your clients stand. You're saying, "This space will hold you consistently, ethically, and with care." Good administration promotes safety and trust. It ensures the healing work can happen without distraction. Building administrative strength is a skill, not a personality trait. You don't have to be a born organizer. You just have to be willing to treat the "unseen work" with the same reverence you give to the "seen work." In this chapter, we show you how to build systems that serve you so you can keep showing up for your clients in the ways that matter most.

## Financial Management and Billing

Money might not be your *favorite* part of the job, but if you're in this field, managing it well is part of the job. Whether you're solo or building a team, your financial systems are what keep the lights on, the doors open, and the stress down. You don't have to be a spreadsheet wizard or a certified public accountant (CPA) to run your practice responsibly, but you do need to know where your money is going, how to track it, and how to clearly and ethically bill clients. When your finances are in order, you feel steadier. When clients understand what to expect, they feel safer. This section walks you through the core financial habits and systems every counselor needs.

### Creating a Financial System That Works for You

If you're running a counseling practice, you're running a business. Financial systems are the foundation that allows you to build thriving clinical work. You need consistency, clarity, and a willingness to treat this part of your business with the same care you give to your clients.

You can use free tools like Wave, paid platforms like Intuit QuickBooks (n.d.), or even a well-designed spreadsheet. Robust accounting software improves accuracy and timeliness in financial reporting (Nwankwo et al., 2025). Regularly using any of these options will get you most of the way there. The point isn't to obsess over every penny—it's to build a clear picture of how your money moves so you can make thoughtful decisions. Research in behavioral finance has shown that creating mental "buckets" for your expenses, like taxes, continuing education, or office upgrades, improves long-term financial self-control and reduces stress (Byrne & Brooks, 2008).

One of the smartest habits you can build early on is automatic savings. Open a separate savings account connected to your business checking account, and every time you get paid, move 25–30%, or whatever you can responsibly spare, of that payment into the savings account for taxes. This simple routine protects you from panic when quarterly taxes are due and keeps you in good standing with the Internal Revenue Service (IRS). Studies on automatic savings plans, even outside of small business contexts, have shown that defaulting into savings increases follow-through and cushions financial anxiety (Beshears et al., 2024).

While you're at it, create another savings bucket for professional development. Continuing education units (CEUs), certifications, and conference registrations shouldn't feel like financial emergencies. You're investing in your growth, and that investment needs a line in your budget. Research on financial stress among helping professionals has shown that proactive financial planning can help buffer burnout and role overload (Britt et al., 2016). When your finances are stable, your mind is clearer, and your presence is sharper. That stability and clarity provide enough space for you to do the work that really matters.

## Billing Clients and Insurance Properly

If it's clear and consistent, billing won't be a nightmare. For private-pay practices, using an invoicing feature built into electronic health record (EHR) platforms like SimplePractice (n.d.) or TherapyNotes (n.d.) ensures clients receive receipts promptly (American Counseling Association [ACA], 2020). Including fees, cancellation policies, and payment expectations in your informed consent is ethically mandated. The *ACA Code of Ethics* (2014, Standard A.2.b) states that counselors must clearly inform clients about fees, billing, and cancellation policies as part of the informed consent process. Research has shown that financial transparency enhances client trust and satisfaction while reducing billing disputes and missed sessions (Polaris, 2019). When accepting insurance, billing becomes more complex, but not unmanageable. You will need to track clients' copays, interpret explanation of benefits (EOBs), and submit claims either manually or via an EHR-integrated clearinghouse.

Recent legislation like the No Surprises Act, most of which took effect January 1, 2022, requires good-faith cost estimates and prohibits surprise out-of-network bills in many situations (Hoadley et al., 2020; U.S. Department of Labor, n.d.). Studies have suggested that these transparency laws reduce patient financial shocks and enhance trust in the care process (Schechter & Sklar, 2022). If insurance billing becomes a drain, or your caseload grows, it may be time to outsource. A trained biller can handle denied claims, timely resubmissions, and detailed reporting. When interviewing potential biller candidates, ask about their experience with mental health billing, denial and error rates, and frequency of client reports.

Smart billing cultivates a trustworthy financial partnership. Clear billing signals to clients and to yourself that your work is rooted in integrity as much as in care.

## Client Record-Keeping and Documentation

We do not know about y'all, but we were hooked on this field the second we saw a Subjective, Objective, Assessment, and Plan (SOAP) note template—just kidding! That being said, documentation is one of the most important clinical tools in our toolbox. Good documentation keeps clients safe, supports ethical decision-making, and protects your professional future. It also sharpens your clinical thinking by helping you track patterns, adjust treatment plans, and communicate clearly with other providers. You don't need to write essays after every session, but you do need to create a record that respects the client, protects the process, and reflects your clinical judgment.

### *The Legal and Ethical Importance of Good Records*

Client records are the backbone of ethical, legal, and clinical integrity in your practice. When your notes are accurate, timely, and purposeful, they protect your clients and your practice, especially if you're audited, subpoenaed, or face a complaint. They also sharpen your clinical thinking, helping you spot trends, measure progress, and coordinate care with other providers. The *ACA Code of Ethics* (2014, Standard A.1.b) emphasizes the importance of thorough documentation, and federal regulations such as the Health Insurance Portability and Accountability Act (HIPAA) require confidentiality and secure handling of client information.

The impact of good documentation goes beyond compliance. In a study, Baumann et al. (2018) found that thorough, routine documentation supports better diagnosis, continuity of care, and risk mitigation. Poor documentation, in contrast, can compromise treatment decisions, continuity, and even client safety (Baumann et al., 2018). Clear records are also essential for clinicians: Progress notes written with structure in mind, using templates such as SOAP or Data, Assessment, Plan (DAP), support better reasoning and communication while improving efficiency (Cifuentes et al., 2015; Reiter, 2023).

## Structuring Your Client Files

A well-organized client file is easy to navigate and supports ethical care. Core components include the following.

- **Informed consent and intake forms:** Signed documents covering confidentiality, fees, and session logistics.
- **Assessments:** Standardized tools or clinical impressions from intake.
- **Treatment plans:** Client-centered goals, objectives, and strategies.
- **Progress notes:** Session summaries that include experience, interventions, observations, and plans.
- **Termination summaries:** When counseling ends, note why and outline any recommended follow-up.

Whether you're working with paper files or an EHR, consistency is key. Templates can help maintain quality and completeness. Many EHRs offer customizable formats like SOAP or streamlined options like DAP, which clinicians appreciate for balancing efficiency with thoroughness (Reiter, 2023; Adhikary et al., 2025).

Research supports structured note formats. SOAP notes are ideal for intricate clinical reasoning and cross-provider communication, while DAP notes can save time and keep documentation aligned with payer standards (Reiter, 2023; Twofold Health, 2025). Templates save effort and support clear, auditable notes—a benefit demonstrated by improved documentation quality in mental health settings (Baker et al, 2000).

## Keeping Up Without Burning Out

Rather than feeling like a grind, documentation can be a sustainable, integrated part of your workflow with a few smart strategies:

### Commit to the 24-Hour Window

Finish your session notes within 24 hours to ensure that your observations are fresh and the details are vivid. This simple habit aligns with best-practice guidelines and reduces the risk of forgotten details or clinical errors (Zur Institute, 2023).

### Use Structured Templates (SOAP and DAP)

Templates help you focus on what matters: interventions, progress, and plans. Counselors using formats like SOAP or DAP often write notes faster and more consistently than those relying on free text (Reiter,

2023; Sudarsan et al., 2021). Set up dropdown menus in your EHR for commonly used languages. This cuts down on typing and maintains standardization (Ebbers et al., 2022).

**Batch Your Documentation**

Block out one or two daily slots to write multiple session notes at once instead of doing them between appointments. Research on batching has shown that it reduces decision fatigue and improves focus, both of which are useful in emotionally demanding work (Baumeister et al., 2007).

**Optimize Your EHR Tools**

Fully leverage your system's capabilities. Use smart templates and macros; pre-populate fields from intake or prior notes; and explore AI-based helpers that auto-summarize sessions or pull previous session data (ClinicTracker, n.d., Chew & Ngiam, 2025). Clinicians retrained to use EHR efficiencies report less burnout and higher note quality (Alobayli et al., 2023; Rao et al., 2017).

**Keep It Clinically Focused**

Your notes shouldn't read like a diary. Stick to the client's key presentation, the interventions you used, progress toward their goals, and any risk or safety issues. Cut out small talk, lengthy personal anecdotes, and unrelated tangents. Documentation is about capturing the therapeutic "gold" and letting the rest go.

**Know When to Delegate**

If documentation still piles up, consider delegating intake forms or task summaries to support staff. In medical settings, asking a medical assistant to handle parts of documentation has been shown to greatly reduce clinician workload (AAFP, 2022).

## *Why It Matters*

Heavy documentation demands are linked to stress and burnout in behavioral health professionals (Mentalyc, n.d.; Rosso, 2024). Overdocumentation not only steals time from clients but also diminishes clinical energy and can compromise care (Sadeh-Sharvit & Hollon, 2025). By documenting quickly, using structured tools, batching efficiently, optimizing technology, and delegating when possible, you reclaim time, reduce emotional drain, and serve clients more effectively.

## Hiring and Managing Staff

By the time you're thinking about hiring, you've probably already felt the strain. Your calendar is packed, your paperwork is backlogged, and the systems you once managed independently now demand more than one person can reasonably handle. That's not failure; it's growth, but growth without structure leads straight to burnout.

Hiring expands your vision. Building a team that reflects your values, operates with integrity, and protects the clinical space you've worked so hard to cultivate can make your dreams grow larger than you may have thought possible. Building and expanding your practice with more employees will grow your reach and improve your long-term potential.

### When It's Time to Expand

The right time to grow your counseling organization, whether it's an agency or private practice, often doesn't announce itself with fanfare. It sneaks up on you. One minute, everything feels manageable; the next, you're booked three months out, feeling frazzled, and wondering if weekends are just a myth. That exhaustion is a red flag for burnout, a condition experienced by up to 67% of mental health professionals (Morse et al., 2012; Salyers et al., 2019). Recognizing these signs early and hiring before burnout peaks is essential. Here are a few indications that you may be ready to expand your team.

- You are consistently turning away referrals due to a lack of availability.
- You're working far more hours than intended without seeing proportional revenue.
- Administrative tasks are encroaching on your clinical time.
- You want to offer new specialties (e.g., trauma counseling, group work, testing services), but can't safely manage the added workload.

Studies have shown that excessive caseloads and administrative burdens are core drivers of burnout in clinicians, with burnout linked to reduced quality of care and increased turnover (SAMHSA, 2022; Morse et al., 2012).

### Employees (W-2) versus Independent Contractors (1099)

When you hire, you must decide if you want to bring on employees or independent contractors. There's no one-size-fits-all answer. Employees give you more control over schedules, methods, and benefits, but they also come with payroll, labor law, insurance, and tax responsibilities (Dowling, 2001; McGurk, 2009). Misclassification can result in fines, back taxes, and penalties (U.S. Department of Labor, 2024).

Independent contractors offer flexibility and fewer overhead costs. They manage their schedules, taxes, and benefits, but you can't legally oversee their clinical methods, training, or performance (Beidas et al., 2016). For mental health practices, this distinction isn't merely academic: one study found that using independent contractors correlated with lower adherence to evidence-based practices compared to clinicians classified as employees (Webb et al., 2010).

If you need someone embedded in your team who is aligned with your values and clinical methods, and you're ready to handle payroll, hiring them as W-2 employees often makes sense (McGurk, 2009). If you need fractional help or have inconsistent demand, contractors are a good choice. Keep in mind that this requires meeting legal requirements and planning for your contractors' time independence.

## *Legal and Financial Considerations When Hiring*

Hiring means finding the right people and onboarding them the right way. Relationships matter, but so does compliance. Whether you're bringing on your first team member or expanding an existing staff, there are nonnegotiables you will need to handle on the front end. If you're hiring W-2 employees, set up a formal payroll system, draft clear employment agreements, and ensure you're following federal and state labor laws, including wage standards, overtime rules, and nondiscrimination policies. For independent contractors, you need a legally sound contractor agreement and must avoid exerting control over their schedule, methods, and training, or risk misclassification.

You are also responsible for filing the right tax paperwork. W-2s are for employees, and 1099s are for contractors. Partnering with a payroll service like Gusto (n.d.) or Intuit QuickBooks (n.d.) can take a lot off your plate. These platforms help manage deductions, filings, and payments accurately and on time. Unless you're ready to spend serious time learning IRS and Department of Labor regulations, you likely need to invest in payroll and compliance assistance. Your team deserves a leader who values both heart and structure. That starts with getting the foundational business practices right.

# Building a Healthy Practice Culture

The culture of a workplace, whether it's a private practice, a community agency, a university clinic, or a group practice, is shaped day by day. Your work environment is influenced as much by what you model as by what you put in writing. It starts with setting clear expectations from the beginning through job descriptions, contracts, or onboarding materials that reflect your values and operational standards. Define how your team communicates, how decisions are made, and what kind of behavior is encouraged or discouraged.

Regardless of your setting, offering regular supervision or mentorship—formally required or not—fosters a sense of safety, accountability, and connection. Teams don't just need direction; they need support. A culture where people know the boundaries and feel safe to ask questions is a culture where people grow (Bernard & Goodyear, 2019).

Well-run systems—ones that have structured feedback loops, clear time-off policies, transparent billing or productivity metrics, and reliable internal communication—can prevent burnout, confusion, and resentment. People do better when they know where they stand and what to expect. A healthy workplace culture needs predictability, fairness, and a sense of belonging.

## *Tips for Effectively Managing a Counseling Practice Team*

The buck stops with you when you're the leader. If you're wondering why your team feels dysfunctional, look in the mirror. If you're struggling to retain counselors or clients of color, you might not be creating a safe environment in your practice. If you're frustrated with the new generation of counselors who just don't "get it," you're probably not adequately communicating your expectations. The culture of your organization will reflect your values, your blind spots, your priorities, and your limitations. You're not just the boss. You're the model. You set the tone for how your team communicates, handles conflict, sets boundaries, and shows up for clients.

An effective leader creates the kind of environment where good clinicians can do great work. That means setting expectations clearly, offering real support, and following through with consistency and fairness. When the culture is right, everything else works better. Retention improves, clients feel safer, and you can take pride in your team.

**Trust Through Transparency**

Be open about policies, pay scales, and performance criteria. Studies have shown that transparent leadership practices increase job satisfaction and reduce turnover among mental health professionals (Brenner et al., 2022).

**Regular Check-Ins and Feedback Loops**

Schedule consistent one-on-one check-ins—ideally monthly or quarterly. These conversations should not only celebrate strengths, but also address small concerns early. Research has shown that structured feedback systems are effective ways to support staff well-being and professional growth (Koivu, 2013).

**Invest in Development**

A crucial element of good leadership is investing in the development of your employees. Implement professional development plans, complete with goal-setting and annual reviews. Providing ongoing training is strongly linked to higher clinician engagement, reduced burnout, and improved client outcomes (Konstam et al., 2015).

**Small Acts, Big Culture**

Culture grows from consistent, intentional actions. Show up to meetings on time, acknowledge wins big and small, model respect, and follow through on promises. These habits build psychological safety, increasing trust and openness (Edmondson, 2018).

# A Healthy Practice

When financial, administrative, and clinical systems run smoothly, your team has the emotional clearance they need to fully show up. A healthy practice isn't built overnight. It's the result of intentional leadership: clarity, empathy, fairness, and reliability. Don't sweat too much about having all the answers. Intending to lead well and regularly checking in with your team goes far. When you build that foundation, the healing work out front flourishes.

Administrative work makes clinical work possible. Clean systems, strong documentation, sustainable schedules, and healthy teams are the scaffolding that holds your practice and your well-being together. Whether you're working alone, managing a small team, or leading an entire agency, your back-end structure shapes your front-line presence.

It's what lets you show up clear, grounded, and fully available for your clients. Take the time to build it right.

It's easy to fall in love with the idea of private practice, but as many of us find out, the business side of that dream can come with unexpected weight. In this reflection, Alicia Prachar, Licensed Professional Counselor Supervisor (LPC-S), trained eye-movement, desensitization, and reprocessing (EMDR), and Founder of Chasing Grace Therapy in Georgetown, Texas, shares a real story of what happens when the dream collides with responsibility, and how to rebuild a practice that truly sustains the counselor as much as it serves the client. Her story is a powerful reminder that private practice doesn't have to be a one-size-fits-all model, and it certainly doesn't have to cost your well-being.

## Voices from the Field

### ALICIA PRACHAR, LPC-S

When I began my private practice, it was driven by both passion and vision. After working in schools, hospitals, and community agencies, I was done being boxed in by bureaucracy. I longed for freedom, for a space that felt safe, meaningful, and wholly aligned with my values. I wanted to choose my clients, craft my days, and build a healing space that honored the kind of care I was trained to give.

For a while, it was everything I hoped it would be. I filled my office with calming décor, set flexible hours, and served clients deeply, especially those navigating relational trauma, anxiety, and perfectionism. I was finally doing the work I loved in the way I believed it should be done.

I didn't realize how complex the business side of things would become. Being a strong clinician is one thing. Being a competent entrepreneur is another.

As the practice grew, so did my responsibilities. I had to hire staff, manage billing, respond to crises, and keep up with insurance. Suddenly, I wasn't just holding space for clients; I was holding the entire business together. I hired people who didn't always match my dedication. They missed notes, took ethical shortcuts, and skipped protocols. Every misstep landed on my desk. When people left without notice or accountability, I carried the weight. Billing became a second full-time job. Claims were delayed for months. Clients showed up without the means to pay. Office staff entered the wrong codes. It was draining and lonely.

Eventually, I realized I wasn't alone in this. So many practice owners burn out doing too much with too little support. The classic model—back-to-back sessions five days a week—becomes stifling. You lose creativity. You lose joy.

That realization was my turning point. The first thing I did was hire a billing specialist. I had been spending hours every week chasing insurance claims and correcting coding errors, and I finally admitted that my time was worth more than the billing fee. The relief was immediate.

Next, I started over with my team. I rewrote our policies, clarified expectations, and learned to interview for values, not just experience. Letting go of the wrong fit was hard, but it opened space for people who shared my vision and integrity.

I also began blocking off one week each quarter as an "admin reset"—no clients, just systems, reflection, and rest. It changed everything.

Luckily, burnout wasn't the end of my story, and it doesn't have to be the end of yours, either. We don't have to abandon private practice when the back-end work becomes overwhelming; we just have to rethink it. Counseling doesn't have to mean a couch and a clock. We can teach workshops, host retreats, create courses, offer walk-and-talk sessions, and run virtual groups. We can build practices that include art, movement, and sensory integration—practices that center on our well-being as much as our clients'.

I know counselors who lead weekend retreats on art counseling and mindfulness. Others run healing intensives or offer coaching packages that blend somatic work and adventure. These are not just income streams; they are energy sources. They bring life back to the work.

We can also rethink the counseling space itself. Not every client needs a chair across from us. Some need a walk. Others need silence and a coloring book. Counseling is a living, adaptive process, and our practices should reflect that. Technology opens doors, too. Online groups, coaching intensives, webinars, and CEU courses expand your reach and reduce burnout.

And we need self-care systems that are built into the business, not overstuffed calendars. Real breaks, vacations, administrative help, billers, and vacant weeks are all lifesavers. We've inherited a model that treats burnout as normal. It shouldn't be.

We don't serve clients better by sacrificing ourselves. We serve better when we are rested, inspired, and whole. This isn't about lowering standards. It's about raising the bar on what kind of life and business this work can offer. Private practice doesn't have to cost you your joy or your future. Done right, it can fuel both.

There's power in permitting yourself to evolve. Alicia's story reminds us that success in counseling isn't just about helping others. It is also about building a life from which you do not need to escape. What could your practice look like if it truly reflected your values, your energy, and your vision for a sustainable career?

# References

Adhikary, P. K., Singh, S., Singh, S., Sharma, P., Soni, P., Choudhary, R., Saxena, C., Chauchan, P., Gupta, S. K., Deb, K. S., Singh, S. M, & Chakraborty, T. (2025). *Towards richer AI-assisted psychotherapy notemaking and performance benchmarking.* MedRxiv. https://doi.org/10.1101/2025.06.25.25330252

Alobayli, F., O'Connor, S., Holloway, A., & Cresswell, K. (2023). Electronic health record stress and burnout among clinicians in hospital settings: A systematic review. *Digital Health, 9*, Article 20552076231220241. https://doi.org/10.1177/20552076231220241

American Counseling Association. (2014). *ACA code of ethics.* ACA. https://www.counseling.org/docs/default-source/default-document-library/ethics/2014-aca-code-of-ethics.pdf

Baker, J. G., Shanfield, S. B., & Schnee, S. (2000). Using quality improvement teams to improve documentation in records at a community mental health center. *Psychiatric Services, 51*(2), 239–242. https://doi.org/10.1176/appi.ps.51.2.239

Baumann, L. A., Baker, J., & Elshaug, A. G. (2018). The impact of electronic health record systems on clinical documentation times: A systematic review. *Health Policy, 122*(8), 827–836. https://doi.org/10.1016/j.healthpol.2018.05.014

Baumeister, R. F., Vohs, K. D., & Tice, D. M. (2007). The strength model of self-control. *Current Directions in Psychological Science, 16*(6), 351–355. https://doi.org/10.1111/j.1467-8721.2007.00534.x

Beidas, R. S., Stewart, R. E., Benjamin Wolk, C., Adams, D. R., Marcus, S. C., Evans, A. C., Jr., Jackson, K., Neimark, G., Hurford, M. O., Erney, J., Rubin, R., Hadley, T. R., Barg, F. K., & Mandell, D. S. (2016). Independent contractors in public mental health clinics: Implications for use of evidence-based practices. *Psychiatric Services, 67*(7), 710–717. https://doi.org/10.1176/appi.ps.201500234

Bernard, J. M., & Goodyear, R. K. (2019). *Fundamentals of clinical supervision* (6th ed.). Pearson.

Beshears, J., Blakstad, M., Choi, J. J., Firth, C., Gathergood, J., Laibson, D., Notley, R., Sheth, J. D., Sandbrook, W., & Stewart, N. (2024). Does pension automatic enrollment increase debt? Evidence from a large-scale natural experiment [NBER working paper 32100]. *National Bureau of Economic Research.* https://doi.org/10.3386/w32100

Brenner, M. J., Hickson, G. B., Boothman, R. C., Rushton, C. H., & Bradford, C. R. (2022). Honesty and transparency, indispensable to the clinical mission—part III: How leaders can prevent burnout, foster wellness and recovery, and instill resilience. *Otolaryngologic Clinics of North America, 55*(1), 83–103. https://doi.org/10.1016/j.otc.2021.08.004

Britt, S. L., Mendiola, M. R., Schink, G. H., Tibbetts, R. H., & Jones, S. H. (2016). Financial stress, coping strategy, and academic achievement of college students. *Journal of Financial Counseling and Planning, 27*(2), 172–183. https://files.eric.ed.gov/fulltext/EJ1161821.pdf

Byrne, A., & Brooks, M. (2008). *Behavioral finance: Theories and evidence*. The Research Foundation of CFA Institute. https://www.cannonfinancial.com/uploads/main/Behavioral_Finance-Theories_Evidence.pdf

Chew, B.-H., & Ngiam, K. Y. (2025). Artificial intelligence tool development: What clinicians need to know? *BMC Medicine, 23*(1), 244. https://doi.org/10.1186/s12916-025-04076-0

Cifuentes, M., Davis, M., Fernald, D., Gunn, R., Dickinson, P., & Cohen, D. J. (2015). Electronic health record challenges, workarounds, and solutions observed in practices integrating behavioral health and primary care. *The Journal of the American Board of Family Medicine, 28*(Suppl. 1), S63–S72. https://doi.org/10.3122/jabfm.2015.S1.150133

ClinicTracker. (n.d.). *ClinicTracker* [Behavioral health EHR documentation automation]. ClinicTracker. Retrieved November 3, 2025, from https://www.clinictracker.com

Dowling, D. C., Jr. (2001). The practice of international labor & employment law: Escort your labor/employment clients into the global millennium. *The Labor Lawyer, 17*, 1–23.

Ebbers, T., Kool, R. B., Smeele, L. E., Dirven, R., den Besten, C. A., Karssemakers, L. H. E., Verhoeven, T., Herruer, J. M., van den Broek, G. B., & Takes, R. P. (2022). The impact of structured and standardized documentation on documentation quality; a multicenter, retrospective study. *Journal of Medical Systems, 46*, Article 46. https://doi.org/10.1007/s10916-022-01837-9

Edmondson, A. C. (2018). *The fearless organization: Creating psychological safety in the workplace for learning, innovation, and growth*. Wiley.

Gusto. (n.d.). *Gusto* [Payroll and HR for small businesses]. Retrieved November 3, 2025, from https://www.gusto.com

Hoadley, J., Keith, K., & Lucia, K. (2020, December 18). Unpacking the No Surprises Act: An opportunity to protect millions. *Health Affairs Blog*. https://doi.org/10.1377/forefront.20201217.247010

Intuit QuickBooks. (n.d.). *Intuit QuickBooks* [Payroll software]. Retrieved November 3, 2025, from https://quickbooks.intuit.com/payroll

Koivu, A. (2013). *Clinical supervision and well-being at work: A four-year follow-up study on female hospital nurses* [Doctoral dissertation, University of Eastern Finland]. Publications of the University of Eastern Finland Dissertations in Health Sciences. https://erepo.uef.fi/items/5238bd36-b1e3-40e9-867c-e33309708f2c

Konstam, V., Cook, A. L., Tomek, S., Mahdavi, E., Gracia, R., & Bayne, A. H. (2015). What factors sustain professional growth among school counselors? *Journal of School Counseling, 13*, n3. https://files.eric.ed.gov/fulltext/EJ1051090.pdf

McGurk, M. M. (2009). *A payroll business model for the future* [Unpublished master's thesis]. University of Chester. https://chesterrep.openrepository.com/handle/10034/73256

Mentaylc. (n.d.). *Mentalyc* [Clinical intelligence platform]. Retrieved November 3, 2025, from https://www.mentalyc.com

Morse, G., Salyers, M. P., Rollins, A. L., Monroe-DeVita, M., & Pfahler, C. (2012). Burnout in mental health services: A review of the problem and its remediation. *Administration and Policy in Mental Health and Mental Health Services Research, 39*(5), 341–352. https://doi.org/10.1007/s10488-011-0352-1

Nwankwo, P. E., Igwe, A. O., & Nnamani, C. O. (2025). Effect of automated accounting software on the efficiency of Nigerian SMEs' financial operations. *Global Journal of Auditing and Finance, 7*(1), 1–17.

Polaris, J. (2019). *Financial transparency: The key to patient satisfaction*. Medical Economics. https://www.medicaleconomics.com/view/financial-transparency-key-patient-satisfaction

Rao, S. K., Kimball, A. B., Lehrhoff, S. R., Hidrue, M. K., Colton, D. G., Ferris, T. G., & Torchiana, D. F. (2017). The impact of administrative burden on academic physicians: Results of a hospital-wide physician survey. *Academic Medicine, 92*(2), 237–243. https://doi.org/10.1097/ACM.0000000000001461

Reiter, M. D. (2023). *A therapist's guide to writing in psychotherapy: Assessment, documentation, and intervention*. Routledge.

Rosso, S. (2024, August 29). The overlooked documentation burden threatening mental health services. *Forbes*. https://www.forbes.com/sites/forbeseq/2024/08/29/

the-overlooked-documentation-burden-threatening-mental-health-services/

Rupert, P. A., & Morgan, D. J. (2005). Work setting and burnout among professional psychologists. *Professional Psychology: Research and Practice, 36*(5), 544–550. https://doi.org/10.1037/0735-7028.36.5.544

Sadeh-Sharvit, S., & Hollon, S. D. (2025). AI integration in behavioral healthcare: A practical framework for clinicians. *Journal of Technology in Behavioral Science,* 1–11. https://doi.org/10.1007/s41347-025-00532-z

Salyers, M. P., Garabrant, J. M., Luther, L., Henry, N., Fukui, S., Shimp, D., Wu, W., Gearheart, T., Morse, G., York, M. M., & Rollins, A. L. (2019). A comparative effectiveness trial to reduce burnout and improve quality of care. *Administration and Policy in Mental Health and Mental Health Services Research, 46*(2), 238–254. https://doi.org/10.1007/s10488-018-0908-4

Schechter, R. M., & Sklar, D. E. (2022). No surprises act and the provider/patient/payor dynamic backdrop. *American Bankruptcy Institute Journal, 41*(2), 8–55. https://www.abi.org/abi-journal/no-surprises-act-and-the-providerpatientpayor-dynamic-backdrop

SimplePractice. (n.d.). *SimplePractice* [Practice management software]. Retrieved November 3, 2025, from https://www.simplepractice.com/

Sudarsan, P., Balakrishna, A. G. M., Asir, J. A. R., Balu, D., Krishnamoorthy, S. G., & Borra, S. S. (2021). Development and validation of A-SOAP notes: Assessment of efficiency in documenting patient therapeutic records. *Journal of Applied Pharmaceutical Science, 11*(10), 001–006. https://doi.org/10.7324/JAPS.2021.1101001

TherapyNotes. (n.d.) *TherapyNotes* [EHR platform]. TherapyNotes. Retrieved November 3, 2025, from https://www.therapynotes.com/

U.S. Department of Labor. (2024, January 10). Employee or independent contractor classification under the Fair Labor Standards Act. *Federal Register, 89*(7), 1638–1718. https://www.federalregister.gov/documents/2024/01/10/2024-00067/employee-or-independent-contractor-classification-under-the-fair-labor-standards-act

U.S. Department of Labor. (n.d.). *No Surprises Act.* Employee Benefits Security Administration. Retrieved November 3, 2025, from https://www.dol.gov/agencies/ebsa/laws-and-regulations/laws/no-surprises-act

Webb, C. A., Derubeis, R. J., & Barber, J. P. (2010). Therapist adherence/competence and treatment outcome: A meta-analytic review. *Journal of Consulting and Clinical Psychology, 78*(2), 200–211. https://doi.org/10.1037/a0018912

Zur, O. (n.d.). *Introduction to informed consent in psychotherapy, counseling, and assessment*. Dr. Ofer Zur. Retrieved November 3, 2025, from https://drzur.com/informed-consent/

# 9

# Marketing Strategies for Counselors

We know marketing can feel uncomfortable, but if people don't know you exist, they cannot find you. They cannot show up for your help. They will never experience the warmth, training, and healing space you have worked so hard to build. At its best, marketing is an act of service (Knapp & VandeCreek, 2008). It's more than slick slogans or flashy posts. It makes it easier for the people who need your help to find you.

This chapter shows you how to clearly, consistently, and ethically show up. It demonstrates that marketing is a tool for connection, not just self-promotion. We detail practical strategies for both traditional outreach and digital visibility, including how to build a client-friendly website, how to use social media without selling out, and how to form referral relationships that feel good on both sides.

You do not have to be a marketing expert, but you must speak clearly and in a way that aligns with your values about what you do, who you serve, and how you can help. Marketing done well promotes clarity. In counseling, clarity builds trust (ACA, 2014; Barnett, 2019).

## Ethical Self-Promotion in Your Community

The *ACA Code of Ethics* (2014, Standard C.3.a) affirms that counselors must avoid false, misleading, or deceptive statements, but it does not discourage visibility or outreach. If you intend to provide accurate information, offer support, and let people know where to find you, you are still well within ethical bounds. Ethical promotion is rooted in your commitment to transparency, competence, and cultural responsiveness (Kaplan & Gladding, 2011).

To keep your marketing ethical, keep these guidelines in mind.

- Avoid promising outcomes or using language that implies guaranteed results. Stay away from "pain-point" marketing that manipulates emotional vulnerability (Kotler et al., 2021).
- Focus on educating, not selling.
- Use respectful language that upholds client dignity, especially when speaking about mental health conditions (Kotler et al., 2021).

## Traditional Marketing Techniques

For many counselors, traditional marketing strategies feel more natural than digital ones. They reflect what we do best—build relationships. Long before social media feeds and search engine rankings, counselors connected with their communities through trust, visibility, and word-of-mouth. These strategies still work. They can be especially powerful in smaller towns or communities where personal referrals carry more weight than online reviews.

Traditional marketing positions you in places where your ideal clients already live, work, and gather. Engaging in traditional marketing methods demands showing up consistently so that when someone does need support, your name is the first one they remember. In this section, we detail several time-tested strategies that remain relevant and effective today.

Business cards and printed materials may seem outdated, but they still hold power in face-to-face interactions. A well-designed card or brochure reinforces credibility and gives people something tangible to pass along. Whether you are attending a local event, meeting someone at church, or getting introduced through a mutual friend, having a physical card can create a lasting impression. Design tools like Canva (n.d.) or services like Vistaprint (n.d.) make it easy to create professional-looking materials that reflect your brand.

Public speaking to local audiences is one of the most efficient ways to establish credibility and attract clients. Consider offering a 30-minute talk at a local school, church, or community group on topics like anxiety in teenagers, communication in marriage, or managing grief. Research has shown that when counselors position themselves as community educators, they increase visibility and perceived expertise (Corrigan et al., 2012).

Hosting workshops and free information sessions are both marketing tools and acts of service. Whether you are offering parenting strategies, mental wellness check-ins, or coping skills for burnout, you are not only helping attendees but also introducing them to your counseling style and philosophy. According to Corrigan et al. (2012), community-based workshops help reduce stigma and increase help-seeking behaviors, particularly when presented in familiar, accessible settings.

Never underestimate the power of a well-placed flyer on a community bulletin board. These are the places people visit regularly and linger long enough to notice announcements. Small-town bulletin boards, YMCA newsletters, and church lobbies are often overlooked marketing gold. They can also signal that you are someone who understands and serves the local community.

If you have the confidence, time, and opportunity, a local radio spot or a recurring column in the city paper can be powerful visibility builders. Topics should be practical, down-to-earth, and non-clinical in tone. Think "How to Talk to Your Kids About Stress" rather than "Cognitive Behavioral Therapy for Adolescent Anxiety." You are building trust, not showing off credentials.

## *Measuring What Works*

The challenge with traditional marketing is that it can be hard to track impact. Unlike website clicks or social media analytics, you will not always know how many people saw your flyer or read your newspaper column, but there are still ways to monitor effectiveness.

Make it a habit to ask new clients how they heard about you. You can add a simple line to your intake form: "How did you find out about us?" Keep notes on outreach efforts. Track which organizations you have partnered with, where you have posted flyers, and when you hosted your last event. Tracking referral sources helps you follow up and identify what is gaining traction.

Look out for patterns as you track your referrals. If several clients say they saw your flyer at the local gym or heard you speak at the parent-teacher conference, you will know that the strategy is paying off. Evaluate cost versus return. Even low-cost marketing efforts take time. Reflect on which ones are generating connection and which ones feel like busywork. Over time, traditional marketing can build a strong, local referral network that works even when you are not actively promoting. It might be slow progress, but it can lead to more sustainable, values-aligned growth.

## Digital Marketing Strategies

In today's world, having an online presence is not optional. It is one of the primary ways people look for services, counseling included. A potential client might hear about you from a friend or colleague, but the next step they often take is a quick online search. If they cannot find you easily, or if your online presence is unclear or outdated, they are likely to move on. While traditional marketing strategies help build trust in your immediate community, digital strategies expand your visibility and provide legitimacy.

This section focuses on four key elements of digital marketing: search engine optimization (SEO), Google Business Profiles, paid advertisements, and review platforms. Together, these practices help people find, see, and trust you.

### Search Engine Optimization

SEO helps your website show up when someone searches for counselors in your area. Google tries to match people's search phrases (like "anxiety counselor near me" or "couples counseling Belton, TX") with the most relevant websites (Google, 2025). If your site includes these key phrases in the right places, you are more likely to show up in search results.

- Clearly state your specialty areas, office location, and credentials on your homepage and service pages.
- Use headers (H1, H2 tags) with search-friendly phrases like "Counseling for Teens in Lafayette" or "Counselor for Grief and Loss."
- Write blog posts answering common questions your clients might have. Search engines love helpful, relevant content.
- Optimize your site speed and make sure it works well on mobile. Google ranks mobile-friendly sites higher (Bansal, 2024).

SEO takes time, but it is one of the most sustainable ways to attract clients without constantly having to push out new content or spend money on ads.

## Google Business Profiles

If you only do one thing digitally, create (or claim) your Google Business Profile (n.d.). It is free, easy to set up, and directly connects you to local people searching for counseling services. It also helps you show up in the "map pack" (the top three results that appear on the map when you search) (SOCI, 2025).

- Ensure your name, phone number, address, and hours are accurate.
- Add photos of your office, headshots, and video introductions if you are comfortable being on camera.
- Encourage satisfied clients to leave honest reviews. A strong review profile builds credibility and increases clicks (Chen et al., 2022).

## Know When to Use Paid Ads

Paid advertising, Google Ads, and social media ads can be powerful, but they are not always necessary for solo or small group practices. If your schedule is already full, or you are in a low-competition area, you may not need to advertise at all. However, if you are just starting or trying to grow quickly, targeted online ads can help drive traffic. Here are some things to consider.

- Google Ads (2023) work best when targeted by location and keyword (e.g., "trauma counselor Austin"). You only pay when someone clicks.
- Facebook and Instagram ads allow you to target based on interests and demographics, but they work best for workshops or psychoeducational services, not necessarily one-on-one counseling (Sunhouse Marketing, 2025).
- Set a clear budget and track results. If you are spending money and not getting inquiries, pivot quickly.

Paid advertising can be effective, but it is rarely a long-term solution. Think of it as a temporary boost, not your primary marketing strategy (Sunhouse Marketing, 2025).

## Review Platforms

When someone is considering counseling, they often want to know what others think of them before reaching out. Review and referral platforms provide that extra element of trust. You do not need to be on every platform, but having a presence on one or two can help. Psychology Today (n.d.) is one of the most recognized platforms for counseling searches. Registering is not free, but the exposure can be worth the monthly fee, especially in high-volume areas. TherapyDen (n.d.) and Mental Health Match (n.d.) are alternatives with a more socially conscious focus. Google reviews are often the most visible and trusted. Encourage reviews, but never incentivize or coach clients on what to say. Just ask them to be honest. Research has shown that clients often read multiple reviews before contacting a counselor, and they place a high value on warmth, relatability, and professionalism in what others write (Sillence et al., 2007).

## Create a Professional Website

There is growing evidence that a counselor's website plays a significant role in whether a potential client reaches out. Research continues to show that the look and feel of digital spaces deeply influence user engagement. In their work on moderated online social counseling, Lederman et al. (2014) found that technology design plays a crucial role in whether users perceive an online mental health service as credible, supportive, and trustworthy. The same principle applies to counseling websites—when a site feels outdated, impersonal, or difficult to navigate, potential clients are less likely to reach out. A well-designed website that communicates warmth, clarity, and professionalism can foster an immediate sense of safety and connection, setting the tone for the therapeutic relationship long before the first session.

Another study found that websites that clearly stated fees, described therapeutic approaches in plain language, and offered online scheduling led to significantly higher client engagement and initial inquiries compared to those that did not (Fogg et al., 2003). Simply put, your website does not only inform—it persuades. Clients are looking for someone who understands what they are going through, offers hope, and makes it easy to start the process. If your website makes them feel confused or unseen, they will likely keep looking.

### *Guiding Philosophy for Your Website*

Whether you are in private practice, working as part of an agency, or leading a group practice, your website should reflect your core values and the experience you want clients to have when they visit. Think about your site as an extension of your therapeutic presence. What you communicate visually and verbally should mirror the safety, clarity, and professionalism you offer in session. When building or updating a website, counselors should consider the following perspectives.

- **Client-first design:** Ask yourself what a first-time visitor might need to feel safe, informed, and empowered. Clear language, transparent fees, and easy scheduling options are often more important than bells and whistles.
- **Authenticity over perfection:** A simple site with relatable language and a warm tone outperforms an overly polished one that feels stiff or disconnected. Clients want to get a feel for *you*, not just your credentials (Chou et al., 2009).
- **Representation and inclusion:** Your site should reflect the people you serve. This includes the photos you use, the language you choose, and the accessibility of your design. Clients often scan for signs that a counselor will understand and respect their identity (Love, 2017).
- **Action over information:** The goal of your website is not to educate people about every possible mental health topic. It is to help the right people feel ready to take the next step with you. Keep it focused, concise, and actionable.

This mindset keeps your website aligned with the heart of your work: creating safety, clarity, and connection for people in distress.

## Choosing a Platform

There are several easy-to-use platforms that counselors commonly use to build their websites. Each one comes with its pros and cons, and the right one often depends on how comfortable you are with technology and how much customization you want.

- **Squarespace:** Known for its modern templates and user-friendly interface. Great for DIYers who want something clean and professional without needing to write any code (Squarespace, n.d.).
- **Wix:** Offers more design flexibility than Squarespace, but can be a little more cluttered. Good for people who want more creative control (Wix, n.d.).
- **WordPress:** The most customizable option, but also the most complex. Best suited if you plan to blog regularly or want to integrate more advanced features. Many professional designers use WordPress because of its scalability (WordPress, n.d.).

Each of these platforms has templates made specifically for counselors, and many include drag-and-drop builders, mobile responsiveness, and integrations with scheduling software and email marketing (Chou et al., 2009).

## What to Include on Your Website

In our experience, simple websites tend to help people stay focused and navigate easily. At a minimum, make sure your site includes the following elements.

- **A brief, humanizing bio:** Share who you are as a person and a professional. Mention your credentials, but do not lead with them—people want to know who they are talking to, not just what degrees you hold.
- **A clear list of services:** Let visitors know what you offer, whether it's individual counseling, couples work, eye-movement desensitization and reprocessing (EMDR), group counseling, etc. Use client-friendly language, not jargon.
- **Fees and payment information:** You do not need to post your full fee schedule, but be transparent. Include a general pricing system, like "My standard rate is $120 per session. I offer a limited number of sliding scale slots." This helps avoid awkward conversations down the road.
- **Location and telehealth availability:** Make it easy for clients to know where you are located and whether you offer online sessions.
- **Contact information and a call-to-action:** Use simple language like "Ready to schedule? Call or email me today." Include your phone number and a contact form on every page.

Clients often decide within 30 seconds if they will reach out. If they have to dig to find your phone number or cannot tell if you are accepting new clients, they may move on to someone else.

## Use Tone and Imagery to Make It Human

Your site should represent your personality and style. Counselors often default to overly formal or vague language that feels safe, but is ultimately forgettable. Instead, write like you speak. If you are warm and calm in session, your website should sound the same way. Avoid language like "mental health solutions for individuals seeking psychological support." Instead, write, "I help people who feel stuck, anxious, or overwhelmed find clarity and connection."

Use images that reflect your actual client population, values, and personality. Avoid stock photos of people in distress unless they are balanced with imagery that communicates hope and support. If possible, include real photos of your office and yourself. This builds connection and trust.

## DIYing It Versus Hiring a Designer

If your budget is tight, building your own website is a completely viable option. Platforms like Squarespace (n.d.) and Wix (n.d.) make it possible to create a professional-looking site in a weekend. If you have the resources, working with a designer, especially one who specializes in counselor websites, can save time and elevate your brand.

DIY if you are comfortable with tech, want full control, and have time to invest. Expect to pay $12–$30 per month for hosting and services. Hire a designer if you want a polished look, have specific needs (like branding or integrations), or just do not want to deal with it. Costs typically range from $750 to $3,000, depending on scope. Either way, you are not locked in forever. Websites evolve with your practice. Start simple, and refine over time.

## The Difference Between What Looks Good and What Works

Many counselors invest in beautiful websites that do not actually convert visitors to clients. A well-designed site can look clean and professional but fail to guide the visitor toward action. Prioritize making it easy for potential clients to understand who you are, what you offer, and how to contact you, rather than only trying to impress. To maximize conversions, make sure your website utilizes clear navigation; simple language about who you help and how you help them; obvious contact buttons on every page; and, if ethical and appropriate, testimonials, credentials, and a warm, inviting tone.

It is okay to start small. A one-page website with essential information and a Google Business Profile (n.d.) is better than waiting months to launch something perfect. Progress over perfection always wins in digital marketing.

## Common Website Mistakes Counselors Make

Here are some common pitfalls that can make even the most credentialed counselor fade into the background online.

- Hiding behind vague language (e.g., "I support a variety of mental health needs").
- Failing to include a clear way to schedule or reach out.
- Using clinical jargon instead of client-centered descriptions.
- Having a cluttered or outdated design.
- Not optimizing for mobile users. A majority of counseling searches happen on mobile devices (Love, 2017).

Effective websites do not try to do everything. They make it easy for the right client to feel seen, understood, and confident enough to reach out.

## Utilizing Social Media

Social media is one of the most powerful tools for visibility in the modern world, but it can also become a trap. Don't focus on chasing trends, racking up followers, or turning yourself into a personal brand. Instead, prioritize offering meaningful, accessible content that helps people understand what you do and why it matters. Done well, social media can humanize your work, build trust, and strengthen your referral network. Done poorly, it can blur boundaries, drain your energy, and create ethical headaches. So, should counselors be on social media? The answer depends on your comfort level, your boundaries, and your goals. For many clinicians, especially those in private or small group practice, a thoughtful social media presence can make a real difference.

### Choosing the Right Platform

Each platform serves a different purpose and attracts a different kind of audience. Rather than trying to master all of them, it is better to pick one or two and engage meaningfully.

- **Instagram:** Great for visual storytelling and short, digestible psychoeducation. Ideal if your audience is millennial or Gen Z and you're comfortable using images, quotes, or reels. Use Instagram to normalize counseling and share helpful, client-facing content (Instagram, n.d.).
- **LinkedIn:** More professional and networking-focused. Best for connecting with other counselors, referral sources, and potential supervisees. Share reflections on your practice, research, or community impact (LinkedIn, n.d.).

- **TikTok:** Growing rapidly as a platform for mental health awareness, especially among younger audiences. Requires more time and creativity, but can build trust quickly through authentic, short-form videos. If you go this route, make sure you are ready to navigate the fine line between personal expression and professional responsibility (TikTok, n.d.).
- **Facebook:** Still relevant, especially for local community marketing, event promotion, and connecting with older demographics. Groups can be especially powerful for referral building or niche specialties such as parenting, faith-based counseling, or trauma support (Meta, n.d.).

Whatever platform you choose, make sure it aligns with your voice and your values. You do not have to dance, disclose, or overshare to have an impact.

## Balancing Professionalism and Relatability

Clients are not necessarily looking for your credentials on social media. They are looking for clarity, warmth, and a sense of what it would be like to work with you. Research has suggested that mental health professionals who maintain an authentic yet professional online persona are more likely to be perceived as trustworthy and competent (Lonappan et al., 2023).

Social media allows you to "show, not tell" who you are. Speak in a human voice, not textbook language. Let your personality come through in your captions and tone. Avoid being overly polished or robotic, and know your boundaries. You are not there to be liked; you are there to be findable and helpful. Always keep in mind that every post contributes to how others perceive your clinical presence.

## Creating Value-Driven Content

Posting consistently is less important than posting intentionally. Every post should seek to educate, normalize, inspire, or inform. Aim to provide small wins for your audience, not overwhelm them with theory or advice. Examples of value-driven content include:

- Normalizing emotions (e.g., "Feeling stuck is not failure—it's a signal that something needs attention.");
- Sharing skills or techniques (e.g., grounding exercises, journaling prompts);

- Addressing common questions or misconceptions about counseling; and
- Highlighting your specialty areas in language your ideal clients use.

Content that centers the client experience—rather than promoting your services—builds connection and credibility (Lonappan et al., 2023). Don't stress about going viral. Instead, focus on helping people understand what you do and why it matters.

## Know Your Ethical Boundaries

Social media blurs the lines between personal life and professional life. That is why ethical clarity is essential. According to the *ACA Code of Ethics* (2014, Standard A.5), counselors must avoid multiple relationships that could impair objectivity or risk harm. Social media is one of the easiest places for those lines to get crossed. Keep these guidelines in mind.

- **Avoid engaging with clients through direct messages:** If someone reaches out with a clinical concern, redirect them to secure communication channels or intake procedures.
- **Be cautious with self-disclosure:** Some personal context is fine, especially if it builds trust or normalizes mental health, but over-disclosing can undermine your role or confuse boundaries.
- **Do not give clinical advice in comments or posts:** General education is fine. Personalized guidance is not.
- **Ensure privacy and separation:** Make sure privacy settings are secure, and business profiles are separate from personal ones.

Sustaining ethical clarity on social media is less about hard rules and more about consistent alignment with your clinical values and your scope of practice (Stoll et al., 2020).

## Does It Actually Help?

When used strategically, social media can expand your reach and deepen your referral relationships. Many of our strongest referral networks come from a mix of in-person networking and consistent, clear online presence. Social media also allows you to stay visible to former clients who may refer others down the road, even if you never hear from them directly. That said, it is not for everyone. If social media creates more stress than value, you are not obligated to participate.

You can run a thriving practice without ever posting a reel. If you do decide to use it, treat it like a tool, not a measure of your worth or a requirement for success.

## Networking with Other Professionals

Counseling is a referral-based profession. Whether you are working in private practice, at an agency, or building a group model, your professional relationships will likely shape your caseload more than your website ever could. When someone is looking for help, they often turn to someone they already trust, like a doctor, a school counselor, a pastor, or even a friend for advice or recommendations. The strength of your network often determines whether your name is the one they mention. People refer to clinicians who are competent, reliable, and easy to work with. If you can become someone others feel confident recommending, your practice will grow both in scale and quality.

### Referring and Being Referable

One of the best ways to build a referral network is to start by referring out. When you send someone a great referral, it positions you as someone who understands community care. More often than not, those referrals come back around. To be referable in your own right, keep these three elements in place.

1. **Clarity:** People need to understand what you do and who you help. A vague specialty like "individual counseling" won't stick. Be specific. Defining your scope using language like "I work with young adults who feel stuck in transition" is more memorable.
2. **Consistency:** Respond promptly, follow up after referrals, and be clear about your availability. You do not need to be always available, but you do need to communicate your availability clearly.
3. **Collaboration:** When appropriate, share updates (with client consent), check in with other professionals, and let them know you appreciate their trust.

Research has shown that clinicians who make it easy to refer by being both responsive and specific are the most likely to stay top of mind (Haworth & Gallagher, 2004).

## With Whom Should You Be Networking?

Some of your best referral sources may not be other counselors. The most powerful connections often come from professionals who work adjacent to mental health. Here are a few examples of people to add to your network.

- **Doctors and nurse practitioners:** They're often the first to hear about stress, trauma, and anxiety.
- **School staff:** Teachers, school counselors, and administrators interact daily with children, teenagers, and parents.
- **Faith leaders:** Pastors, rabbis, priests, imams, and spiritual counselors walk with people through grief, marital issues, and mental health struggles, but may need a trusted referral for counseling.
- **Wellness professionals:** Trainers, yoga instructors, and wellness coaches may see signs of burnout, trauma, or self-image issues before anyone else.
- **Nonprofit and community organizers:** People in service agencies often have strong networks and are looking for ethical, approachable mental health partners.

You do not need to know everyone. Just focus on building 3–5 solid relationships and let them grow over time.

## Creating a Simple Follow-Up System

It is easy to meet someone once and then disappear from their radar. Most referrals happen not after the first introduction but after the second or third touchpoint. You do not need customer relationship management software or a marketing campaign to stay connected. A little intention can go a long way. Here is a low-effort system that works.

1. After meeting a new contact, send a short follow-up email within 48 hours using language like this:
    a. "It was great connecting with you. I appreciated hearing about your work with [population]. I'd love to stay in touch. Let me know if I can ever support you or your clients."
2. Set a calendar reminder to check in 1–2 months later with a helpful resource or casual note.
3. Track your contacts—just a basic spreadsheet with name, role, last contact, and potential next step can go a long way in keeping those relationships warm.

According to Haworth and Gallagher (2004), consistent follow-up is one of the strongest predictors of referral flow—often more important than credentials or years of experience.

## Super-Connectors and How to Spot Them

In every community, there are a few people who seem to know everyone. These are your super-connectors. They are people who, if they don't have a referral for you, know someone who does. Look for school leaders or guidance directors, physicians who serve on local nonprofit boards, clergy who host regular events or support groups, and small business owners who are deeply involved in the community.

Connecting with one super-connector can multiply your exposure and get your name into conversations you were never in the room for. These people can be powerful allies, not just for referrals, but for understanding the pulse of your community.

## How to Ask for Referrals Without Feeling Desperate

Asking for referrals does not have to be awkward if it's rooted in service. You are not begging for clients. You are letting people know you are available to help. You can use language like:

- "If you ever have someone navigating [your specialty], I'd be happy to support them."
- "I'm building out my practice with a focus on [population]. If you know anyone who could use a counselor in that space, feel free to pass my info along."
- "Would it be helpful if I sent you a one-sheet that outlines what I offer and how to get in touch?"

These are invitations, not sales pitches. Most people appreciate the clarity and will be more likely to refer to you because you made it easy for them.

## What You Bring to the Table

In a referral relationship, what you offer is not just your availability—it's your professionalism. Show people they can trust you by being

- **Reliable:** do what you say you will do;
- **Collaborative:** share insights (ethically), ask for feedback, and show gratitude; and

- **Consistent:** make space for ongoing connection, even if it is just a brief check-in a few times a year.

You do not need to impress anyone. You just need to show up, follow through, and keep the relationship focused on shared care for the people you serve.

## Niche Marketing and Demographics

One of the biggest mistakes counselors make when it comes to marketing is trying to speak to everyone. When your message is too broad, it fades into the background. When you speak directly to the clients you are uniquely equipped to serve, something clicks. People feel seen, and that connection is often the reason they choose to reach out. Niche marketing clarifies who you help best and makes it easy for those people to find you. In this section, we explore how to identify your ideal client, speak to them in ways that feel authentic and inclusive, and align your marketing with your values, especially when serving marginalized or underserved communities.

### *Identifying Your Ideal Client*

Finding your niche starts with getting clear on your most meaningful work. Think about the clients you feel energized by, the issues you're passionate about, and the populations you understand deeply. That's your sweet spot. Some helpful questions to clarify your ideal client include:

- Who do you feel most drawn to serve?
- What issues do you feel most competent and effective working with?
- Whose stories feel familiar, like you "get it" on a deeper level?

Your niche might be a population (e.g., new moms, Black men, LGBTQIA+ teens), a life stage (e.g., college transitions, midlife crises), or an issue (e.g., anxiety, grief, identity development). The clearer you are about who you serve, the more your marketing can become an invitation rather than a broadcast. When people see themselves in your language, they are more likely to feel that you are *their* counselor—not just *a* counselor.

## Inclusive, Culturally Responsive Messaging

Marketing that works is marketing that respects people's complexity. Culturally responsive language is more than being politically correct; it's also human-centered. Clients come from different cultural backgrounds, faith traditions, languages, gender identities, and socioeconomic realities. If your website, bio, or content assumes a one-size-fits-all experience, you're likely missing the mark with many of the people who need you most. Inclusive marketing involves

- Using language that avoids assumptions (e.g., saying "partner" instead of "husband/wife");
- Naming systems of oppression when relevant to your niche (e.g., trauma-informed support for BIPOC professionals navigating workplace discrimination); and
- Speaking directly to community-specific experiences in a way that honors, not exploits, identity.

According to Love (2017), clients are significantly more likely to initiate contact with counselors whose materials reflect cultural awareness and identity-affirming language. Representation matters—and not just in photos, but in tone, values, and messaging.

## Marketing to Specific Populations

Niche marketing necessitates crafting messages that speak to lived experiences as well as diagnoses. For example:

- Men may not resonate with language like "emotional processing," but might connect with terms like "stress management," "focus," or "showing up in your relationships."
- Couples often want to know you understand both sides—not just the "problem partner." Use language that invites both people in without assigning blame.
- BIPOC communities may seek counselors who understand cultural code-switching, intergenerational trauma, or the pressure to perform in majority spaces.
- Veterans may connect more with messaging around transitions, identity shifts, or navigating civilian life, rather than generic terms like "adjustment issues."

Your job is to speak the language of your people. What are their worries? What questions are they searching online at midnight? Use that language. If you are not a member of the population you are serving, take extra care to ensure your words are informed by real learning, humility, and experience, rather than assumptions or savior narratives.

### Accessibility and Representation

Inclusive marketing is also about how your practice looks and functions. Your clients should feel welcomed both in what they read and in what they see. Ask yourself:

- Do the images on your website reflect the diversity of the clients you want to serve?
- Is your site accessible (e.g., readable fonts, image descriptions, translation options)?
- Can people of different income levels access your services or understand your fees?
- Do you use plain, welcoming language, or does it feel academic and distant?

Representation and accessibility are signals, and clients are paying attention. Research shows that cultural cues and representation play a significant role in how clients of color evaluate potential counselors. Meyer and Zane (2013) found that clients' perceptions of cultural responsiveness and identity awareness within mental health services directly influence their willingness to engage and remain in treatment. In the same way, a counselor's website or marketing materials can communicate whether a practice is inclusive, respectful, and attuned to diverse client experiences long before the first session ever begins.

## Aligning Your Marketing with Your Values

Your marketing should express your values and ethics. If you say you are inclusive, your content should reflect that. If you value trauma-informed care, your tone should be spacious and non-triggering. If you claim to be LGBTQIA+ affirming, that should be evident in your images, forms, and intake process. Aim for congruence rather than perfection. Your marketing should feel like an extension of the thoughtful, attentive, and grounded ways you show up in the counseling room.

As counselors, we are in a profession built on trust, connection, and care. Our marketing should reflect that. Whether we are handing out business cards at a community event, writing a blog post for our website, or sharing an Instagram post about anxiety, we are doing more than promoting services. We are extending an invitation to healing.

Throughout this chapter, we have explored the many ways counselors can ethically and effectively market their work. From traditional methods like community partnerships and local workshops to modern tools like SEO, social media, and niche branding, the options are broad, but the goal is always the same: visibility with purpose.

The most effective marketing strategies come from alignment. When your message reflects your actual work, when your tone reflects your therapeutic presence, and when your visibility reflects your values, your marketing becomes an extension of your clinical integrity. Clients are looking. Make it easy for them to find you.

## References

American Counseling Association. (2014). *ACA code of ethics*. ACA. https://www.counseling.org/docs/default-source/default-document-library/ethics/2014-aca-code-of-ethics.pdf

Bansal, D. (2024). How SEO makes websites load faster and helps in user engagement. *International Journal for Multidisciplinary Research, 6*(2). https://doi.org/10.36948/ijfmr.2024.v06i02.15291

Barnett, J. E. (2019). The ethical practice of psychotherapy: Clearly within our reach. *Psychotherapy, 56*(4), 431–440. https://doi.org/10.1037/pst0000272

Canva. (n.d.). *Canva* [Graphic design platform]. Retrieved November 3, 2025, from https://www.canva.com

Chen, T., Samaranayake, P., Cen, X., Qi, M., & Lan, Y. C. (2022). The impact of online reviews on consumers' purchasing decisions: Evidence from an eye-tracking study. *Frontiers in Psychology, 13*, Article 865702. https://doi.org/10.3389/fpsyg.2022.865702

Chou, W. Y., Hunt, Y. M., Beckjord, E. B., Moser, R. P., & Hesse, B. W. (2009). Social media use in the United States: Implications for health communication. *Journal of Medical Internet Research, 11*(4), Article e48. https://doi.org/10.2196/jmir.1249

Corrigan, P. W., Morris, S. B., Michaels, P. J., Rafacz, J. D., & Rüsch, N. (2012). Challenging the public stigma of mental illness: A meta-analysis of outcome studies. *Psychiatric Services, 63*(10), 963–973. https://doi.org/10.1176/appi.ps.201100529

Fogg, B. J., Soohoo, C., Danielson, D. R., Marable, L., Stanford, J., & Tauber, E. R. (2003). How do users evaluate the credibility of websites? A study with over 2,500 participants. In *Proceedings of the 2003 Conference on Designing for User Experiences*, 1–15. https://doi.org/10.1145/997078.997097

Google. (2025). *Search engine optimization (SEO) starter guide*. Google Search Central. https://developers.google.com/search/docs/fundamentals/seo-starter-guide

Google Ads. (2023, March). *What is paid search? Basics of online marketing*. Google Ads. https://business.google.com/us/resources/articles/what-is-paid-search/

Google Business Profile. (n.d.). *Google Business Profile* [Business platform]. Retrieved November 3, 2025, from https://business.google.com/en-all/business-profile/

Haworth, R., & Gallagher, T. (2004). Referrals: Clinical considerations and responsibilities. In R. Tribe & J. Morrissey (Eds.), *Handbook of Professional and Ethical Practice for Psychologists, Counsellors and Psychotherapists* (1st ed., pp. 137–148). Routledge.

Instagram. (n.d.). *Instagram* [Social media platform]. Meta Platforms, Inc. Retrieved November 3, 2025, from https://about.instagram.com.

Kaplan, D. M., & Gladding, S. T. (2011). A vision for the future of counseling: The 20/20 principles for unifying and strengthening the profession. *Journal of Counseling and Development, 89*(3), 367–372. https://doi.org/10.1002/j.1556-6678.2011.tb00101.x

Knapp, S., & VandeCreek, L. (2008). The ethics of advertising, billing, and finances in psychotherapy. *Journal of Clinical Psychology, 64*(5), 613–625. https://doi.org/10.1002/jclp.20475

Kotler, P., Kartajaya, H., & Setiawan, I. (2021). *Marketing 5.0: Technology for humanity*. John Wiley & Sons.

Lederman, R., Wadley, G., Gleeson, J., Bendall, S., & Álvarez-Jiménez, M. (2014). Moderated online social therapy: Designing and evaluating technology for mental health. *ACM Transactions on Computer-Human Interaction, 21*(1), 1–26. https://doi.org/10.1145/2513179

LinkedIn. (n.d.). *LinkedIn* [Social media platform]. LinkedIn Corporation. Retrieved November 3, 2025, from https://about.linkedin.com

Lonappan, J., Aithal, P. S., & Jacob, M. (2023). E-professionalism as a professional identity in the digital era of medical education. *International Journal of Health Sciences and Pharmacy, 7*(2), 35–48. http://dx.doi.org/10.2139/ssrn.4729068

Love, K. (2017, November 7). *How to welcome diversity on your therapist website.* EmpathySites. https://empathysites.com/how-to-welcome-diversity-on-your-therapist-website/

Mental Health Match. (n.d.). *Mental health match* [Therapist platform]. Mental Health Match. Retrieved November 3, 2025, from https://mentalhealthmatch.com

Meta. (n.d.). *Meta*. Meta Platforms, Inc. Retrieved November 3, 2025, from https://about.meta.com.

Meyer, O. L., & Zane, N. (2013). The influence of race and ethnicity in clients' experiences of mental health treatment. *Journal of Community Psychology, 41*(7), 884–901. https://doi.org/10.1002/jcop.21580

Psychology Today. (n.d.). *Psychology Today* [Therapist platform]. Retrieved November 3, 2025, from https://www.psychologytoday.com/us/therapists

Sillence, E., Briggs, P., Harris, P. R., & Fishwick, L. (2007). How do patients evaluate and make use of online health information? *Social Science and Medicine, 64*(9), 1853–1862. https://doi.org/10.1016/j.socscimed.2007.01.012

SOCI. (2025, May 28). *What is the Google Map Pack?* SOCI. https://www.soci.ai/knowledge-articles/what-is-google-map-pack/

Squarespace. (n.d.). *Squarespace* [Website platform]. Squarespace, Inc. Retrieved November 3, 2025, from https://www.squarespace.com.

Stoll, J., Müller, J. A., & Trachsel, M. (2020). Ethical issues in online psychotherapy: A narrative review. *Frontiers in Psychiatry, 10*, Article 498439. https://doi.org/10.3389/fpsyt.2019.00993

Sunhouse Marketing. (2025, April 18). *Winning with Meta ads: A Facebook ads playbook for ABA therapy.* Sunhouse Marketing. https://sunhousemarketing.com/meta-ads-aba-therapy/

TherapyDen. (n.d.). *TherapyDen* [Therapist platform]. TherapyDen. Retrieved November 3, 2025, from https://www.therapyden.com

TikTok. (n.d.). *TikTok* [Social media platform]. TikTok Pte. Ltd. Retrieved November 3, 2025, from https://www.tiktok.com/about.

Vistaprint. (n.d.). *Vistaprint* [Custom marketing materials and printing services]. Vistaprint. Retrieved November 3, 2025, from https://www.vistaprint.com

Wix.com. (n.d.). *Wix* [Website platform]. Wix.com, Ltd. Retrieved November 3, 2025, from https://www.wix.com.

WordPress. (n.d.). *WordPress* [Website platform]. Automattic, Inc. Retrieved November 3, 2025, from https://wordpress.com.

# 10

# Taking Advantage of Counseling Innovation

Some of y'all don't know what it's like to stare down a Subjective, Objective, Assessment, and Plan (SOAP) note six hours after your first session—with a permanent ink pen in your hand—and it shows.

Y'all don't know the stress of wondering what a friction fire would do to your client files. You don't know the pure chaos of trying to fax a chart to another provider. *Faxing*. It was basically launching paper airplanes and praying the trade winds delivered them to the right provider.

Some of us remember walking across campus with a DVD of a recorded session for supervision, scanning for ethics police like we were smuggling state secrets. When did Titanium show up in the training clinic? You would think we needed a cognate course in computer science just to sign a termination note.

For all of these reasons, we need to discuss innovation, but not like it's some abstract tech buzzword. We have lived through many awkward updates, glitchy rollouts, and ethically gray workarounds, and we have also seen all the good that came from those times of innovative transition. Innovation in counseling makes our work more accessible, more sustainable, and more human.

In this chapter, we discuss the tools, trends, and tensions that come with 21st-century counseling. We explore how to integrate technology into your workflow without losing your therapeutic presence. We name the risks, such as privacy breaches and Zoom fatigue, and give you strategies to mitigate them. We also remind you that innovation exists outside of technological advancements. Creativity, collaboration, and courage are all forms of innovation, too.

Counseling has always been innovative. Every time you sit with a client and adapt to their needs, you're innovating. Every time you rework a metaphor, co-create a new ritual, or respond to silence with something that shifts the air, you're innovating. The tools may change, but the heart of the work doesn't.

## A New Era of Counseling Tools

If you're still juggling paper calendars, sticky notes, and email chains, it's time to streamline. Today's counseling tools—from practice management systems like SimplePractice (n.d.) and TherapyNotes (n.d.) to AI-supported note generators—protect your time, presence, and peace of mind (Cavanagh et al., 2023). These platforms automate the back-end work. They handle scheduling, reminders, billing, intake forms, and even documentation (Maheu et al., 2019). Some now include dashboards to track client progress, suggest treatment plans, or generate draft notes using AI—features that support your clinical decisions without replacing your intuition (Luxton, 2014; Denecke et al., 2021).

On the client side, mindfulness and journaling apps like Reflectly (2025) have become increasingly popular tools to help clients stay engaged between sessions. These apps support mood tracking, guided meditation, and self-reflection, and some even allow for data-sharing with providers (with client consent), enhancing continuity of care and supporting therapeutic outcomes (Linardon et al., 2019; Miralles et al., 2020). A comprehensive review by Miralles et al. (2020) highlighted these platforms as examples of how mobile mental health apps can supplement traditional counseling by increasing self-awareness and reinforcing therapeutic practices.

No app can replace attunement, but the right tools can support it (Marshall et al., 2020). Before adopting anything new, ask yourself: "Does this help the client?" "Does it align with my style?" "Does it simplify my workflow or reinforce my values?" Innovation is already here. Thriving in it doesn't mean doing everything. It means doing the right thing on purpose.

## Telehealth Counseling Is Not New, But It's Definitely Now

One of the most transformative innovations in counseling has been telehealth. While it existed well before the onset of COVID-19, the pandemic made it mainstream. What started as a crisis workaround has become a permanent and powerful way to reach clients across distance, barriers, and lived realities. Whether you're serving rural communities, parents juggling childcare, or folks with limited mobility or inflexible work hours, telehealth counseling expands access, and it is here to stay (Bailenson, 2021).

Of course, it's not flawless. Some clients struggle to stay focused in home environments or find video-based interaction draining. Others may miss the nuance of in-person communication. That's why *how* you show up virtually matters. Good lighting, clear sound, a clean background, and intentional pacing go a long way. Treat your virtual office like a real one, and you will help clients do the same.

Still, some work needs to happen in the room. Clients with dissociation, psychosis, or high-risk concerns often need the groundedness, safety planning, and immediacy that only in-person work can offer (American Counseling Association [ACA], 2014). The same goes for younger clients who need art, movement, or play; or for trauma survivors whose healing relies on subtle co-regulation, body language, or physical presence. Certain modalities like eye movement, desensitization, and reprocessing (EMDR), sandtray counseling, or somatic work don't tend to translate well on screen.

Cultural factors matter, too. Some clients, particularly those from collectivist cultures, need shared rituals, presence, and relationship-building that feel more natural face-to-face (Sue et al., 2012). The point of these distinctions is to ensure your practice stays client-centered within innovative counseling spaces. That means knowing when to shift formats, offer hybrid models, or revisit the structure as needs evolve.

A well-designed hybrid practice can offer the best of both worlds. Start by organizing your week to avoid jumping between modes. Maybe this looks like designating some days for telehealth sessions, and others for in-person sessions. Answer potential client questions clearly from day one. Explain how clients can switch between modalities, what happens if tech fails, and any differences in fees or protocols. Put it in writing. Set expectations.

Above all, don't lower your standards just because you're online. Telehealth counseling still requires documentation, informed consent, Health Insurance Portability and Accountability Act (HIPAA) compliance, and ethical presence. You also need to confirm licensure in the client's location and make sure your insurance covers telehealth sessions. The logistics matter nearly as much as the heart of the work.

Offering hybrid care provides flexibility for your clients and sustainability for you. You can travel, handle emergencies, protect your family time, and still offer consistent care. When designed intentionally, a hybrid setup supports your practice and protects it. That kind of structure is more than innovative. It's good business.

## *Integrating Innovative Technology into Your Counseling Practice*

Being a good counselor extends beyond what happens in session. It's also about what holds your practice together behind the scenes. Practice management platforms like TherapyNotes (2025) and SimplePractice (2025) help you stay organized, handle billing, send reminders, and store notes securely (Maheu et al., 2019).

Artificial intelligence (AI) is also starting to play a role in the counseling field. Some electronic health records (EHRs) now include tools that suggest treatment plans or generate draft notes. Used intelligently, they support your clinical judgment, rather than threaten it (Luxton, 2014; D'Alfonso, 2020). With clients using mindfulness and journaling apps like Headspace or Reflectly (2025) between sessions, some of that work can loop into counseling, giving you a clearer picture of how they're doing outside the counseling room (Linardon et al., 2019).

Don't feel pressured to use everything. Choose tools that simplify, rather than complicate, your work. If an app helps you stay present and your client stays engaged, it's worth considering. The right tech isn't a replacement for good counseling. It's a backup.

Tech should make your practice lighter. The "best" tools aren't the trendiest ones—they're the ones that reduce stress, simplify care, and fit how *you* work. A trauma counselor might use somatic tracking. A teen counselor might rely on journaling apps. If it doesn't match your theory or style, skip it. Audit your pain points, test one tool at a time, and look for platforms that earn their keep (Maheu et al., 2019).

Innovative technology can help with administrative tasks as well. The clutter of unfinished administrative tasks is dangerous. Administrative overload contributes to burnout, missed details, and diminished presence (Rupert & Morgan, 2005). But when you use systems that simplify administrative labor for you and your clients, you have more space to focus on the counseling work.

Utilizing innovative technology can make your practice more efficient and ethically sound. We have a responsibility to use technology that's secure, appropriate, and client-centered (American Psychological Association [APA], 2024). Know the risks, explain them clearly, and check in on your client's comfort with the process. Some clients will love the digital tools. Others might feel overwhelmed. Your ability to simplify and adapt is part of cultural competence.

## Confidentiality in a Tech-Heavy World

Confidentiality is sacred in counseling. These days, confidentiality isn't as simple as locking a filing cabinet. Now, you have to protect client information in emails, smartphones, payment systems, cloud backups, and scheduling apps (Bada, 2023). Technology is baked into nearly every part of our workflow, and every tool adds both opportunity and risk.

From EHR systems to encrypted emails, HIPAA-compliant texting apps, and even AI-powered note generators, each platform you use needs to be evaluated through the lens of client safety. Data can be intercepted, misrouted, or exposed if not properly secured (Zur, n.d.). Billing records, cloud-stored notes, voice memos, and even app integrations carry risks.

Using encrypted email platforms like Paubox (n.d.) is useful, but your clients need to know what those platforms entail. If you're texting, only use secure apps, and keep your conversations concise. Use texting and voicemails to schedule sessions, and nothing else. Keep it professional and never leave personal details in messages. Client portals remain the gold standard for security. They centralize communication, paperwork, billing, and message tracking, all in one protected hub.

Even the most secure tools won't help if your client doesn't know how to use them safely. That's why informed consent must cover all your digital tools (Bada, 2023). Let clients know what technology you use, what risks come with it, and what they're responsible for, like creating strong passwords, using private devices, and never communicating private information over public Wi-Fi. Revisit this agreement yearly or when platforms change.

Even with precautions, things can occasionally go wrong. If there's a breach, follow HIPAA's notification rules and communicate openly. Transparency builds trust. Clients usually don't expect perfection, but they do expect accountability. In the end, confidentiality is a policy that creates a secure presence. It's what tells your client that they're safe, even in a digital space. As you add more digital platforms to your counseling practice, your backend actions must evolve accordingly.

Keep learning. Keep adapting. Let every tech decision reflect your deepest ethical commitment to doing this work right.

### Cybersecurity Is Clinical

Cybersecurity is part of your clinical responsibility. Every digital touchpoint in your practice—email, EHR, texting, billing, backups—is a potential vulnerability. When you handle sensitive client info, protecting that data is just as important as protecting the client in session (McCord et al., 2020).

The basics still matter. Use strong, unique passwords stored in a secure password manager like Bitwarden (n.d.). Enable two-factor authentication, or multifactor authentication, everywhere you can. Keep all of your work devices updated, encrypted, and secured (Stotts, 2020). Never store client data locally if you can avoid it; use HIPAA-compliant cloud platforms instead.

Only use EHR systems that encrypt data at rest and in transit. Backups should also be encrypted and stored separately from your main system. Free platforms like Dropbox or Google Drive are not secure unless you have upgraded and configured them specifically for HIPAA compliance. Privacy filters, locked cabinets, and secure Wi-Fi should all be part of your setup, whether you are at home or in a shared office.

Create a data recovery plan before you need it. Know how to restore your records, what to tell clients if systems go down, and how to pivot to phone or alternate care if needed. Run a "digital fire drill" annually so you're not caught off guard.

If there's a breach, transparency matters. Follow HIPAA's notification rules (Office for Civil Rights, 2013). Contact your malpractice provider. Let clients know what happened, what you've done, and how you're protecting them moving forward. A calm, professional response builds trust, even when mistakes happen (Zur, n.d.).

Finally, stay teachable. Schedule an annual cybersecurity review. Update your informed consent. Read the latest on data safety or take a continuing education course. You don't need to become an expert, but you do need to stay alert and proactive. Protecting your clients' data is another way of saying, "You matter, and I've got you."

## Innovation Isn't Always Digital

When we hear the word "innovation," our minds often jump straight to technology like apps, platforms, AI tools, and virtual delivery systems. However, the truest form of innovation in counseling isn't limited to the digital world. It's about thinking differently, meeting people where they are, and using unconventional pathways to create a therapeutic connection. In many cases, the most transformative innovations happen in movement, nature, community, and culture. This section explores the powerful ways that counselors are reimagining counseling through embodied, experiential, and non-digital approaches.

## Outdoor Counseling and Walk-and-Talk Sessions

Outdoor counseling, sometimes referred to as ecocounseling or walk-and-talk counseling, moves the counseling session out of the traditional office setting and into parks, trails, or other natural environments. For some clients, especially those with anxiety, trauma, or depression, being outside can have an immediate regulatory effect on the nervous system. Research has shown that time in nature reduces cortisol levels, improves attention, and supports emotional processing (Revell & McLeod, 2016).

Walking side-by-side rather than sitting face-to-face can also reduce social pressure. Many clients report feeling more open and less "watched" when walking. The rhythm of movement can enhance bilateral stimulation and unlock emotional insight (EMDR theory; see Laliotis et al., 2024; Shapiro, 2001/2002), while the changing scenery offers organic metaphors that can be woven into the therapeutic dialogue. Even brief outdoor sessions can literally and figuratively breathe life into the therapeutic process.

Of course, outdoor work requires additional planning. Counselors must consider client safety, confidentiality (e.g., passing others on a public trail), weather conditions, and physical accessibility. It also requires updating informed consent forms and discussing with clients what to do if the session is interrupted, observed, or impacted by the environment. When done thoughtfully, outdoor counseling can restore vitality to both client and clinician alike.

## Equine-Assisted and Animal-Assisted Counseling

Animal-assisted interventions tap into the therapeutic power of relationships. Horses, dogs, and other counseling animals offer opportunities for emotional healing through attunement, mirroring, and nonverbal connection. Equine-assisted counseling is particularly powerful for clients working through attachment trauma, anxiety, or relational struggles. Horses are hyper-attuned to emotional energy. (Yorke et al., 2013) They respond immediately to human affect, body language, and intention. This real-time feedback provides powerful material for clients learning to manage boundaries, assert needs, or sit with vulnerability (Yorke et al., 2013).

Counselors can use these interactions to explore metaphor, raise insight, and practice new relational skills. Similarly, trained counseling dogs can be integrated into sessions to reduce anxiety, encourage grounding, and build rapport. For neurodiverse clients or those with posttraumatic stress disorder (PTSD), the presence of an animal can offer a level of safety and co-regulation that accelerates therapeutic progress (O'Haire, 2013; Dietz et al., 2012). Animal-assisted work requires specialized training, liability coverage, and ethical documentation. It has the potential to open doors to connections that talk therapy alone sometimes cannot.

## *Community-Based and Culturally Embedded Interventions*

Innovation also means stepping beyond the four walls of the counseling room to engage clients in their communities, families, and cultural contexts. This might entail offering services in settings where clients already gather, like schools, churches, barbershops, community centers, or even correctional facilities (Bernal & Domenech Rodríguez, 2012; Metzger et al., 2021). It might also mean embedding counseling within cultural rituals, storytelling traditions, or spiritual practices that reflect a client's worldview and lived experience.

In collectivist cultures, for example, healing often happens across generations and through shared symbolic acts. Family sessions, community circles, or rites of passage may resonate more than one-on-one verbal processing (Gone, 2013; Sue et al., 2012). Culturally congruent counseling is respectful and effective. When clients feel seen in their full cultural identities, they're more likely to engage consistently and benefit from the process (Zhang et al., 2022).

Community-based approaches also expand access. For clients who mistrust formal institutions, lack transportation, or can't afford private counseling, meeting them where they physically and emotionally are creates critical bridges. It redefines what counseling can look like and where healing is allowed to happen.

## *Therapeutic Storytelling and Creative Expression*

Narrative practices, art counseling, music, and movement are powerful clinical tools—innovative not because they're new, but because they help clients access what words often can't. These creative modalities support emotional integration, identity development, and trauma processing in ways that talk therapy alone sometimes cannot (Malchiodi, 2020).

Storytelling, in particular, can be transformative. Whether spoken, written, or performed, stories help clients make meaning out of chaos. They give shape to pain, create distance from internalized shame, and allow space for reframing and reauthoring identity, especially for those recovering from trauma (Neimeyer, 2000). In groups, narrative sharing fosters connection and empowerment through shared humanity and collective healing (Denborough, 2014).

Art-based interventions such as painting, making music, moving, or sculpting can be especially effective for children, adolescents, and anyone who has experienced early or preverbal trauma. These tools engage sensory and somatic pathways that language-based approaches often miss (Cohen-Yatziv & Regev, 2019). For neurodiverse clients or those with communication differences, creative work can also feel more accessible and emotionally safe (Slak, 2023).

The key is to skillfully use these tools. Clinicians trained in expressive modalities can unlock a deeper level of work, offering clients more ways to process, explore, and heal.

### Public Education and Creative Outreach as Clinical Work

Podcasts, blogs, workshops, and social media aren't distractions from counseling. They can be extensions of it. These platforms help demystify mental health, reduce stigma, and give people tools to reflect and grow, sometimes long before they ever book a session (Naslund et al., 2016; Reavley & Jorm, 2012). When clinicians use them with clear boundaries, protected confidentiality, and evidence-informed content, they become a kind of public service.

Someone might hear a counselor talk about grief on a podcast and finally feel seen, or read a blog post about boundaries and realize what's been off in their relationships. These moments matter. They plant seeds. They spark change. While they aren't substitutes for counseling, they're often the first bridge to it.

This kind of outreach is cultural intervention, advocacy, and innovation. When done ethically, it helps us meet people exactly where they are—scrolling, listening, wondering—and remind them they're not alone.

## Redefining the Work, Reimagining the Space

Innovating counseling often entails asking, "What else is possible?" Moving beyond rigid definitions of counseling creates spaces where healing fits real people with real lives. Whether you're walking through a park, sitting beside a horse, co-facilitating a family circle, or recording a 60-second video that helps someone feel less alone, you're doing counseling. You're just doing it with flexibility, courage, and creativity (Comas-Díaz, 2012; Malchiodi, 2020).

Not every counselor needs to offer these alternatives, but we all need to recognize them as legitimate, necessary, and often more accessible forms of care. Innovation expands how we live out our professional values in an evolving world (Zhang et al., 2022).

The future of counseling may be screen-based. But it will also be sidewalk-based, barn-based, community-based, and artroom-based. Healing isn't confined to a couch, and it never was. Our job is to meet it wherever it shows up.

# References

American Counseling Association. (2014). *ACA code of ethics*. ACA. https://www.counseling.org/docs/default-source/default-document-library/ethics/2014-aca-code-of-ethics.pdf

American Psychological Association. (2024). *Guidelines for the practice of telepsychology*. APA. https://www.apa.org/about/policy/telepsychology-revisions

Bada, M. (2023). A clinician's guide to cybersecurity and data protection: How to ensure client confidentiality?. In C. Knibbs & G. Hibberd (eds.), *A Practitioner's Guide to Cybersecurity and Data Protection* (pp. 25–37). Routledge.

Bailenson, J. N. (2021). Nonverbal overload: A theoretical argument for the causes of Zoom fatigue. *Technology, Mind, and Behavior, 2*(1). https://doi.org/10.1037/tmb0000030

Bernal, G., & Domenech Rodríguez, M. M. (Eds.). (2012). *Cultural adaptations: Tools for evidence-based practice with diverse populations.* American Psychological Association. https://doi.org/10.1037/13752-000

Bitwarden. (n.d.). *Bitwarden* [Password manager]. Retrieved November 3, 2025, from https://bitwarden.com/

Cavanagh, R., Gerson, S. M., Gleason, A., Mackey, R., & Ciulla, R. (2023). Competencies needed for behavioral health professionals to integrate digital health technologies into clinical care: A rapid review. *Journal of Technology in Behavioral Science, 8*(3), 446–459. https://doi.org/10.1007/s41347-022-00242-w

Cohen-Yatziv, L., & Regev, D. (2019). The effectiveness and contribution of art therapy work with children in 2018—What progress has been made so far? A systematic review. *International Journal of Art Therapy, 24*(3), 100–112. https://doi.org/10.1080/17454832.2019.1574845

Denborough, D. (2014). *Retelling the stories of our lives: Everyday narrative therapy to draw inspiration and transform experience.* W. W. Norton & Company.

Denecke, K., Abd-Alrazaq, A., & Househ, M. (2021). Artificial intelligence for chatbots in mental health: Opportunities and challenges. In M. Househ, E. Borycki, & A. Kushniruk (Eds.), *Multiple perspectives on artificial intelligence in healthcare: Opportunities and challenges* (pp. 115–128). Springer. https://doi.org/10.1007/978-3-030-67303-1_10

Dietz, T. J., Davis, D., & Pennings, J. (2012). Evaluating animal-assisted therapy in group treatment for child sexual abuse. *Journal of Child Sexual Abuse, 21*(6), 665–683. https://doi.org/10.1080/10538712.2012.726700

Gone, J. P. (2013). Redressing First Nations' historical trauma: Theorizing mechanisms for indigenous culture as mental health treatment. *Transcultural Psychiatry, 50*(5), 683–706. https://doi.org/10.1177/1363461513487669

Linardon, J., Cuijpers, P., Carlbring, P., Messer, M., & Fuller-Tyszkiewicz, M. (2019). The efficacy of app-supported smartphone interventions for mental health problems: A meta-analysis of randomized controlled trials. *World Psychiatry, 18*(3), 325–336. https://doi.org/10.1002/wps.20673

Luxton, D. D. (2014). Artificial intelligence in psychological practice: Current and future applications and implications. *Professional Psychology: Research and Practice, 45*(5), 332–339. https://doi.org/10.1037/a0034559

Maheu, M. M., Callan, J. E., & Hilty, D. M. (2019). *Telebehavioral health: Foundations in theory and practice for graduate learners.* Cognella Academic Publishing.

Malchiodi, C. A. (2020). *Trauma and expressive arts therapy: Brain, body, and imagination in the healing process.* Guilford Press.

Marshall, J. M., Dunstan, D. A., & Bartik, W. (2020). Apps with maps—anxiety and depression mobile apps with evidence-based frameworks: Systematic search of major app stores. *JMIR Mental Health, 7*(6), e16525. https://doi.org/10.2196/16525

Metzger, I. W., Anderson, R. E., Are, F., & Ritchwood, T. (2021). Healing interpersonal and racial trauma: Integrating racial socialization into trauma-focused cognitive behavioral therapy for African American youth. *Child Maltreatment, 26*(1), 17–27. https://doi.org/10.1177/1077559520921457

Miralles, I., Granell, C., Díaz-Sanahuja, L., Van Woensel, W., Bretón-López, J., Mira, A., Castilla, D., & Casteleyn, S. (2020). Smartphone apps for the treatment of mental disorders: Systematic review. *JMIR mHealth and uHealth, 8*(4), e14897. https://doi.org/10.2196/14897

Naslund, J. A., Aschbrenner, K. A., Marsch, L. A., & Bartels, S. J. (2016). The future of mental health care: Peer-to-peer support and social media. *Epidemiology and Psychiatric Sciences, 25*(2), 113–122. https://doi.org/10.1017/S2045796015001067

Neimeyer, R. A. (2000). Narrative disruptions in the construction of the self. In R. A. Neimeyer & J. D. Raskin (Eds.), *Constructions of disorder: Meaning-making frameworks for psychotherapy* (pp. 207–242). American Psychological Association. https://doi.org/10.1037/10368-009

O'Haire, M. E. (2013). Animal-assisted intervention for autism spectrum disorder: A systematic literature review. *Journal of Autism and Developmental Disorders, 43*(7), 1606–1622. https://doi.org/10.1007/s10803-012-1707-5

Office for Civil Rights. (2013). *HIPAA Breach Notification Rule, 45 CFR §§ 164.400–414*. U.S. Department of Health & Human Services. https://www.hhs.gov/hipaa/for-professionals/breach-notification/index.html

Paubox. (n.d.). *Paubox* [HIPAA-compliant email]. Retrieved November 3, 2025, from https://www.paubox.com/

Reavley, N. J., & Jorm, A. F. (2012). Public recognition of mental disorders and beliefs about treatment: Changes in Australia over 16 years. *The British Journal of Psychiatry, 200*(5), 419–425. https://doi.org/10.1192/bjp.bp.111.104208

Reflectly. (2025). *Reflectly: Journal & AI Diary* (Version 4.14.4) [Mobile app]. Reflective Technologies. Apple App Store. https://apps.apple.com/us/app/reflectly-journal-ai-diary/id1241229134

Rupert, P. A., & Morgan, D. J. (2005). Work setting and burnout among professional psychologists. *Professional Psychology: Research and Practice, 36*(5), 544–550. https://doi.org/10.1037/0735-7028.36.5.544

SimplePractice. (n.d.). *SimplePractice* [Practice management software]. Retrieved November 3, 2025, from https://www.simplepractice.com/

Slak, A. (2023). Creative therapies for autism: Movement, music, and sandplay. *The Crown: Syracuse Honors Research Journal, 1*, Article 8. https://surface.syr.edu/cgi/viewcontent.cgi?article=1007&context=thecrown

Stotts, R. H. (2020). *Cyber security in mental health: An assessment of current practice and behavioral intent* [Doctoral dissertation, St. Mary's University]. St. Mary's University Dissertations. https://commons.stmarytx.edu/dissertations/40/

Sue, D. W., Rasheed, M. N., & Rasheed, J. M. (2012). *Multicultural social work practice: A competency-based approach to diversity and social justice* (2nd ed.). Wiley.

TherapyNotes. (n.d.) *TherapyNotes* [EHR platform]. TherapyNotes. Retrieved November 3, 2025, from https://www.therapynotes.com/

Yorke, J., Nugent, W., Strand, E., Bolen, R., New, J., & Davis, C. (2013). Equine-assisted therapy and its impact on cortisol levels of children and horses: A pilot study and meta-analysis. *Early Child Development and Care, 183*(7), 874–894. https://doi.org/10.1080/03004430.2012.693486

Zhang, H., Watkins, C. E., Jr., Hook, J. N., Hodge, A. S., Davis, C. W., Norton, J., Wilcox, M. M., Davis, D. E., DeBlaere, C., & Owen, J. (2022). Cultural humility in psychotherapy and clinical supervision: A research review. *Counselling and Psychotherapy Research, 22*(3), 548–557. https://doi.org/10.1002/capr.12481

Zur, O. (n.d.). *Introduction to informed consent in psychotherapy, counseling, and assessment*. Dr. Ofer Zur. Retrieved November 3, 2025, from https://drzur.com/informed-consent/

# 11

# A Trainer's Paradise

This chapter demonstrates how to design training and workshops that actually teach, rather than merely filling a time slot. A counselor who is being paid to give a lecture or lead a workshop should not be standing at a podium reading word-for-word from a slideshow. That is not what they were hired to do. Your audience already has the slides. They can read. Nobody signs up for a workshop buzzing about the transition from slide 87 to 88. Nobody's placing bets on the font choice.

If you've been counseling, supervising, or teaching for a while, you've probably picked up expertise worth sharing. Maybe it's a strategy that works. Maybe it's a way of explaining concepts that helps people understand. Either way, it's time to consider teaching it.

Turning your hard-earned knowledge into something others can learn from can be a great revenue stream without quitting your job or selling out. Teaching is part of the work of counseling. It helps the field grow, supports your business, and protects your energy (Moate & Cox, 2015).

You don't need a PhD or a stage. You need clarity. What do you know? Who needs it? How can you deliver it in a way that is helpful, grounded, and counselor-focused (Hays & Erford, 2010)?

The field doesn't need more fluff. It needs wisdom—practical, honest insight from people doing the work. That's where you come in. In paying your experience forward, you offer others a service, create sustainability within your own practice, and show up for the profession in a way that supports both your mission and your income.

## Finding a Training Topic That Actually Lands

If you're going to teach, choose a subject or idea that you know well and that people actually need. Great training topics live at the intersection of what you care about, what you're good at, and what others are asking for. That's your sweet spot. That's your lane.

### *What's Your Bread and Butter?*

Chances are that your topic is hiding in plain sight. What do friends, supervisees, or colleagues keep coming to you for help with? What do clients or interns say "finally makes sense" when you explain it? Those are your cues. If the same question keeps surfacing, it probably points to a real gap in the field (Knowles et al., 2014).

### *Spot Gaps in the CEU Landscape*

You've probably sat through a continuing education unit (CEU) that felt outdated, too broad, or disconnected from clinical reality. Those feelings are your opportunities. The best trainings are born from frustration—when you know something can be done better (Bierema et al., 2025). Ask yourself: "What training do I wish I had five years ago?" If you needed it then, someone needs it now.

### *Why Niching Down Works*

Trying to appeal to everyone usually ends in forgettable content. Specificity builds trust. It shows your audience you see them, and it sharpens your teaching. Instead of offering a "trauma-informed care" course, teach one about "Using somatic interventions with adult survivors of childhood abuse." Instead of leading a workshop on "cultural issues in counseling," lead one about "Supporting Latino clients through immigration-related grief." Instead of writing a leaflet about "mental health in schools," write one about "Helping school counselors manage burnout during times of crisis."

Niche doesn't mean narrow-minded. It means focused, applicable, and real. Adult learners want training that speaks to their world and offers usable strategies, not abstract theory (Hays & Erford, 2010; Taylor & Marienau, 2016).

## Ideas to Get You Started

Some powerful topics might include teaching supervision strategies for first-generation graduate students, helping clinicians recognize trauma in high-achieving teens, business systems for counselors in group practice settings, and integrating faith-based frameworks into ethical clinical work. None of these requires you to be a celebrity expert. You just need lived experience, clarity, and the ability to make something teachable.

## If You're Stuck, Try This Test

The hardest part of creating a workshop or presentation is narrowing the focus. You might have ten good ideas swimming around in your mind, but no clear sense of which one actually connects with an audience. When that happens, try this quick clarity test. Ask yourself: "Is my topic too broad, or is it specific enough that people immediately know what they'll walk away with?"

- **Too broad:** "Cultural humility in counseling."
- **Sharper:** "Avoiding microaggressions in supervision with BIPOC interns."
- **Too broad:** "Anxiety in teens."
- **Sharper:** "Helping anxious perfectionists break the burnout cycle in high school."

Clarity isn't just for your marketing—it's for you. It tells you what to build, how to structure it, and who it's for.

## You Don't Need Permission, You Need a Voice

Impostor syndrome gets loud when you start teaching. That's normal, but remember that readiness isn't always a feeling. It's often a decision. You don't need to have it all figured out. You just need to start where you are. Your story, your skill set, and a real need in the field are what build a solid foundation for meaningful, counselor-focused training (Moate & Cox, 2015).

# Designing Educational Content that Sticks

Good training guides people through a meaningful learning experience that leaves them thinking differently, feeling empowered, and ready to take action. When you design content that sticks, you're creating something that can ripple outward into dozens, hundreds, or even thousands of client sessions down the line. That's why careful planning matters. Whether you're designing a one-hour webinar or a multiday intensive, your structure, delivery, and style all influence whether your message lands.

## *Structuring Your Training for Maximum Impact*

Before you ever build a slide deck, start with three simple questions:

1. What do I want people to know after this? (e.g., understand a specific clinical concept.)
2. What do I want them to feel? (e.g., confident, equipped, curious.)
3. What do I want them to do? (e.g., implement a skill, change a practice, seek more training.)

These three anchors help shape your curriculum objectives. Research has shown that adult learners are most engaged when they can immediately connect new knowledge to action (Taylor & Marienau, 2016). They're not looking for abstract theories; they want tools they can use the next day. Once you're clear on outcomes, you can sequence your material logically.

1. **Start with the "why":** Why does this topic matter? What problems does it solve?
2. **Teach the "what":** Define your concepts clearly. Avoid jargon unless you explain it.
3. **End with the "how":** Show practical application through steps, stories, or demonstrations.

This sequencing mirrors how adults naturally learn: context first, knowledge second, action last.

Delivery method matters, too. Some content works better in person, where experiential exercises can happen in real time. Other material may lend itself to digital formats, especially if your audience needs flexibility. Consider what kind of environment will best serve the material and your teaching style.

## *Make Learning Engaging, Not Exhausting*

Slideshows have their place, but they aren't the heartbeat of good teaching. To really engage adult learners, your training needs to include moments of reflection, interaction, and real-world application (Knowles et al., 2014). Here are a few ways to do that.

- **Tell stories:** Share personal stories, anonymized client vignettes, and case studies to bring concepts to life.
- **Ask real questions:** Build in opportunities for participants to reflect or discuss, even in webinars (chat boxes and breakout rooms work wonders).
- **Use experiential exercises:** Activities like role-plays, guided imagery, or worksheet tasks shift participants from passive to active learners.
- **Model transparency:** When you share your learning curves or mistakes, you build credibility and connection.

Good trainers are facilitators of experience, not just deliverers of content. Your goal is to get participants thinking critically, practicing new skills, and seeing how the material fits into their world.

## Aligning with CEU Board Requirements (When Needed)

If you want your training to offer CEUs, it has to meet specific board requirements. Even if you're not seeking CEU approval, designing your workshop with those expectations in mind will make it stronger, more structured, and easier to market. Licensing bodies like the National Board for Certified Counselors (NBCC), state boards, or the Association of Social Work Boards (ASWB) have slightly different criteria, but most share a core set of standards (NBCC, 2014; ACA, n.d.).

First, you need clear learning objectives, written in measurable terms like, "Participants will be able to identify three signs of burnout in supervisees." Objectives help clarify the scope of your training and keep your content focused. Next, you will need a timed agenda, breaking down how you will use each part of the session. This demonstrates intentional pacing and outcomes-based design, which is key to adult learning (Bierema et al., 2025).

You should also support your material with evidence-based references. Use peer-reviewed sources or recognized frameworks to back up your teaching (Knowles et al., 2014). Finally, most boards require an assessment component: a short post-test, evaluation form, or participation check to show learners are engaged with the material and have met the objectives.

Checking your state or national board's website is essential. They often have downloadable CEU provider checklists or approval criteria.

Planning with these requirements in mind from the beginning will save you major revisions later. Even if you're not submitting for formal CEU approval, following this structure gives your training more credibility. It tells participants, "This isn't just helpful—it's professional, vetted, and worth your time."

## Pricing and Packaging Your Program

When it comes to training, there's a natural temptation to focus only on content: what you will teach, how you will explain it, and what resources you will create. An equally important concern is how you will package and price it.

Pricing and packaging are business strategies and boundary-setting tools (Nagle et al., 2023). They help define the relationship between you, your content, and the people you're serving. Done well, they create sustainability. Done poorly, they create burnout, resentment, and missed opportunities.

Pricing begins with recognizing that your training is not just "nice information." It is a bridge you built through years of education, practice, trial, and error that helps others get somewhere faster, safer, and with more clarity than they would on their own. Pricing should reflect the value of transformation, not just the time spent delivering it.

### Picking the Right Delivery Model

The first step is choosing the format that fits both your material and your energy. Not every training needs to be a full-day event. In fact, some of the most effective adult learning happens in short, focused sessions that are easy to digest and apply (Bierema et al., 2025). Your delivery model should reflect the depth of your content, the level of support you want to offer, and how much time and energy you realistically have to give. It also sets the tone for how your participants experience you, not just as an expert, but as a teacher and guide (Knowles et al., 2014). Here are a few formats to consider.

- **One-hour webinar ($29–$49):** Ideal for one clearly defined topic, like "Five Common Ethical Pitfalls New Supervisors Miss." These are easy to deliver and great for visibility.
- **Half-day workshop (3–4 hours, $99–$149):** Best for hands-on skills training, such as "Integrating Somatic Techniques for Anxiety" or "Creating Your First Supervision Contract." Adult learners benefit from interactive, scenario-based content in this format (Taylor & Marienau, 2016).

- **Weekend intensive ($250–$600):** Higher ticket, immersive experiences that may offer CEUs or certification hours. These are great for deeper content like "Trauma-Informed Play Therapy" or "Advanced Clinical Supervision Practices."
- **Cohort-based programs (4–6 weeks, $400–$1,000):** Mix of live teaching, group support, and individualized feedback. They're especially useful for training that builds professional identity or requires guided implementation over time (Brown & Green, 2019).

The delivery model you choose shapes the relational and educational experience for your learners. Thoughtful structure, pacing, and learner engagement are central to effective adult education (Knowles et al., 2014; Bierema et al., 2025).

**Thinking Strategically About Pricing**

Not every training needs to be priced the same way. Offering a free webinar can be a smart move when you're building visibility, introducing a new topic, or creating an on-ramp into a larger program (Brown & Green, 2019). For example, a free 45-minute session on "Understanding Burnout in Counselors" can build trust and naturally point toward a deeper paid training.

Low-cost trainings—typically priced between $25 and $99—help make valuable material accessible without undercutting its worth. These formats are great for "lunch and learn" events or niche, skill-specific topics that don't require a full transformation experience (Bierema et al., 2025). Offering affordable, short-format content aligns well with what adult learners want: relevant, focused, and immediately usable material (Knowles et al., 2014).

Premium trainings (starting around $150 and reaching $500 or more) are designed for deeper work—trainings that strengthen professional identity, build confidence, or help learners make meaningful shifts in how they practice. A six-week course like "Building a Private Pay Counseling Practice from Scratch," paired with coaching, templates, and live Q&A, easily warrants a $500–$750 price point. These costs of these kinds of offerings reflect the value of the outcome, not just the time spent.

When setting your price, ask:

- What's the real value of what I am teaching?
- Can participants apply it immediately?

- Will it serve them long-term?
- How much access and feedback am I providing?

More depth, more access, and more transformation all justify a higher investment. You're offering a guided path past the years of trial and error you had to work through yourself.

## Creating Simplified Tiered Options

One way to serve a broader audience while honoring different levels of commitment is by offering tiered packages. Instead of locking yourself into a one-size-fits-all price, you can create options, including

- A basic access package for $49 that offers live training and a recording;
- A plus package for $99, adding a 15-page downloadable workbook, access to additional templates, and a private resource list; and
- A VIP package for $199–$249, offering everything above, plus a 30-minute consultation call or access to a private Q&A group.

Tiered options allow participants to self-select how deeply they want to engage, without requiring you to change the core content. It's a way to honor both beginners and more seasoned professionals within the same training structure. Still, simplicity matters. Two or three options are plenty. More than that, and you risk confusing your audience, which can lead to hesitation or abandonment at the purchase decision point.

## Pricing to Reflect Your Expertise and Energy

Finally, it's critical to price your training in a way that protects your energy. Undercharging doesn't just hurt your bank account. It can subtly chip away at your motivation and satisfaction. When you spend weeks preparing, delivering, and supporting a training only to net a few hundred dollars, it's easy to start questioning whether it was worth it. Healthy pricing meets three objectives:

1. It honors the depth of your knowledge and experience.
2. It protects the energy and enthusiasm you bring to your work.
3. It frames your training as a real investment for participants, not a casual "add-on."

Building in post-training recovery time is a vital part of this equation. After a major workshop, block a day for rest and decompression. If you're running an intensive training group, limit enrollment to what feels manageable. Pricing high enough to give yourself space to breathe is a long-term investment in the sustainability of your whole career.

At the end of the day, you are not just selling information. You're offering transformation. Pricing and packaging thoughtfully ensure that both you and your participants are set up to experience the full value of what you've built.

### Marketing Your Training with Integrity

Marketing your training lets people know you have something that could help. For counselors, this can feel foreign at first. We're wired to listen, not promote. Marketing done with clarity and care is just another form of service (Brown & Green, 2019). The key is knowing who your training is for and speaking directly to them. Don't try to appeal to everyone. Speak to the counselor who's struggling with documentation, or the new supervisor who's second-guessing their feedback. The more specific your message, the more it lands.

Skip the fluff. Instead of promising "new skills," show them the actual outcome: "Walk away with three templates you can use tomorrow." Keep it human. A personal message, like "Hey, I thought of you when I built this," will do more than any polished ad. Use platforms that match your energy, whether it is LinkedIn, email, or just word of mouth. You don't need to shout; you just need to be clear. Marketing with integrity means remembering that you're not stepping outside your identity as a counselor; you're extending it.

## Scaling and Sustaining Educational Income Streams

Building a single training is a big deal, and it deserves credit. However, stopping there can limit both your income and your reach. One of the smartest things a counselor-educator can do is think beyond the live event. Scaling means building something that continues to serve others and sustains you, even when you're not in the room. It's not about building an empire. It's about creating systems where your best ideas keep working long after you've delivered them.

In a profession where burnout is a tangible risk, scaling your work is a sustainability strategy. Repackaging content into evergreen formats like on-demand courses or downloadable bundles allows you to keep making an impact without constantly reinventing the wheel (Bierema et al., 2025). A recorded webinar, for example, can be turned into a self-paced course that people can purchase anytime. Add a downloadable workbook, templates, or reflection prompts, and it becomes a full experience that learners can return to on their own schedule (Knowles et al., 2014).

Let's say you offer a three-hour live workshop priced at $129. With a bit of preparation, you can later sell the recording as a $99 on-demand course. It's still valuable and relevant, but no longer tied to your calendar. Over time, even modest, consistent sales can add up to meaningful passive income. To make the most of this approach,

- record with quality audio and visuals (even basic upgrades like a USB microphone and clean slides help);
- provide tools that encourage application (e.g., checklists, worksheets, or client-ready resources); and
- offer a certificate of completion if CEU credit or proof of learning is relevant to your audience.

Smart scaling repurposes what already works. It turns the effort you've already made into something that can keep delivering value long after the Zoom call ends.

## Collaborating With Organizations to Expand Your Reach

Partnering with organizations that already have established audiences is another way to scale without exhausting yourself. Many counseling associations, community mental health centers, universities, and private training companies are looking for new, relevant training to offer their members or staff.

Instead of selling individual tickets, you can license your training to an organization for a flat fee. For example, an agency might pay $2,000–$5,000 for the rights to use your recorded 4-hour trauma training across all their clinician teams for a year. Partnerships like these allow you to amplify your impact without multiplying your workload. They also position you as a respected educator whose material has broader professional value.

## Developing Licensing or Certification Programs

For trainings that delve deeper or offer a specialized method, consider creating a facilitator or certification program. This allows other professionals to license your framework, run your curriculum, or even teach it under your brand. While building a certification track is a bigger investment of time and planning, it creates opportunities for ongoing licensing fees or royalties, expanded brand recognition, and a growing network of professionals trained under your model

Certification programs aren't necessary for every training, but when done thoughtfully, they can turn a personal expertise into a legacy that scales far beyond what one person could do alone.

## Staying Grounded as Your Influence Grows

Visibility often invites self-doubt. Many counselors hesitate to step into thought leadership roles because they worry, they aren't "expert enough." Impostor syndrome tends to grow louder the more visible we become. It's important to remember that leadership in counseling doesn't demand flawless expertise. All you need to do is offer your voice thoughtfully and recognize that your perspective adds value simply because it's informed by real work, reflection, and care.

As your reach grows, consistency becomes more important than perfection. Thought leaders don't have to post daily or be on every social platform, but they do need to show up regularly and stay anchored to a few core principles:

- Center your learners. Focus on what your audience needs, not just what you want to say.
- Be transparent about your learning process. Vulnerability builds trust.
- Prioritize real conversations over polished marketing. Thought leadership is relational, not transactional.

Over time, people will begin to associate your name with a particular kind of wisdom, insight, or challenge. They won't remember every post or presentation, but they will remember how your work made them feel smarter, stronger, or more hopeful about their own journey. Ultimately, stepping into thought leadership is an act of stewardship. It's recognizing that your experiences—the messy, hard-earned, beautiful parts of your counseling life—are not just for you. They're meant to light the path for others, just as others once lit the way for you.

## Teaching, Sharing, Leading

The opportunity to train others in our field is one of the quiet privileges of counseling. It is a way to extend the best parts of our experience—what we've learned, what we've struggled through, what we've tested and refined—and offer it to others in a form they can carry forward.

Throughout this chapter, we have explored how to identify your training niche, design educational content that sticks, price and package your offerings thoughtfully, market your work with integrity, and step into your role as a thought leader. We have also looked at how to scale your efforts in ways that allow your work to keep growing without draining you dry.

The skills, insights, and frameworks you have developed through your own clinical work, supervision, or research are needed by others. Sharing them through trainings, workshops, courses, or speaking engagements is both a business move and a contribution to the profession.

As you continue building your educational offerings, remember that success isn't defined by reaching everyone. It's defined by serving the right people with depth and authenticity. Focus on creating experiences that genuinely help your participants grow, and the reputation you build will be far more enduring than any short-term marketing push.

Teaching allows us to leave fingerprints on the next generation of counselors, supervisors, and educators. It invites us to see our work not just in terms of client outcomes or caseload numbers, but in the ongoing growth of the profession itself. In becoming a trainer and thought leader, you are stepping into a role that sustains both the field and yourself.

Your voice is needed. Your experiences matter. The future of counseling is shaped by what we teach, how we lead, and who we empower along the way.

# References

American Counseling Association. (n.d.). *Continuing education*. ACA. Retrieved November 3, 2025, from https://www.counseling.org/events-education/continuing-education

Bierema, L. L., Fedeli, M., & Merriam, S. B. (2025). *Adult learning: Linking theory and practice* (2nd ed.). John Wiley & Sons.

Brown, A. H., & Green, T. D. (2019). *The essentials of instructional design: Connecting fundamental principles with process and practice* (4th ed.). Routledge. https://doi.org/10.4324/9780429439698

Hays, D. G., & Erford, B. T. (Eds.). (2010). *Developing Multicultural Counseling Competence: A Systems Approach*. Pearson.

Knowles, M. S., Holton, E. F., III, & Swanson, R. A. (2014). *The adult learner: The definitive classic in adult education and human resource development* (8th ed.). Routledge. https://doi.org/10.4324/9781315816951

Moate, R. M., & Cox, J. A. (2015). Learner-centered pedagogy: Considerations for application in a didactic course. *The Professional Counselor*, 5(3), 379–389. https://doi.org/10.15241/rmm.5.3.379

Nagle, T. T., Müller, G., & Gruyaert, E. (2023). *The strategy and tactics of pricing: A guide to growing more profitably*. Routledge.

National Board for Certified Counselors. (2014). *NBCC Continuing Education Provider Policy*. NBCC. https://nbcc.org/assets/ceprovider/nbcc_continuing_education_provider_policy.pdf

Taylor, K., & Marienau, C. (2016). *Facilitating learning with the adult brain in mind: A conceptual and practical guide*. Jossey-Bass.

# 12

# The Business of Supervision

Not all good clinicians make good supervisors, and not all good supervisors are great clinicians. No matter how many years you've been in the field, that 40-hour supervision training course does not automatically make you skilled at holding space for someone else's growth. We all know someone practicing who has no business being a counselor, let alone a clinical supervisor. The truth is, the first step in turning supervision into a business is being good enough at it that people seek you out, not just for the hours, but for the quality of the experience.

Supervision isn't a checklist or a weekly chat. It's a deeply layered professional relationship that carries clinical, legal, and ethical weight. You're not just reviewing notes and giving feedback. You're shaping how future counselors think, work, and show up for clients. It's mentorship, gatekeeping, consultation, and evaluation all wrapped into one role. It takes skill to hold all of that well (Borders et al., 2014; Bernard & Goodyear, 2019).

Supervision is also a business. It involves scheduling, billing, contracts, liability, marketing, and documentation. If you're charging a fee, taking on risk, and providing a structured service, then you're running a business, whether you call it that or not. Yet, most of us enter supervision roles without any real preparation for this side of things (Watkins et al., 2021). We wing it. We piece together old templates. We meet at coffee shops. We undercharge. We avoid the uncomfortable conversations. Over time, that lack of structure can lead to burnout, blurred boundaries, and even legal trouble.

Research has shown that high-quality supervision significantly improves counselor development, confidence, and retention (Rousmaniere, 2025). Poor supervision, especially when it is inconsistent or under-structured, can undermine growth and cause real harm to clients and supervisees alike (Ellis et al., 2015). While our clinical skills matter, they're not enough. To do this work well and sustainably, we have to build something clear, ethical, and financially viable.

This chapter lays the groundwork for a supervision practice that works, reflects your values, protects your time, and respects your expertise. We discuss the characteristics of good supervision. We show you how to build the infrastructure: contracts, policies, systems, and documentation that protect both you and your supervisees. We break down what to charge, how to talk about money with confidence, and how to manage boundaries without losing connection. We share what we've learned through trial, error, and years of figuring it out on the fly.

Supervision is a clinical service and should be treated as such. The business side doesn't have to take away from the heart of the work. In fact, when done right, it protects it.

## What Makes a Good Supervisor

Supervision is a distinct skill set that blends leadership, clinical reasoning, emotional regulation, and professional mentoring (Falender & Shafranske, 2004). At its best, supervision helps counselors-in-training (CITs) internalize the ethical standards, clinical decision-making, and reflective habits they will need throughout their careers. Good supervision is structured, intentional, and accountable.

Effective supervisors balance warmth with structure. They create a safe enough space for supervisees to be honest, but hold the line when boundaries or ethical codes are crossed. Research has shown that high-quality supervision improves counselor confidence, identity development, and overall clinical competence (Rousmaniere, 2025; Borders et al., 2014). That being said, it's not just about being supportive; it's also about being consistent, clear, and grounded in a supervision model.

Good supervisors use an articulated theoretical framework. Whether it's developmental, discrimination-based, or reflective-relational, the model provides structure to track growth, frame feedback, and resolve ruptures when they arise (Bernard & Goodyear, 2019). Supervisors also stay organized. They document sessions, track goals, log hours, and complete evaluations in a timely, professional manner. These habits protect the supervisor and teach supervisees what professionalism looks like behind the scenes.

Cultural responsiveness is also central to quality supervision. A strong supervisor doesn't avoid discussions of identity, power, or systemic inequities. They name dynamics when they show up, invite dialogue, and model how to navigate discomfort without shutting down (Hernández & McDowell, 2010). Supervision is one of the first places where counselors learn how to talk about race, gender, and power in the clinical space. If it doesn't happen here, it often doesn't happen at all.

Finally, good supervisors keep growing. They seek consultation. They reflect on their own reactions. They revisit the literature and refine their approach. Supervision is a living process, shaped by the needs of the supervisee, the demands of the setting, and the wisdom of the field.

If you want to be a good supervisor who is sought out and referable, don't focus on being perfect. Instead, prioritize being present, ethical, and engaged. Your role is to hold space, hold standards, and hold the line. Do that well, and you will shape not just better counselors, but a better profession.

## Establishing a Supervision Practice

Starting a supervision practice is more than a natural next step in a counselor's career. It's an intentional shift in identity, responsibility, and business orientation. While many clinicians are excited to support early-career professionals, few are fully prepared for what it means to launch and sustain a supervision practice that is legally compliant, financially sound, and ethically robust.

## Licensing and Credentialing Requirements

The first step in offering clinical supervision is ensuring that you're credentialed to do so. Each state has specific requirements regarding who can supervise, how many years post-licensure they must have, and what supervision-specific training is required. In many states, this means obtaining a formal credential such as LPC-S (Licensed Professional Counselor Supervisor) or LMFT-S (Licensed Marriage and Family Therapist Supervisor).

These designations often require completion of board-approved continuing education units (CEUs), a certain number of post-licensure practice hours (often 3–5 years), and, in some cases, submission of a supervision philosophy or sample contract. The process can be rigorous, but that is for your own protection. Credentialing ensures that supervisors understand not only clinical theory but also the legal, ethical, and educational dimensions of guiding developing counselors. Clinicians should consult their state licensing board, professional associations, and peer-reviewed guidance (Borders et al., 2014) to ensure their qualifications and training meet current standards.

## Establishing Policies and Paperwork

Before you meet with your first supervisee, you need a comprehensive supervision agreement that lays the foundation for a clear, structured, and ethical relationship. This agreement should outline,

- Frequency and format of meetings;
- Goals and evaluation benchmarks;
- Roles and responsibilities;
- Confidentiality and its limits;
- Documentation expectations;
- Emergency and crisis protocols; and
- Policies on cancellations, payment, and grievances.

This document protects everyone involved. It should reflect your supervision model, your ethical responsibilities, and your business policies (Borders et al., 2014; Ellis et al., 2015). Alongside the agreement, you should create a supervision log (for both you and your supervisee), evaluation forms, and a professional disclosure statement that details your clinical background, theoretical orientation, and supervision philosophy. These tools promote transparency, reduce liability, and foster professional trust. Supervisees report greater satisfaction, clarity, and growth when expectations are established clearly at the outset, not after problems arise (Romans et al., 1995; Bernard & Goodyear, 2019).

## Insurance and Liability Protection

Supervising other clinicians increases your professional risk. If a supervisee becomes the subject of a complaint, grievance, or lawsuit, you may be named, especially if supervision documentation is subpoenaed or your oversight is called into question (Munson, 2001). That's why liability protection is not optional.

Every supervisor should review their malpractice insurance and make sure it explicitly covers clinical supervision. Some policies exclude supervision unless you purchase a specific rider or upgrade your premium. If you supervise through your private practice, make sure the practice entity itself is insured, not just you personally. It's also your responsibility to confirm that all supervisees carry their own professional liability insurance throughout the supervisory relationship (Lawson & Cook, 2017).

Even with insurance, supervision carries inherent exposure. You can't eliminate the risk, but you can manage it. Document supervision sessions thoroughly. Include topics discussed, clinical decisions reviewed, ethical concerns addressed, and follow-up plans. Comply with your state's record-keeping and supervision documentation requirements. Seek consultation when something feels unclear or risky. Staying within your scope, documenting consistently, and leaning on peer support are three of the most reliable ways to protect yourself while doing meaningful work.

## Marketing and Visibility

Just like counseling, supervision needs marketing. If you want supervisees, go where the supervisees are. That might mean reaching out to your local graduate counseling programs and offering to lead a free weekend training for their honor societies or practicum students on anything you're confident teaching. In order to grow your supervisee pool, you must show up with value, build trust, and let folks know that you supervise and that you'd love to work with them when they are ready.

You also need a professional presence that communicates your supervision style, who you work best with, and how to get in touch. That might include adding a supervision-specific page to your website, creating a digital brochure outlining your services and fees, and getting listed in directories like TherapyDen (n.d.), Psychology Today (n.d.), or SupervisionTracker (n.d.). Be clear about who you best supervise. Are you great with interns who need lots of structure? Postgrad associates who want more autonomy? School counselors navigating complicated systems? Speak to your ideal supervisee; clarity builds connection (Borders et al., 2014).

Supervisors who build professional visibility also report stronger alignment with their supervision values and fewer mismatched supervisees. When supervisees know what to expect, they're more likely to thrive and stay (Gibson et al., 2019). So, treat this like you would marketing your counseling practice. Show people what it's like to work with you, and they'll find their way to your door.

## Creating a Space for Learning and Accountability

Remember that supervision is not counseling; it's a professional learning relationship. Establish a tone that balances warmth with boundaries, flexibility with consistency. Provide feedback early and often. Use your own supervision and consultation to stay grounded, especially when supervisees bring their clinical and personal struggles into the room. Supervisees are learning the technique and how to carry the weight of this work. Your role is to help them build internal resources, ethical muscles, and clinical confidence. A supervision practice is a reflection of your identity as a mentor, a leader, and a business owner. Done well, it's one of the most meaningful, growth-promoting, and generative choices you can make in your counseling career.

## Financial Aspects of Supervision

Supervision takes time, training, emotional energy, and legal risk. Like any professional service, it has substantial costs. Whether you're reviewing documentation, showing up to crisis calls, or writing evaluations for licensure boards, you're investing in your supervisee's future and using your expertise to do it.

This section treats that investment with the same seriousness you give to your clinical work. We cover the financial side of supervision: what you're actually being paid for, what it costs to do it well, and how to structure your fees so they're fair, ethical, and sustainable.

You will learn how to set rates that reflect your time and risk, how to account for hidden costs like insurance and administrative hours, and how to build a model that allows you to supervise without burning out or going broke.

### *How Much Should You Charge?*

Rates vary based on geography, experience, and credentials, but in 2024, most LPC-S and LMFT-S providers charge between $90 and $160 per hour (Kim, 2025). Some charge less for interns, more for post-master's associates, and offer group supervision at a reduced per-person rate. Many supervisors admit that their fee-setting practices are often guided more by emotion, such as guilt or fear of overcharging, than by a clear financial strategy (Myers, 2012; Grodzki, 2015). Supervisors think, "They're just starting—I should help them." Access matters, but so does sustainability. Undercharging doesn't make you more ethical. It makes your work less sustainable and increases your risk of burnout (Thompson et al, 2012).

Supervision is a professional service that involves legal liability, emotional labor, and administrative oversight. Setting rates that reflect those realities isn't greedy. It's responsible. Research has shown that when supervisors feel undercompensated, they're more likely to experience fatigue, boundary erosion, and reduced supervision quality (Slanzi & Sellers, 2023). Pricing supervision fairly helps you stay in this role long enough to actually make a difference, and models healthy business practice for your supervisees.

## What Most Supervisors Forget to Include in Their Budget

Supervision has tangible, recurring costs. If you don't plan for them, you will end up covering them out of pocket. If you want your supervision practice to last, you need to treat it like the professional service it is. That starts with knowing where your money's going.

### Risk and Liability

If you're supervising provisionally licensed clinicians, your risk exposure goes up. Most malpractice insurance policies don't automatically cover supervision, and if they do, it's often in limited situations. You will likely need a supervisor-specific rider. It's not flashy or exciting, but it's necessary. Always add it to your budget.

### Technology and Systems

Supervision documentation must be secure. That means Health Insurance Portability and Accountability Act (HIPAA)-compliant email, encrypted cloud backups, and maybe even access to an electronic health record (EHR) system to store notes and evaluations. Google Workspace (n.d.) (with the right settings) and SimplePractice (n.d.) aren't free. These tools are your infrastructure, and they come with a monthly cost. Be sure to price them in.

### Professional Development

Being a supervisor isn't a one-and-done certification. Most states require renewal every 2–5 years, and that includes CEUs in areas like ethics, multicultural supervision, and legal standards. Staying current is a necessary part of the job. Those trainings aren't free. If you're going to require your supervisees to grow, you've got to model that yourself.

**Unseen Administrative Time**

There's a ton of unpaid labor baked into supervision, including reviewing recordings, documenting sessions, writing licensure evaluations, emailing back and forth, and consulting on cases. If you're not building that time into your fee structure, you're working for free, and that adds up fast. Your calendar and your energy will feel it long before your bank account does.

**Marketing and Visibility**

Even if you get supervisees by word-of-mouth, you still need a professional presence. That might mean a page on your website, a digital brochure, a listing on SupervisionTracker (n.d.), or a few social media posts. You don't need to become an influencer, but you do need to showcase yourself in some way. Otherwise, people won't know you're available.

**Taxes and Bookkeeping**

Supervision income is business income. That means tracking your earnings, estimating quarterly taxes, filing 1099 forms if needed, and possibly hiring an accountant. If you don't plan for this from the start, it'll catch up with you, and it won't be pretty.

Supervision runs on structure, preparation, and respect for your time and energy. If you want to do this well, you've got to build your business like it matters, because it does.

## *Supervision as a Scalable, Sustainable Income Stream*

More than just a professional obligation, supervision can become a reliable, rewarding, and sustainable source of income. What many supervisors don't realize is how scalable this work can be compared to counseling. Ten supervisees paying $100 per week adds up to $4,000 per month. That's significant revenue, especially when the emotional load of supervision tends to be lighter than clinical work filled with crisis or trauma cases (Thompson et al, 2012; Borders & Brown, 2022).

In fact, many supervisors find supervision to be more collaborative and less draining than counseling. The dynamic is different. It's often more reflective, more collegial, and more energizing. Supervision supports professional identity development and counselor retention, while also benefiting the supervisor's own growth and career longevity (Bernard & Goodyear, 2019; Borders et al., 2014).

Supervision also opens the door to financial diversification. Group supervision, for example, is a common and smart way to scale. A 90-minute group with five supervisees paying $50 each brings in $250 in a single session, often with less preparation and emotional demand than individual counseling. It's also pedagogically rich: Supervisees learn from each other while you facilitate deeper reflection and peer feedback.

Beyond face-to-face supervision, your knowledge and systems can also be monetized. If you've built evaluation forms, onboarding packets, or remediation templates, consider packaging them for purchase. Many early-career supervisors are looking for those exact tools. You can also teach workshops or webinars that count toward supervision-specific CEUs, which adds another income stream while building your credibility.

Supervision is also intellectual property. Your tools, processes, and frameworks can be turned into offerings that serve others and sustain you. Supervision may not make you rich, but it absolutely can be a meaningful, recurring, and values-aligned part of your business portfolio that leverages your experience, strengthens your impact, and creates income that doesn't depend solely on counseling hours.

# Managing Supervisees

When people think about becoming a clinical supervisor, they often picture the conversations: the case conceptualizations, ethics consults, and theoretical explorations. Once you begin supervising, you quickly realize that one of the hardest parts isn't what happens in the room—it's setting up everything around it. This includes deciding what to charge, how to track progress, how to handle no-shows, and how to address difficult dynamics before they derail the relationship. It's part clinical, part administrative, and part emotional labor. If you don't build it with intention, it builds itself around you.

### *Managing No-Shows, Cancellations, and Boundaries*

Every supervisor should have and enforce their late cancellation and no-show policies. This models professional boundaries. If your supervisee is regularly canceling last minute or skipping sessions without consequence, they're learning to disrespect the very framework we're trying to teach. A 24- or 48-hour cancellation policy is standard. If a supervisee cancels late more than once, address it directly. Remind them that this is part of preparing them for real-world practice. Include the policy in writing in your supervision agreement and restate it during onboarding. Also, be clear about boundaries around contact outside of scheduled sessions. Are you available by phone or text? During which hours? What constitutes an emergency? Just like with clients, creating a supervisory container supports safety, structure, and professionalism.

## *Effectively Tracking Supervisee Progress*

Supervision is part art and part accountability. You will need a system for tracking how your supervisees are growing. This serves you, them, and the licensing board. Keep a log of every session: date, time, major topics, goals addressed, ethical issues discussed, and any follow-up items. This documentation protects you legally and helps you reflect on trends. It also serves as a professional record if you're ever asked to verify a supervisee's hours or performance.

Consider using quarterly evaluations. You can co-create this with the supervisee. Set 3–5 core goals, rate progress collaboratively, and reflect together on what's going well and what still needs support. Some supervisors also use tools like supervision genograms, journaling prompts, or structured feedback forms. These tools deepen the work and keep it from becoming overly casual.

## *Addressing Underperformance or Ethical Concerns*

Not every supervision relationship goes smoothly. Some supervisees struggle with time management, resistance to feedback, poor documentation, or blind spots around ethical practice. As a supervisor, it's your job to support and intervene. First, document the concerns early. Don't wait until they escalate. Use clear, behavioral language. Instead of writing that a supervisee "seems checked out," write that they "missed three supervision sessions in a month and submitted documentation late twice." Second, give the supervisee a chance to respond. Sometimes, life circumstances interfere, or the expectations are unclear. If there's still a pattern after redirection, you may need to create a formal remediation plan: clear goals, check-ins, timelines, and consequences. If the issues persist, or if client welfare is at risk, you have a duty to report the concern to your licensing board or the supervisee's program director. This is one of the most emotionally taxing parts of supervision, but it's also one of the most critical. When we avoid conflict, we protect comfort instead of protecting clients.

## Ending Supervision Well

Termination isn't just something that happens when the hours are complete. It's a clinical process that deserves reflection, closure, and celebration. Ideally, you will have a final session that reviews the supervisee's progress, future goals, and key lessons learned. But sometimes, supervision ends early due to fit issues, ethical concerns, or life transitions. Regardless of the reason, supervisors should provide written confirmation of hours completed, any evaluations or recommendations, and appropriate referrals if ongoing support is needed. Ending supervision is part of modeling what it means to complete a professional relationship well.

## Ensuring the Relationship Is Professional, Not Parental

Many supervisors fall into the trap of becoming parental. They carry their supervisees emotionally. They over-function when the supervisee under-functions. They confuse empathy with enabling. You are not their counselor. You are not their rescuer. You are a developmental partner. That means being supportive, but also means setting boundaries and being consistent and willing to sit with discomfort. Supervisees don't just learn from what we say. They learn from how we show up. Your fee structure, your policies, and your feedback style teach them how to be a professional. When they leave your supervision, they will carry your voice with them. Make sure it's one that taught both compassion and structure.

## Holding the Future, Holding the Line

Clinical supervision is one of the most meaningful ways to give back to the profession. It's not just mentorship, it's leadership, and leadership requires structure. We hope this chapter inspired you to supervise and equipped you to treat supervision as a legitimate income stream and business branch. Done well, supervision can be a cornerstone of your practice. It provides consistent income, professional stimulation, and a meaningful way to stay sharp and connected to the next generation of clinicians.

# References

Bernard, J. M., & Goodyear, R. K. (2019). *Fundamentals of clinical supervision* (6th ed.). Pearson.

Borders, L. D., & Brown, L. L. *(2022). The New Handbook of Counseling Supervision.* Routledge. https://doi.org/10.4324/9781003251583

Borders, L. D., Glosoff, H. L., Welfare, L. E., Hays, D. G., DeKruyf, L., Fernando, D. M., & Page, B. (2014). Best practices in clinical supervision: Evolution of a counseling specialty. *The Clinical Supervisor, 33*(1), 26–44. https://doi.org/10.1080/07325223.2014.905225

Ellis, M. V., Creaner, M., Hutman, H., & Timulak, L. (2015). A comparative study of clinical supervision in the Republic of Ireland and the United States. *Journal of Counseling Psychology, 62*(4), 621–631. https://doi.org/10.1037/cou0000110

Falender, C. A., & Shafranske, E. P. (2004). *Clinical supervision: A competency-based approach.* American Psychological Association. https://doi.org/10.1037/10806-000

Gibson, A. S., Ellis, M. V., & Friedlander, M. L. (2019). Toward a nuanced understanding of nondisclosure in psychotherapy supervision. *Journal of Counseling Psychology, 66*(1), 114–121. https://doi.org/10.1037/cou0000295

Google Workspace. (n.d.) *Google Workspace* [Online productivity and collaboration tools]. Google. Retrieved November 3, 2025, from https://workspace.google.com/

Grodzki, L. (2015). *Building your ideal private practice: A guide for therapists and other healing professionals* (2nd ed.). Norton Professional Books.

Hernández, P., & McDowell, T. (2010). Intersectionality, power, and relational safety in context: Key concepts in clinical supervision. *Training and Education in Professional Psychology, 4*(1), 29–35. https://doi.org/10.1037/a0017064

Kim, J. J. (2025). *Supervisees' payment for clinical supervision: Supervisor shortage and changing practice trend* [Preprint]. Rutgers, the State University of New Jersey. https://doi.org/10.13140/RG.2.2.19149.70889

Lawson, G., & Cook, J. M. (2017). Wellness, self-care, and burnout prevention. In J. S. Young & C. S. Cashwell (Eds.), *Clinical mental health counseling: Elements of effective practice* (pp. 313–335). Sage Publications, Inc. https://doi.org/10.4135/9781071801253.n14

Munson, C. (2001). *Handbook of clinical social work supervision* (3rd ed.). Routledge.

Myers, K. (2012). Show me the money: (The "problem" of) the therapist's desire, subjectivity, and relationship to the fee. In B. Berger & S. Newman (Eds.), *Money talks: In therapy, society, and life* (pp. 143–163). Routledge/Taylor & Francis Group.

Psychology Today. (n.d.). *Psychology Today* [Therapist platform]. Psychology Today. Retrieved November 3, 2025, from https://www.psychologytoday.com/us/therapists

Romans, J. S., Boswell, D. L., Carlozzi, A. F., & Ferguson, D. B. (1995). Training and supervision practices in clinical, counseling, and school psychology programs. *Professional Psychology: Research and Practice, 26*(4), 407–412. https://doi.org/10.1037/0735-7028.26.4.407

Rousmaniere, T. (2025). *Deliberate practice for psychotherapists: A guide to improving clinical effectiveness* (2nd ed.). Routledge.

SimplePractice. (n.d.). *SimplePractice* [Practice management software]. Retrieved November 3, 2025, from https://www.simplepractice.com/

Slanzi, C. M., & Sellers, T. (2023). Paying for supervision: Barriers, solutions, and opportunities. *Behavior Analysis in Practice, 16*(2), 363–373. https://doi.org/10.1007/s40617-022-00727-3

SupervisionTracker. (n.d.). *SupervisionTracker* [Supervision management platform]. Retrieved November 3, 2025, from https://supervisiontracker.org/

TherapyDen. (n.d.). *TherapyDen* [Therapist platform]. TherapyDen. Retrieved November 3, 2025, from https://www.therapyden.com

Thompson, E. H., Frick, M. H., & Trice-Black, S. (2012). Counselor-in-training perceptions of supervision practices related to self-care and burnout. *The Professional Counselor, 1*(3), 152–162. https://doi.org/10.15241/eht.1.3.152

Watkins, C. E., Vîşcu, L. I., & Cadariu, I. E. (2021). Psychotherapy supervision research: On roadblocks, remedies, and recommendations. *European Journal of Psychotherapy & Counselling, 23*(1), 8–25. https://doi.org/10.1080/13642537.2021.1881139

# 13

# Evaluating and Improving Your Business

Running a counseling business isn't just about setting goals and hoping for the best. It's about learning how to listen to your clients, to the work itself, and to your community. It's about paying attention to what's really happening, measuring progress, and having the humility to change course when needed.

Good clinical work doesn't guarantee a successful practice. You could be doing deeply meaningful counseling and still miss signs that things aren't working. If you're not evaluating your outcomes, gathering feedback, and reflecting on your approach, you're essentially steering a ship without a compass. You might not notice you've drifted off course until clients start disappearing—or worse, you start burning out.

## Survival Skills, Not Bonus Skills

Evaluation is how you stay sharp, grow, and ensure you're still helping. Counselors who thrive over the long haul don't just work harder; they also pay attention. They're willing to ask tough questions, make small corrections, and evolve with their clients and the field.

This chapter shows you how to steer your business on purpose using data, feedback, and honest reflection. You will learn how to build systems that keep you aligned with what works. When something stops working, you will know how to shift without capsizing the whole ship.

## The Cost of Standing Still

There's a myth in our field that once you're licensed and have a steady caseload, the hard part's over. The truth is, clients, culture, and mental health are changing. If we don't adapt to it, we risk becoming ineffective or even harmful. When counselors stop evolving, subtle issues start popping up. Clients are no-showing more often. Referrals dry up. Sessions feel flat. Burnout creeps in. We lose the edge, the presence, and the clarity that made us good at this in the first place.

This chapter isn't about scrapping what's already working. It's about building a living, breathing practice that stays grounded in your values but keeps evolving to meet the real-world needs of your clients. In other words, this is the chapter about becoming a skilled captain, not a passive passenger. It's about learning how to adjust the sails without losing your direction.

## Four Core Skills That Keep You Growing

In this chapter, we break down four essential areas that help you keep your business—and your clinical work—on track.

1. **Assessing client outcomes:** How to measure whether your work is helping, and how to choose the tools you will use.
2. **Gathering and using feedback:** How to invite honest input from clients and apply it in ways that deepen the work.
3. **Staying informed about new research:** How to keep up with the field without drowning in articles, and how to translate research into action.
4. **Continuously improving:** How to train your clinical ear to hear more, help more, and grow into the kind of counselor you're proud of.

### *Assessing Client Outcomes*

#### Gut Feelings Aren't Enough

You might think you will know when counseling is working. Clients smile, open up, and say "thank you." Unfortunately, feelings are a terrible business metric. If you want your counseling practice to stay effective over time, you must measure outcomes using data (Boswell et al., 2013). This is not to say that data is more important than people, but without it, we risk believing our own hype and missing signs that a client is quietly disengaging, plateauing, or not connecting the way we think they are.

## The Necessity of Reliable Outcome Tracking

Outcome tracking enables you to more reliably catch when elements of your practice aren't clicking for clients. It helps you see what's working, what's not, and what needs adjusting. It keeps your instincts honest and helps you stay aligned with what your clients actually need, not just what you hope will work.

## Simple Tools That Actually Work

You don't need a PhD in statistics to track outcomes. Most counselors use a few simple, research-backed tools that offer quick insights for both counselor and client. Here are two of the most practical examples.

- **Outcome Rating Scale (ORS):** This scale is a four-item questionnaire filled out at the beginning of each session. Clients rate their well-being, relationships, social functioning, and life satisfaction. It takes less than 30 seconds and correlates well with longer clinical assessments (Miller et al., 2003).
- **Session Rating Scale (SRS):** Administered at the end of sessions, the SRS taps into the client's perception of the alliance, goals, approach, and connection with you. Alliance quality is one of the best predictors of counseling outcomes (Flückiger et al., 2018), so this tool gives you real-time feedback where it matters most.

## Symptom-Specific Measures

For clients with clear clinical diagnoses, it can be helpful to add condition-specific tools, like Patient Health Questionnaire-9 (PHQ-9) for depression (Kroenke et al., 2001) and Generalized Anxiety Disorder-7 (GAD-7) for generalized anxiety (Spitzer et al., 2006). These offer a more structured way to track symptom reduction over time, especially in agency settings or when required for insurance compliance. Other options include behavior checklists for children or family systems, or even progress note reviews that look for stuck points or signs of growth across sessions.

### Track Your Presence, Too

Client-focused measures matter, but so does how you show up in the room. The Therapeutic Presence Inventory (TPI) is a powerful self-assessment tool for counselors. It measures your capacity to be grounded, present, and fully attuned to your clients, and is especially useful for spotting drift caused by fatigue or distraction (Geller & Greenberg, 2012). Checking in with yourself regularly can help prevent disconnection before it affects your work.

### How These Tools Fit In Different Contexts

Here's how outcome tracking might look in different practice environments.

- **Private practice:** Use the ORS every few sessions, the SRS after tough conversations, and check your TPI monthly to self-audit your presence.
- **Agencies:** PHQ-9 and GAD-7 might be required at intake, every 90 days, and at discharge. You can still layer in ORS/SRS to enhance your feedback-informed care model.
- **University counseling centers:** ORS can help track progress across a semester, with data aggregated for both individual care and program evaluation.
- **Telehealth practices:** Assessments can be digitized through Health Insurance Portability and Accountability Act (HIPAA)-compliant portals, giving you easy snapshots before and after sessions, even from afar.

### How to Use These Tools Ethically and Effectively

Outcome measurements aren't for grading clients or yourself. They're conversation starters. A drop in an ORS score is your cue to check in. Say something like, "I noticed you marked a lower score today. What's been going on lately?" or "I want to make sure this still feels helpful. Is there anything you'd like us to shift?"

Thoughtful outcome tracking invites collaboration and reinforces that counseling is something you do *with* your clients, not *to* them (Lambert & Shimokawa, 2016). Adding outcome tracking to your practice makes you more grounded, a better listener, a more precise clinician, and a more faithful guide. Choose tools that match your setting and style. Start small, be consistent, and let the data make you better.

## Gathering and Using Feedback

### Creating a Culture of Feedback

One of the most important, and most overlooked, parts of running a successful counseling practice is learning how to actively seek out and use client feedback. Don't wait passively for compliments or assume silence means satisfaction. Instead, create a consistent space for honest reflection and use that information to improve how you work.

Research has consistently supported the value of client feedback in improving counseling outcomes and preventing early dropout (Anker et al., 2009; Lambert & Shimokawa, 2016). Feedback-informed treatment is a sign of respect. It shows clients that their experience matters, not just their symptoms. It signals that counseling is a shared process, not something being done to them. It also positions you, the counselor, as someone committed to ongoing growth.

### Practical Ways to Invite Honest Input

Asking for feedback can feel vulnerable. No one likes hearing that they've missed the mark, even if the message is delivered with care. Questions like "How am I doing?" can feel loaded for both you and the client. Clients may feel pressure to say something positive or stay quiet if they don't feel safe enough to be honest (Bohart & Wade, 2013). That's why the way we invite feedback matters.

Instead of waiting for feedback or hoping for it to surface naturally, experienced counselors build it into the rhythm of their sessions. Here are a few practical approaches.

- **Normalize it from day one:** Let clients know during intake that you will check in about how counseling feels, and that their feedback helps you serve them better.
- **Use micro check-ins:** Don't wait for ruptures. Ask short, simple questions during sessions:
- "Was today's pace good for you?"
- "Are we focusing on what matters most right now?"
- "Anything you wish we were doing differently?"
- **Employ structured tools:** Tools like the SRS allow clients to rate their session experience in a non-confrontational way (Miller et al., 2003). These brief scales consistently correlate with stronger alliance and better outcomes when used regularly (Anker et al., 2009).

- **Give ongoing permission:** Don't just ask once. Remind clients throughout the work: "If anything ever feels off, too fast, or not helpful, I hope you will let me know. It's not rude; it's actually super helpful."

When these habits are built into the process from the start, feedback stops feeling like a confrontation. It becomes a normal, welcome part of the work.

### Formal Versus Informal Feedback

There's more than one way to gather feedback from clients, and the best practices use both formal and informal measures. Formal feedback involves structured tools and surveys. Informal feedback is woven into the everyday flow of the session. Each catches something different, and together they give you a fuller picture of how your clients are experiencing counseling.

Formal feedback uses validated tools like the SRS or anonymous satisfaction surveys to give clients a non-threatening way to express how things are going. These systems are especially useful in a group or large practice, in which aggregated feedback across clients or clinicians can highlight trends and systemic issues (Lambert & Shimokawa, 2016); in grant or contract work, in which funders often want clear outcome or satisfaction data that has been formally collected and cleanly reported (Anker et al., 2009); or when refining your brand or marketing because feedback patterns can reveal what's actually resonating with your clients, not just what you think is working.

Informal feedback is more relational. It shows up in body language, emotional tone, subtle shifts in client engagement, and casual, but intentional, questions you ask in session. Invitations for informal feedback can be as simple as asking, "Did this pace feel right today?" or "What did you find most helpful, or least helpful, about that?"

Informal feedback catches the micro-moments—the pauses, sighs, or energy drops—that formal methods can miss. Research has shown that therapeutic alliance, strengthened by relational sensitivity, continues to be one of the strongest predictors of client outcomes (Norcross & Lambert, 2019).

Here's how feedback methods can play out across settings.

- **Private practices:** You might use an SRS or client satisfaction form every 6–8 sessions and supplement with brief check-ins during sessions.

- **Agency settings:** Feedback might be collected during clinical reviews or at major treatment milestones, like reassessments or discharge.
- **University counseling centers:** These often blend both approaches—semester-end surveys for data, and mid-semester feedback in supervision to catch problems before they escalate.

Formal methods give you patterns. Informal methods give you nuance. Both are necessary. One helps you track trends over time. The other helps you catch the quiet signals in real time.

## What to Do with Feedback

Gathering client feedback is important, but what you do with that feedback matters even more. Ignoring feedback, especially critical feedback, sends the message that your comfort matters more than the client's experience. On the other hand, small, thoughtful responses to feedback build trust, repair ruptures, and deepen the therapeutic alliance (Norcross & Lambert, 2019).

## A Five-Step Internal Checklist

Here's a simple framework for how to respond when a client gives you feedback, especially if it's uncomfortable.

1. **Pause and breathe:** Take a moment. Resist the urge to defend or explain. Most of us are tempted to jump in and "fix" or clarify. Before you do anything, just breathe.
2. **Assume positive intent:** Clients rarely give feedback to hurt us. More often, they're taking a risk by speaking up. See it as a gift, not a threat (Anker et al., 2009).
3. **Clarify when needed:** If the feedback is vague or emotionally loaded, gently ask follow-ups:
4. "Can you tell me more about what that felt like for you?"
5. "What do you wish had been different in that moment?"
6. **Reflect openly, without shame:** Be honest about what you missed without beating yourself up:
7. "Thanks for telling me. I'm hearing that you need more structure/faster pacing/more space to vent. I want to work on that with you."
8. **Adjust collaboratively:** Make it a team effort. Collaborate with the client to shift the counseling process. Even small tweaks

build trust when they're clearly linked to feedback (Lambert & Shimokawa, 2016).

Once you have gone through the five-step checklist, you can integrate your clients' feedback and adjust your practice moving forward. You must touch base with clients and let them know when and how their feedback is being used. Language builds trust, so how you communicate those changes matters. Try phrases like:

- "Would you be open to experimenting with a slightly different focus next session?"
- "Thanks for letting me know—that's something I can adjust starting today."
- "Let's keep checking in to make sure this continues to feel right for you."

These statements normalize the feedback loop and create space for deeper collaboration.

Responding to client feedback with humility and action makes you more likable and makes counseling more effective. Research has shown that clients are more engaged, stay in counseling longer, and report stronger outcomes when their input shapes the process (Anker et al., 2009; Norcross & Lambert, 2019).

**Building Feedback Into Your Business Systems**

High-performing counseling businesses build feedback processes into the actual structure of the practice, not just the counseling room. Here are some examples of how you can do this in your practice:

- Add a "How Was Your Session?" question to online scheduling confirmations.
- Create a brief "Client Satisfaction Check-In" at the end of treatment.
- Survey departing clients (anonymously if needed) about what they appreciated and what could have been better.
- Include "client feedback themes" as part of your quarterly or annual practice review.

Tracking feedback over time helps you refine your intake process, your scheduling policies, your marketing messaging, and your own continuing education needs. Counselors who consistently grow their practice aren't just great at counseling—they are great at listening. Gathering and using feedback helps you become the kind of counselor who evolves on purpose, staying flexible, client-centered, and humble, even as your skills and reputation grow. Feedback is a mirror. The best practices and the best counselors keep looking into it.

## Staying Informed About New Research

You don't need to be a research junkie like one of us (Jude), but if you want to stay sharp and relevant in this field, you can't tune out either. Counseling evolves fast. If your knowledge stalls, your work will, too (Westerhof & Keyes, 2010).

That's not to say you need to read every article or follow every trend. You just need a system that fits your life. Skim a journal once in a while. Subscribe to an email digest. Catch a continuing education unit (CEU) or a podcast that keeps you curious.

When a new method or a new study catches your attention, ask yourself, "Can I use this?" If the answer is yes, try it in a way that fits your style. Mention it to a client as a potential option. Weave it into the work and pay attention to how it lands. Staying informed about new research does not equate to quoting studies in sessions. It's knowing enough to keep your practice effective and your clients safe. You don't have to know everything, but you do have to make a conscious effort to keep learning.

## Continuously Improving

Building a successful counseling practice necessitates committing to constant, intentional growth through deeply refining your clinical craft over time. The best counselors aren't the ones with the flashiest techniques. They're the ones who consistently sharpen their hearing and learn to pick up the subtle signals, contradictions, emotional themes, and unfinished business clients bring into the room. Master counselors aren't made overnight. They're made through decades of disciplined listening.

### How Counselors Can Train Their Ears to Hear More Precisely

Every session you sit in offers an opportunity to sharpen your skills and seek deeper meaning in your clients' words and in the spaces between them. Here are some practical ways to start sharpening your clinical ear.

- **Listen for contradictions:** Notice when a client's words and emotions don't line up.
  - Example: A client says, "I'm fine," while their body slumps and their voice shakes.
- **Track patterns over time:** Pay attention to recurring language, themes, or emotional reactions that show up across multiple sessions.
- **Notice emotional undercurrents:** Listen for what isn't directly said. Grief, anger, longing, and fear often live underneath polished stories.
- **Reflect feelings:** Instead of "You said you're stressed," try, "It sounds like you're carrying a lot alone right now."

Sharpening your hearing takes time. It's like developing a musician's ear. You move from hearing simple melodies to noticing harmonies, dissonances, and rhythms that weren't obvious at first.

### Practical Ways to Keep Improving After Graduate School

Formal education gives you a foundation, but most growth happens when you intentionally build on it throughout your career. Learning is a muscle. If you don't stretch it intentionally, it atrophies. Here are some effective strategies for continual clinical development.

- **Record yourself (ethically) and review:** Listen to audio recordings of your sessions when possible (with proper consent). Notice where you missed cues or rushed moments of emotional depth.
- **Join consultation groups:** Surround yourself with other counselors who value depth and skill-building.
- **Pursue specialized training:** Focus on training that sharpens your depth of hearing and conceptualization, not just technique-heavy certifications.
- **Study the classics and the new:** Read foundational theorists (e.g., Adler, Rogers, Satir) alongside newer evidence-based approaches to deepen both your intuition and your knowledge.
- **Stay curious about yourself:** Notice your own emotional reactions in session—boredom, frustration, or excitement—and treat them as data, not distractions.

### Master the Basics to Become a Master Counselor

A myth in counseling is that mastery comes from collecting more techniques. In reality, becoming a master counselor usually involves listening more deeply, speaking more carefully, intervening more precisely and less often, trusting silence, and honoring client autonomy.

Sharpening your hearing is slow, sometimes invisible work, but it's the work that makes everything else possible. Clients don't always need another exercise or worksheet. Sometimes, they need someone who can hear the crack in their voice and invite them to stay with it instead of running from it. True clinical skill isn't *doing* more, but rather noticing more.

Having a successful career in this field is bigger than getting clients in the door. It's defined by doing work that is actually helping and growing yourself in the process. To evaluate and improve your business over time, prioritize honesty. Be honest about whether clients are getting better. Be honest about what they're experiencing in the room. Be honest about where your own growth edges are.

Assessing client outcomes, gathering and using feedback, staying plugged into new research, and sharpening your clinical hearing aren't one-time tasks. They are lifetime practices. They're what separate counselors who burn out or plateau from those who quietly keep getting better, year after year. If you build evaluation and improvement into the bones of your practice, two things will happen. Your clients will have better, deeper outcomes, and you will become a stronger, more vivid counselor.

The work will stay meaningful. The business will stay sustainable. You will continue growing into the kind of counselor and human being that you would trust to work with. Success in counseling requires starting strong and staying intentional and awake.

# References

Anker, M. G., Duncan, B. L., & Sparks, J. A. (2009). Using client feedback to improve couple therapy outcomes: A randomized clinical trial in a naturalistic setting. *Journal of Consulting and Clinical Psychology, 77*(4), 693–704. https://doi.org/10.1037/a0016062

Bohart, A. C., & Wade, A. G. (2013). The client is in psychotherapy. In M. J. Lambert (Ed.), *Bergin and Garfield's Handbook of Psychotherapy and Behavior Change* (6th ed., pp. 219–257). Wiley.

Boswell, J. F., Kraus, D. R., Miller, S. D., & Lambert, M. J. (2013). Implementing routine outcome monitoring in clinical practice: benefits, challenges, and solutions. *Psychotherapy Research, 25*(1), 6–19. https://doi.org/10.1080/10503307.2013.817696

Flückiger, C., Del Re, A. C., Wampold, B. E., & Horvath, A. O. (2018). The alliance in adult psychotherapy: A meta-analytic synthesis. *Psychotherapy, 55*(4), 316–340. https://doi.org/10.1037/pst0000172

Geller, S. M., & Greenberg, L. S. (2012). *Therapeutic presence: A mindful approach to effective therapy.* American Psychological Association. https://doi.org/10.1037/13485-000

Kroenke, K., Spitzer, R. L., & Williams, J. B. W. (2001). The PHQ-9: Validity of a brief depression severity measure. *Journal of General Internal Medicine, 16*(9), 606–613. https://doi.org/10.1046/j.1525-1497.2001.016009606.x

Lambert, M. J., & Shimokawa, K. (2016). Collecting client feedback. In A. E. Kazdin (Ed.), *Methodological issues and strategies in clinical research* (4th ed., pp. 361–372). American Psychological Association. https://doi.org/10.1037/14805-023

Miller, S. D., Duncan, B. L., Brown, J., Sparks, J. A., & Claud, D. A. (2003). The Outcome Rating Scale: A preliminary study of the reliability, validity, and feasibility of a brief visual analog measure. *Journal of Brief Therapy, 2*(2), 91–100.

Norcross, J. C., & Lambert, M. J. (Eds.). (2019). *Psychotherapy relationships that work: Evidence-based therapist contributions* (3rd ed.). Oxford University Press.

Spitzer, R. L., Kroenke, K., Williams, J. B. W., & Löwe, B. (2006). A brief measure for assessing generalized anxiety disorder: The GAD-7. *Archives of Internal Medicine, 166*(10), 1092–1097. https://doi.org/10.1001/archinte.166.10.1092

Westerhof, G. J., & Keyes, C. L. M. (2010). Mental illness and mental health: The two continua model across the lifespan. *Journal of Adult Development, 17*(2), 110–119. https://doi.org/10.1007/s10804-009-9082-y

# 14

# Generating Wealth Toward Retirement

Written from a place of pure panic and self-preservation, this chapter is a mix of what we've learned about saving for retirement pulled from research, financial advisers, and those "Come to Jesus" moments we've had with each other (like the time we seriously debated whether a home golf simulator counted as a retirement investment—spoiler: It doesn't).

We're in this stage of our careers right now. We have kids, we're finally making enough to save without the pressure of missing a bill, and we've had some hard, honest conversations about what our future needs to look like.

For a lot of counselors, retirement feels more like a dream than a plan. We're not professionals on a corporate track with pensions and bonuses. Most of us piece together income from private practice, supervision, teaching, and agency work. We got into this field for people, not profits. We know how to hold space, not necessarily how to build spreadsheets. Eventually, the question hits: How will I support myself when I stop working?

This chapter is about creating enough wealth to stop working when you want, to be discerning about clients, and to rest without guilt. Wealth, in this context, is not excess—it's the freedom to have options. Many of us work in systems that undervalue what we do. Wages are capped.

Budgets are tight. We're often told that the work itself is the reward, but meaning doesn't pay the mortgage. Financial literacy is not a luxury. It's part of ethical self-care (Barnett et al., 2007).

This chapter provides a straightforward, values-aligned roadmap: how to save, invest, and plan your exit from full-time work. Whether you're just starting or thinking about winding down, you need practical tools and a new story to tell yourself about money. Counselors already have the skills for long-term financial success: goal setting, long-term thinking, and navigating uncertainty. This is just applying those same strengths to your future.

If you haven't been actively planning for retirement, you're not behind. You're not broken. And you're not alone.

## Financial Planning for Retirement

A study by Lusardi and Mitchell (2011) found that mental health professionals often underestimate how much they will need in retirement, primarily because they base their estimates on current income rather than projected living expenses, inflation, and health-care costs. According to the U.S. Department of Labor (2023), the average American will need 70–90% of their pre-retirement income to maintain their current lifestyle after leaving the workforce. For counselors, whose income may fluctuate over time and who often enter the field later in life or with student loan debt, estimating retirement needs must factor in both personal circumstances and professional variability.

### Step One: Create a Retirement Vision Statement

Before you get into numbers, set clear expectations for the life you want to build. Retirement isn't just the absence of work; it's also the presence of something else. What do your ideal days look like when you're no longer seeing clients full-time? Are you traveling? Gardening? Mentoring new counselors? Living in the same house, or downsizing to something simpler? Maybe you're teaching a course once a semester or running an occasional workshop. Maybe you're done altogether.

Create a one-page "retirement vision" that describes the pace, priorities, and values you want in that season of life. Be specific. Where are you living? Who are you around? How do you spend your mornings? What brings you joy?

Counselors are often so focused on caring for others that we don't slow down to ask what *we* want next, but this clarity matters. Research has shown that people who create vivid, detailed visions for retirement are more likely to engage in consistent savings behaviors and experience smoother emotional transitions when the time comes (Lahlouh et al., 2025).

This vision is your compass. Every decision you make, from how much to save to when to stop taking new clients, should align with the life you want to create. You don't need it to be perfectly mapped out, but you do need to start picturing it.

For example, we have a great friend and mentor who has always dreamed of running drama counseling groups that use Bible stories to help people act out and process their trauma. For him, retirement didn't mean not working again; it meant finally having the freedom to do the work he'd always wanted to do, without worrying about whether it paid the bills. His vision was to step into counseling differently, with purpose and without pressure.

## Step Two: Project Your Monthly Expenses

Once you've got a picture of the life you want, it's time to figure out what it costs. Clear numbers will help you retire, not vague dreams. Open a spreadsheet or use a retirement calculator and list out your future monthly expenses. These expenses should reflect future numbers, not what you are paying today. Inflation averages 2–3% per year, so make sure you adjust your anticipated bills to reflect that (U.S. Bureau of Labor Statistics, n.d.). On this spreadsheet, include

- Housing (mortgage, rent, property taxes, HOA fees);
- Utilities (electricity, internet, water, phone);
- Food and groceries;
- Transportation (car payment, insurance, gas, maintenance);
- Health care (premiums, co-pays, prescriptions);
- Travel and entertainment;
- Family support or gifts, and
- Emergency savings.

If you want to travel, budget for it. If you're dreaming of downsizing, put in lower housing costs. If you're retiring before 65, bump up the health-care numbers. You can't plan for what you don't name.

Let's say your retirement dream includes downsizing to a smaller home in a walkable town, traveling a couple of times a year, and doing part-time supervision. You estimate a $1,200 mortgage, $400 for utilities, $800 for groceries and eating out, and $600 for travel. Add in $500 for transportation, $1,000 for health care (if you're retiring at 67, $300 for family giving and gifts, and another $200 for emergencies. That brings your estimated monthly budget to around $5,000, or $60,000 per year.

## Step Three: Inventory Your Current Assets

With this goal in mind, it's time to look at your current financial situation. This is your baseline. Pull together everything, regardless of financial heft, that could support you financially in retirement. In this group, include

- Any 401(k), 403(b), or IRA balances (including old employer accounts);
- Roth IRA accounts;
- Employer pensions (if you have one);
- Savings accounts and emergency funds;
- Real estate equity (like your home or rental property);
- Business equity or income-generating assets;
- Expected Social Security benefits; and
- Other passive income (royalties, book sales, rental income, etc.).

You can check your projected Social Security income by creating an account at ssa.gov. It shows you estimates at different retirement ages (62, 67, and 70).

Let's say your SSA account shows you will receive $2,000 per month if you retire at 67. You have $150,000 in a Roth IRA, $60,000 in a 403(b) from your agency days, and you co-own a rental property that nets $500/month. That's a decent start, and it shows you a full picture of your financial status. With this information, you will be able to calculate the gap between your future expenses and your current assets.

## Step Four: Estimate the Retirement Gap

Once you know how much money you will need each month and how much income (like Social Security) you can expect, the next step is to figure out how much you will need to pull from your savings. Let's say your future monthly budget is $6,000. Social Security will give you $2,000 a month. That means you will still need $4,000 each month from your savings and investments just to break even. Multiply that $4,000 by 12 to get your yearly gap of $48,000.

You need a retirement fund with enough money that you can safely take out that amount every year for the rest of your life. That's where the 4% rule comes in (Bengen, 1994). This rule doesn't mean you save 4% of your income each year; it's about how much you can safely *spend* from your total retirement savings once you stop working. Financial planner William Bengen found that you know you have saved enough for retirement if you can withdraw about 4% of your nest egg each year (adjusting for inflation), and have your money last roughly 30 years. So, if you plan to live on $48,000 a year in retirement, you'd need to have around $1.2 million saved. (That's $48,000 ÷ 0.04, or just multiply $48,000 by 25.)

It sounds like a lot, but now you've got a number to work toward. You're not guessing anymore. You're planning.

## Step Five: Build a Savings Timeline

Now that you know how much you will need in retirement, the next question is how much you should save each month to get there. Start by figuring out how many years you have left until you want to retire. Let's say you're 42 now and want to retire at 67. That gives you 25 years to save. Next, take the total amount you need to save—let's stay with $1.2 million from the previous step—and break it down.

First, multiply your 25 years by 12 months. That gives you 300 months. Now, divide your $1.2 million goal by 300 months. That comes out to $4,000 per month. That number might feel impossible. Don't panic.

The good news is you likely won't need to save that full amount out of pocket because your money will grow over time through interest and investments. Most retirement portfolios grow at about 6–8% per year. So, depending on how early you start and how your investments perform, you may only need to save half that monthly amount, sometimes even less. If you want a more accurate number based on your situation, try a free tool like NerdWallet's Retirement Calculator (n.d.), or talk with a financial planner. You don't have to figure this all out alone.

## Step Six: Automate, Adjust, and Assess

Automate your savings through payroll deduction, bank transfers, or self-employment contributions. Make it invisible. If you're a solo practitioner, set aside a percentage of every paycheck (e.g., 15–20%) to go directly into a retirement account. Review your plan every 6–12 months. Life will shift due to marriage, children, illness, inflation, debt payoff, etc., and your plan should shift with it. Retirement planning is not a one-time event. It's an evolving part of your professional life.

*Step Seven: Build a Retirement-Ready Mindset*

Finally, prepare emotionally. Many counselors identify deeply with their role. Retirement may feel like a loss of identity. Begin integrating reflective practices now: journaling about your future, attending retirement planning workshops, and talking to retired counselors. Wealth is not just about numbers. It's about security, freedom, and the ability to choose how you spend your time.

## Investment Strategies for Counselors

Investing is how your money grows over time. When you invest, you give your money a job and let it work while you live your life. A savings account keeps your money safe, but inflation eats away at its value over time (U.S. Bureau of Labor Statistics, n.d.). Investing helps your money grow faster than inflation.

Here's a simple example: You save $6,000 a year for 25 years. In a regular savings account, you might end up with about $150,000. If you invest that same money in a balanced portfolio averaging a 7% return, you could have over $400,000 by retirement. That's compound growth: earning interest on your interest (Vanguard, 2022). Counselors already understand the value of long-term commitment and patience. Investing is just applying those values to your finances.

*Choosing the Right Investment Account*

Think of investment accounts like different buckets you can use to hold your money. Each bucket serves the same basic purpose—keeping your savings in one place—but the *rules* for how you fill it and take money out differ.

Some buckets (like Roth IRAs) let your money grow tax-free, but you can't touch it until retirement. Others (like traditional IRAs or 401(k) s) give you a tax break now but will be taxed later when you withdraw. Then, there are taxable investment accounts. Those are like open buckets with no lid: easy to access, but you will pay taxes on what you earn each year.

The key is knowing which bucket to fill first. Some help you save on taxes now, whereas others reward your future self later. A good financial plan usually uses a mix of buckets so that your money grows efficiently and you have options at every stage of your career.

Here are a few common retirement-focused accounts that might be useful for counselors.

- **Roth IRA:** You pay taxes now, but growth and withdrawals in retirement are tax-free. This is a great option if you expect your income to grow.
- **Traditional IRA:** You may get a tax break now, but you will pay taxes later when you withdraw.
- **403(b):** This option is available if you work for a nonprofit, school, or hospital. Money goes in before taxes and grows tax-deferred.
- **Solo 401(k):** This is designed for business owners with no employees. As of 2024, you can contribute up to $69,000 if your income supports it (IRS, 2025a).
- **SEP (simplified employee pension) IRA:** This is a simpler option for self-employed counselors. You can contribute up to 25% of your net income, up to $69,000 (IRS, 2025b).

You don't need to master them all. Just choose one that fits where you are. You can always adjust later with a financial adviser (Wang & Shi, 2014).

## Dividing Up Your Investments (Asset Allocation)

Once your money is in an account, you need to decide how to allocate your assets, or spread it out across different investment types such as stocks, bonds, and cash. This is how you manage risk and reward.

Here's a general guide.

- **In your 20s–30s:** Put 80–90% in stocks and 10–20% in bonds.
- **In your 40s:** Put 70% stocks and 30% bonds.
- **In your 50s–60s:** Put 60% stocks and 40% bonds (and increasing bond allocation over time).

Stocks grow your money, but they fluctuate frequently. Bonds are steadier, but they grow more slowly. The younger you are, the more risk you can take because you have time to ride out the market's ups and downs (Fama & French, 2015). Use low-cost index funds or exchange-traded funds (ETFs) like Vanguard's Total Stock Market Index Fund (VTSAX; 2025b) or Fidelity's ZERO Total Market Index Fund (FZROX; 2025b). These track the whole market with minimal fees. Over time, low-fee funds tend to outperform expensive, actively managed ones (Renneboog et al., 2008). Recheck your asset allocation once a year and rebalance if needed.

## Picking a Platform That Works for You

Investing doesn't need to be intimidating. You just need a platform that feels manageable. If you want to manage your own investments and keep fees low, start with Fidelity (2025a) or Vanguard (2025a). If you'd rather not think about it too much, use a robo-adviser like Betterment (n.d.) or Wealthfront (n.d.). These use algorithms to manage your money based on your risk tolerance and goals for a small fee (typically around 0.25%).

Make sure whatever platform you choose offers the accounts you need, such as Roth IRAs or Solo 401(k)s, and carefully walk through their setup process. Many platforms now offer guided onboarding to help you choose your investment mix.

## Automating Your Contributions

The best investment plan is the one that doesn't rely on your memory. Set up automatic monthly transfers into your investment account. Whether it's $50, $200, or more, automation keeps you consistent. If your income is stable, set a fixed dollar amount. If your income fluctuates, set a percentage of your revenue. For example, you might transfer 10% of every deposit into your Roth IRA.

Automation has been shown to significantly increase long-term savings success and reduce the emotional stress tied to manual budgeting (Thaler & Benartzi, 2004). Once it is set up, you won't even miss it, but your future self will benefit from it every day.

## Avoiding Common Mistakes

Even smart, intentional people make investment mistakes. Here are a few you can skip.

- **Trying to time the market is difficult:** Research shows that even professional investors rarely beat the market over the long haul. Stick to your plan (Fama & French, 2015).
- **Holding too much cash:** Inflation eats away at savings. Keep an emergency fund, but invest the rest.
- **Panic selling:** Markets will dip. That's normal. Don't let anxiety guide your decisions.
- **Paying high fees:** Actively managed funds can charge 1–2% or more. That adds up and cuts into your returns. Use low-cost index funds instead.

The best approach is boring and consistent. It's not flashy, but it works.

## Checking In Once a Year

Investing is not a one-and-done task. Life changes. Income shifts. Your retirement vision might evolve. That's why once a year, ideally at the same time, you should ask yourself if you are still on track for your goals, has your income has changed, and does your investment mix still matches your age and risk tolerance.

If things feel off or you're unsure, talk to a fee-only fiduciary financial planner. Look for someone with a CFP (Certified Financial Planner) or AFC (Accredited Financial Counselor) designation who has experience helping professionals. Unlike commission-based advisers, fiduciaries are required to put your interests first (National Association of Personal Financial Advisors, n.d.). You already help people stay grounded through change. You already know how to manage risk, build trust, and think long-term. Investing is just another version of that same skill set.

We know that planning for your retirement can feel overwhelming. If you've made it this far and you are doing some of this on your own, that's admirable. Honestly, we didn't figure this out alone. We hired financial advisers who helped us answer these exact questions and build a plan we could stick to. It's not a sign of weakness to ask for help with money—it's wisdom. Just like our clients trust us to help them work through the tough stuff, we needed someone to help us sort through ours. You do not have to be perfect. You just have to start.

## Building a Retirement Fund

Building a retirement fund as a counselor isn't about finding the one perfect account or hitting some magic number right away. It's about being intentional with the income streams you have and creating layers of savings that work together over time. Start with a Roth IRA or Traditional IRA, then add in options like a Solo 401(k) or SEP IRA if you're self-employed. If you have access to a Health Savings Account, use it. When you've maxed out your tax-advantaged accounts, a regular brokerage account can give you flexible savings you can tap into anytime.

We don't talk enough about how powerful your business can be in funding your retirement. When you run workshops, lead groups, or bring in supervision income, treat those funds like fuel for your future. Set aside a percentage of that profit, maybe 20–30%, and move it straight into a retirement account. Don't wait until tax season or until "things calm down." Make it a line item in your business plan now. Not only does this lower your tax burden, but it shifts your mindset from surviving each year to building long-term freedom.

## Planning for Transition Out of Active Practice

Planning your exit from clinical work demands preparing for a major life shift. Most counselors spend decades building a life around relationships, routines, and being needed. Letting go of that identity requires intentionality. One of the most effective ways to ease into retirement is to create a broad timeline. Don't focus on the exact date. Instead, pick a window and start plotting out when you will reduce your caseload, notify clients, or pivot into supervision or teaching. A phased retirement, where you slowly decrease sessions or shift into consultation or telehealth, has been shown to improve emotional well-being and identity adjustment during retirement (Osborne, 2012). It also gives you and your clients time to transition with care.

Understanding your financial readiness is equally important. Use the numbers you've already worked through in earlier sections of this chapter and build a mock post-retirement budget: housing, health care, food, travel, taxes, and extra expenses. Match that with your anticipated income streams like Social Security, retirement withdrawals, or side work. If you run a practice, begin building a succession plan. Decide whether you will sell, transfer, or close operations and ensure your records, electronic health records, and liability coverage are accounted for. Even after you retire, your clinical decisions still follow you, so do not skip malpractice tail coverage and license transition logistics.

Lastly, don't underestimate the emotional work of stepping away. We've seen colleagues grieve the loss of identity and connection as much as they celebrated their freedom. Talk with others who've retired. Journal about your legacy and what you want to carry forward. Find ways to stay connected—maybe through mentorship, teaching, or even just offering encouragement to younger counselors. When the time comes, mark it. Host a continuing education unit, write a legacy letter, or simply take a quiet moment of gratitude. Retirement is more than the end of your career—it's the next stage of your life. It deserves the same care and thoughtfulness you've given to everyone else.

## Wealth Is Security, Not Excess

Counselors are experts in emotional safety. We help people rebuild, reclaim, and reshape their lives. We hold space for grief, growth, and transformation. However, when it comes to our own financial futures, too many of us check out. We delay, defer, or avoid, telling ourselves we'll figure it out later. But planning for retirement is the wise choice.

It's applying the same intentionality and care to your future that you offer your clients every day.

For us, retirement planning isn't about yachts or early exits. It's about dignity and choice. It's about getting to a place where we can still have purpose, but without pressure. Where we can still contribute, but without the threat of burnout. The counselor who plans for rest models what sustainable living looks like. You are allowed to want ease, flexibility, and peace of mind in the years ahead. You've earned it.

This chapter has shown what wealth-building can look like in our profession: saving consistently, investing intentionally, leveraging your business, building layered accounts, and transitioning out of full-time work with care. These are small moves, but when they stack up, they change everything. For us, wealth isn't flashy; it's freedom. It looks like paying off your mortgage. Taking a month off without guilt. Saying no to a client who isn't a fit—not because you're burned out, but because you have options. Whether your path includes IRAs and real estate or part-time teaching and passive income, what matters is that it's yours. You don't need to know everything today. You just need to make the next right move: Open the account, automate the transfer, hire the adviser, ask the question.

Let this be the moment you stop putting your future at the bottom of your to-do list. You've helped so many others build a life they're proud of. Now it's your turn. You deserve more than survival. You deserve sustainability. You deserve space to rest.

# References

Barnett, J. E., Baker, E. K., Elman, N. S., & Schoener, G. R. (2007). In pursuit of wellness: The self-care imperative. *Professional Psychology: Research and Practice, 38*(6), 603–612. https://doi.org/10.1037/0735-7028.38.6.603

Bengen, W. P. (1994). Determining withdrawal rates using historical data. *Journal of Financial Planning, 7*(4), 171–180.

Betterment. (n.d.). *Betterment* [Investment platform]. Retrieved November 3, 2025, from https://www.betterment.com

Fama, E. F., & French, K. R. (2015). A five-factor asset pricing model. *Journal of Financial Economics, 116*(1), 1–22. https://doi.org/10.1016/j.jfineco.2014.10.010

Fidelity Investments. (2025a). *Fidelity Investments* [Financial planning and investment management]. Fidelity. Retrieved October 23, 2025, from https://www.fidelity.com

Fidelity Investments. (2025b). *Fidelity ZERO Total Market Index Fund (FZROX)*. Fidelity Investments. Retrieved October 23, 2025, from https://fundresearch.fidelity.com/mutual-funds/summary/31635T708

Internal Revenue Service. (2025a). *Retirement plans*. U.S. Department of the Treasury. Retrieved November 3, 2025, from https://www.irs.gov/retirement-plans

Internal Revenue Service. (2025b). *SEP contribution limits (including grandfathered SARSEPs)*. U.S. Department of the Treasury. Retrieved October 23, 2025, from https://www.irs.gov/retirement-plans/plan-participant-employee/sep-contribution-limits-including-grandfathered-sarseps

Lahlouh, K., Lacaze, D., Oumessaoud, A., & Abdelmotaleb, M. (2025). Proactive personality, future time perspective, and career resources as predictors of retirement intentions: A serial mediation. *Career Development International*, 1–17. https://doi.org/10.1108/CDI-12-2024-0550

Lusardi, A., & Mitchell, O. S. (2011). *Financial literacy and planning: Implications for retirement wellbeing* (No. w17078). National Bureau of Economic Research. https://www.nber.org/papers/w17078

National Association of Personal Financial Advisors. (n.d.). *Find a fiduciary financial planner* [Financial planner directory]. Retrieved November 3, 2025, from https://www.napfa.org

NerdWallet. (n.d.). *Retirement calculator – Estimate your retirement savings needs*. NerdWallet. Retrieved October 23, 2025, from https://www.nerdwallet.com/calculator/retirement-calculator

Osborne, J. W. (2012). Psychological effects of the transition to retirement. *Canadian Journal of Counselling and Psychotherapy, 46*(1), 45–58.

Renneboog, L., Ter Horst, J., & Zhang, C. (2008). Socially responsible investments: Institutional aspects, performance, and investor behavior. *Journal of Banking and Finance, 32*(9), 1723–1742. https://doi.org/10.1016/j.jbankfin.2007.12.039

Thaler, R. H., & Benartzi, S. (2004). Save more tomorrow™: Using behavioral economics to increase employee saving. *Journal of Political Economy, 112*(S1), S164–S187. https://doi.org/10.1086/380085

U.S. Bureau of Labor Statistics. (n.d.). *Consumer Price Index (CPI) inflation tables*. Retrieved October 31, 2025, from https://www.bls.gov/cpi

U.S. Department of Labor. (2023). *Taking the Mystery Out of Retirement Planning*. Employee Benefits Security Administration. https://www.dol.gov/agencies/ebsa/about-ebsa/our-activities/resource-center/publications/taking-the-mystery-out-of-retirement-planning

Vanguard. (2022). *Vanguard long-term investing guide*. Vanguard. https://investor.vanguard.com

Vanguard. (2025a). *Vanguard Investments* [Investment platform]. Vanguard. https://investor.vanguard.com

Vanguard. (2025b). *Vanguard Total Stock Market Index Fund (VTSAX)*. Vanguard. https://investor.vanguard.com/investment-products/mutual-funds/profile/vtsax

Wang, M., & Shi, J. (2014). Psychological research on retirement. *Annual Review of Psychology, 65*(1), 209–233. https://doi.org/10.1146/annurev-psych-010213-115131

Wealthfront. (n.d.). *Wealthfront* [Investment platform]. Retrieved November 3, 2025, from https://www.wealthfront.com

# 15

# Having Money on the Mind and Not in the Heart

There's a fine line between building a life and being consumed by it. We live in a world where ambition is heralded like oxygen—essential and endlessly celebrated. Counselors get swept up in it, too. Between private practice dreams, speaking gigs, side hustles, and the pressure of student loans, it's easy to feel like a businessperson who happens to do counseling, instead of a counselor who happens to run a business.

This chapter shows how to keep money where it belongs—in your mind, not in your heart. Yes, this is a career, and yes, it deserves to be financially sustainable, but when financial goals start guiding your clinical decisions—when burnout gets rebranded as "grind"—something's off.

We won't villainize money. Charging what you're worth, building a thriving practice, and saving for the future are acts of resistance, especially in a field that too often expects us to martyr ourselves in the name of compassion. However, we will ask you to take a hard look at how unchecked ambition, a scarcity mindset, and hustle culture might be shaping how you show up for your clients, your family, and yourself.

## When Finances Start Steering the Work

Passion doesn't pay rent, and when money gets tight, financial stress can start subtly steering your clinical choices. You might say yes to clients with whom you're not trained to work. You might keep someone as a client longer than they need because of the income they supply. You might accept low insurance rates just to stay booked, rush sessions, double-book, and stretch your scope. You're probably making these choices not because you're unethical, but because you're under pressure (Barnett & Cooper, 2009; Neff & Germer, 2013).

We aren't interested in placing blame. We hope to build awareness and give you the means to create systems that protect both your values and your livelihood. If you don't put guardrails in place, money will start running the show (Moffatt, 2020). With the right systems and guardrails, you can stop choosing between being broke and passionate or paid and disconnected. Money and meaning can coexist, but only if you make room for both (Ryan & Deci, 2000; Larkin, 2023).

Money should reflect your values, not replace them. It should fund your boundaries, not erase them. It's a tool, not a purpose. Clients can tell when you're there for them and when you're just surviving (Skovholt & Trotter-Mathison, 2016).

Ask yourself: "Am I making decisions that honor both my calling and my capacity?" "Is my work helping people and sustaining my life?" "What would need to change for me to feel proud of both my care and my income?" When you stay rooted in your why, the business becomes sustainable and aligned.

## Hustle Culture and the Counselor

In our modern society, there is an invisible pressure to always be building, posting, scaling, launching, and monetizing. For counselors, there is an expectation that you are a clinician, but also a brand, a content creator, and a hustler.

That pressure to always be working is hustle culture. It's sneaky, y'all. It cloaks itself in noble language: impact, service, visibility, opportunity. It turns overwork into ambition and makes burnout feel like a personal weakness (Maslach & Leiter, 2016). It's crept into our field under the banner of entrepreneurship, even though many of us may have chosen counseling precisely to step away from the corporate grind.

### *The Rise of the Counselor-Entrepreneur*

Much of the pressure to grind and participate in hustle culture is economic in nature. We're trying to make ends meet, support our families, pay off student loans, and find a financial cushion in a field that doesn't always reward the work we put in (Skovholt & Trotter-Mathison, 2016).

Counselors are underpaid, and private practice or side gigs can help close the gap (Barnett & Cooper, 2009). Some of that pressure is cultural. Visibility is treated like currency, and success is often equated with being known, not necessarily effective (Schaufeli et al., 2009). So, we say yes to the extra client, to the podcast interview, to writing the book, to running the group, to launching the webinar, to opening the practice, to training supervisees, and to teaching adjunct on the side.

Before long, we're so busy building our businesses that we don't have time to sit with ourselves. We promote rest while secretly resenting how tired we are. We teach boundaries while ignoring our own. Hustle culture isn't just a personal problem—it's a systemic one. It can't be fixed by working harder. It can only be fixed through honesty (Ryan & Deci, 2000).

## Building a Sustainable Practice That Doesn't Eat Your Life

We bet you can think of some counselors who build businesses that secretly make them miserable. They care so much about their clients, their reputation, and their financial future that they just keep saying yes to everything and everyone. Then one day, they look up and realize they've built a machine that runs on their exhaustion. They're busy, booked, maybe even banked up, but they feel trapped. Their problem isn't ambition. Their problem is ambition that goes unchecked—when there are no brakes on the business plan, no filter for what's sustainable, and no real vision beyond "more."

### *Is Your Business Serving You Or Enslaving You?*

A growing body of research has shown that counselors often internalize unrealistic expectations about what it means to be "successful," especially when they run their own businesses (Skovholt & Trotter-Mathison, 2016; Ryan & Deci, 2000). Many start with healthy intentions, like seeking flexibility, autonomy, and sustainability, but over time, those intentions get buried under the weight of overcommitment, financial pressure, and poor boundaries (Barnett & Cooper, 2009). What begins as freedom turns into a cage made of calendar alerts and performance metrics.

Utilizing intentional design when building your private practice can mitigate that eventuality. Your practice should be built to support your life, not the other way around. You should be able to take time off without guilt, set limits without fear, and scale your work in a way that aligns with your season of life, not society's metric for success.

Counselors often need permission to reimagine their business as a tool for well-being rather than just a vehicle for productivity. You are allowed to change the structure, scope, or speed of your work to reflect who you are now. You're allowed to rest. You're allowed to grow slowly. You're allowed to choose joy over hustle, and connection over constant output (Ryan & Deci, 2000; Neff & Germer, 2013). You didn't enter this profession to be owned by your calendar. You came to help, to heal, to serve, and to live. Let your business reflect that.

## The Money Mirror: How Your Finances Reflect Your Beliefs

You can read all the right books, listen to all the right podcasts, and still find yourself hesitating when it's time to raise your rates or enforce a no-show fee. That's not because you lack knowledge, but because money decisions aren't just about strategy. They're also about story.

The way we approach money is often shaped by internalized beliefs about worth, fairness, generosity, and what it means to care. These beliefs come from many places: our families, our cultures, our training, and our early professional experiences. For many counselors, those influences can carry conflicting messages: to be generous, not to focus on the money, to always be available, but also not to burn out.

That internal conflict is what we call the money mirror. It reflects not just our current financial behaviors but the deeper narratives that drive them. It's not about judging yourself and your behaviors; it's about understanding them, and deciding what still fits and what needs to shift.

### *Scarcity, Abundance, and the Mindset Behind the Work*

One of the most common dynamics that shows up in the money mirror is the tension between scarcity and abundance. A scarcity mindset tends to sound like fear: "There's not enough." "If I charge more, people will leave." "If I take time off, I'll lose momentum." It keeps you overextending, undercharging, and quietly anxious, even when, on paper, your work is thriving.

An abundance mindset doesn't ignore the reality of economic limitations, but it reframes the narrative. It says: "There are clients who value this." "I can charge a fair rate and still make a difference." "Money can be a resource, not a reward for struggle." This shift doesn't happen overnight, but it's powerful when it does.

Research backs this up. In a study of educational counselors, those with an abundance mindset reported higher job satisfaction, greater resilience, and more perceived professional growth than those with scarcity-based thinking (Larkin, 2023). Similarly, Larkin (2023) found that abundance-oriented practitioners demonstrated enhanced creativity and well-being, which translated into both personal and professional sustainability.

You don't need to "manifest" your way to financial health, but it is worth examining whether your business is being led by fear or trust. The answers often show up in places you're not looking, like your calendar, your pricing, your stress level, and your sense of capacity. This doesn't mean you have to become a radically different person. It just means you get to choose the money story you carry forward: one that fits both your values and the life you're trying to build.

## Financial Trauma and Inherited Beliefs

Your money story started in childhood. What did your family say about money? Was it talked about openly, or was it off-limits? Was money used as power or control? Was there always just enough or never enough? Did you hear things like, "We can't afford that," or "People like us don't live like that," or "Rich people are selfish"? Maybe it wasn't what was said, but what was modeled. You saw stress, fear, and arguments. Perhaps you saw relentless generosity that left nothing for the giver. Maybe money was tied to morality or survival.

Layer on any cultural, spiritual, or systemic messages, and you start to see just how complex and deeply embedded these beliefs can become. Many of us carry shame, anxiety, or guilt around money that we've never examined. Those emotions end up running our businesses behind the scenes. If you've ever felt uncomfortable stating your session rate, struggled to believe you're worth paying, or feared losing touch with your roots by succeeding financially, you should examine where that voice originates. Healing your relationship with money means unlearning what you thought was truth, grieving the messages you inherited, or permitting yourself to believe something new, that you can care deeply about people and still get paid well for your work.

The concept of financial trauma has gained attention in recent years. According to Weida et al. (2024), financial trauma encompasses experiences of financial abuse, shaming, and chronic stress, often passed down through generations. This trauma can manifest as anxiety, depression, and other mental health challenges. Weida et al. (2024) emphasized the importance of trauma-informed financial empowerment programs, which integrate financial education with emotional support, leading to improved financial behaviors and confidence among participants.

## Money Beliefs That Keep Counselors Under-Earning

Here are some common money myths we've heard repeatedly in our work with counselors, as well as from ourselves.

- "If I do good work, the money will take care of itself."
- "If I raise my rates, I'm abandoning people who need help."
- "If I want to earn more, I must be in this for the wrong reasons."
- "Talking about money makes me uncomfortable, so I just won't."

These beliefs are powerful, but they're not permanent. You can challenge and replace them. You can believe that doing good work and making good money are not opposites. You can believe that money in the hands of ethical, compassionate, well-trained professionals can do incredible good in the world.

That shift starts by looking in the mirror. We hope you will sit with the following questions.

- "What was I taught about money growing up?"
- "How do those beliefs show up in how I price, plan, or avoid money decisions?"
- "What part of my money story needs to be healed or rewritten?"

You do not need to have perfect money beliefs to move forward, but you do need to know what is shaping your decisions. You cannot build a thriving, values-aligned counseling business with a self-sabotaging narrative playing in the background.

# When Income Goals Compete with Client Care

The moment your financial needs start to affect your clinical decisions is not something we discuss in graduate school. Unfortunately, most counselors eventually experience this. At first, it's subtle. You're doing good work, helping people, managing your caseload, but then there's a dip in clients, rent is due, or your kid needs braces. A slot opens up, and you have to decide whether to fill it based on clinical fit or financial fear. To keep your income goals in line with client care, you must recognize when income pressure starts to shape your clinical choices, understand the ethical boundaries involved, and create systems that keep you manageably rooted in the work.

### Recognizing the Red Flags: When Money Talks Too Loud

If you're like us, you want to believe your decisions are driven by ethics, not economics. In the real world, where your income is often tied directly to your client load, that line can get blurry. Here are some common warning signs.

- You hesitate to discharge a client who has plateaued because you are afraid to lose the weekly income.
- You're tempted to keep someone in weekly sessions when bi-weekly would be more appropriate.
- You refer out less often than you should, holding on to clients outside your scope to maintain full books.
- You agree to see clients at times that hurt your well-being because the time slot pays well.
- You feel anxious when a client is improving because it means fewer sessions, and fewer sessions mean less revenue.

These aren't indictments of your character; they're symptoms of a profession that often pushes you to be both healer and hustler without telling you how to hold both roles with integrity.

## Ethical Billing Is More Than Just Following the Rules

We often reduce ethics to paperwork and codes, but ethical billing is also about intention. You must bill for the time you actually spent with a client, rather than rounding up to maximize reimbursement. You must code your sessions based on what was discussed, not what pays the most. Moreover, you must be transparent with clients about your rates, your policies, and your expectations. More deeply, ethical billing means letting clinical goals—not financial ones—drive the length and frequency of treatment. Ask yourself:

- "Are my treatment plans built around client needs, or around making sure I hit a financial target?"

- "Have I ever suggested a session without a clear therapeutic objective?"
- "Do my documentation practices reflect clinical realities or income protection?"

This is where self-reflection becomes your best ethical safeguard. Most ethical drift doesn't happen all at once. It happens in inches, justified by stress, normalized by the culture of our clinical work, and silently reinforced by financial fear.

## Scheduling With Integrity: Your Calendar Isn't Just a Business Tool

In this field, your calendar becomes your paycheck, but it's also a clinical tool. How you schedule can say a lot about how you're prioritizing care. Are clients being seen at a frequency that reflects clinical progress or revenue loss? Are you padding your schedule to feel "full," even when the work doesn't require it? Are your boundaries around session length and start times holding up?

Even subtle shifts like giving in to frequent cancellations or overbooking can become slippery slopes if not addressed. Clients deserve a counselor who is present, honest, and not quietly resenting them for being their lowest-paying hour of the day. Don't act like you haven't taken in a client at a sliding scale rate only to have them and their partner come into session, raise hell, and pay you a fraction of your typical rate because you didn't want to refer them to a more appropriate agency.

## When You Slip

If you've ever made a financial decision that compromised your clinical instincts, welcome to the club. This doesn't make you unethical. It makes you human. Julius is the captain of this club. Every time he calls me (Jude), I am expecting to hear, "This is a collect call from an inmate at County Jail. To accept the call, press 1." When, not if, you slip, the key is to notice it, own it, and course-correct. Let the mistake teach you what needs to change—whether that's your fee structure, your caseload, your savings plan, or your support system. We are not perfect counselors, but we can be honest ones.

## Telling a New Story: Money and Meaning in Mental Health

Many of us, ourselves included, have a money story problem. For decades, the narrative has been that "real" counselors shouldn't care about money, that profit compromises purity, and that wanting to be financially secure is somehow greedy. Let's call that what it is: a limiting belief rooted in scarcity and martyrdom. The reality is that financially healthy counselors tend to be more grounded, more generous, and more available. They can afford supervision. They can take breaks. They can refer out without fear. They can invest in continuing education, community partnerships, and innovative practices that serve clients more deeply.

Money doesn't corrupt meaning unless you give it that power. What corrupts meaning is when counselors pursue money in ways that betray their values or when they adopt someone else's blueprint for success rather than create their own. Instead, let's tell a new story in which financial stability and deep, meaningful work go hand in hand; your bank account reflects your boundaries, not your burnout; and you can take vacations without guilt, build retirement savings without shame, and charge for your services without apology. This new story doesn't mean you won't work hard. It means you will work from a place of integrity, not insecurity. From purpose, not panic.

You've made it to the end—not just of a chapter, but of a conversation we've been having this whole book: How do you build a business that works for you, not one that quietly works against you? Define success for yourself and don't apologize for it. This doesn't mean you have to reject money, ambition, or growth. It just means those elements of your career need to be aligned with who you are, what you value, and the kind of life you want to live.

There will always be people who are louder, richer, and faster. If your work is honest, sustainable, and true to your values, you're winning in ways that can't be measured in bank statements or followers. That's success.

## References

Barnett, J. E., & Cooper, N. (2009). Creating a culture of self-care. *Clinical Psychology: Science and Practice, 16*(1), 16–20. https://doi.org/10.1111/j.1468-2850.2009.01138.x

Larkin, T. J. (2023). Cultivating a mindset of abundance. *The Journal of Continuing Education in Nursing, 54*(8), 344–346. https://doi.org/10.3928/00220124-20230711-03

Maslach, C., & Leiter, M. P. (2016). Understanding the burnout experience: Recent research and its implications for psychiatry. *World Psychiatry, 15*(2), 103–111. https://doi.org/10.1002/wps.20311

Moffatt, G. K. (2020, February). Voice of experience: Billing guilt. *Counseling Today.* https://ctarchive.counseling.org/2020/02/voice-of-experience-billing-guilt/

Neff, K. D., & Germer, C. K. (2013). A pilot study and randomized controlled trial of the Mindful Self-Compassion program. *Journal of Clinical Psychology, 69*(1), 28–44. https://doi.org/10.1002/jclp.21923

Ryan, R. M., & Deci, E. L. (2000). Self-determination theory and the facilitation of intrinsic motivation, social development, and well-being. *American Psychologist, 55*(1), 68–78. https://doi.org/10.1037/0003-066X.55.1.68

Schaufeli, W. B., Leiter, M. P., & Maslach, C. (2009). Burnout: 35 years of research and practice. *Career Development International, 14*(3), 204–220. https://doi.org/10.1108/13620430910966406

Skovholt, T. M., & Trotter-Mathison, M. (2016). *The resilient practitioner: Burnout and compassion fatigue prevention and self-care strategies for the helping professions* (3rd ed.). Routledge.

Weida, E. B., Carroll-Scott, A., Lê-Scherban, F., Bloom, S. L., & Chilton, M. M. (2024). Trauma-informed financial empowerment programming is associated with improved financial well-being. *Journal of Child and Family Studies, 33*(11), 3541–3550. https://doi.org/10.1007/s10826-024-02927-7

# 16

# Doing Good Business

When we were 15 years old, we spent a lot of time riding around Opelousas, Louisiana, in our dad's old work truck. Every Friday, without fail, we made the rounds with him—dropping off payroll checks to his crew. Our dad, owner of BASS Concrete Construction, had been running his business for decades. His slogan was simple: no job too big or too small. To us, at that age, those Friday routes felt like the biggest waste of time.

We would stop at the bank first, where he knew everyone by name. Then, we'd crisscross the city, pulling up to each employee's house. He'd pay them, sit for a while, talk with their families, lend a hand if something needed fixing, and laugh at the same jokes as last week. Afterwards, we'd get back in the truck and head to the next house and repeat the process over and over again.

In our memories, one Friday stands out. We noticed Dad getting emotional on the drive. We asked him what was up, and he shared how much money he had finally been able to save. He gave us the number, proud and a little teary. We looked around at the busted truck and the worn seats and blurted out, "Why are we still doing this? Pay somebody else to handle it." He smirked, pulled up to the next house, and said, "Nah, boys, this here is good business."

Any good business, including a good counseling business, needs profits, branding, and some level of automation, but it also needs trusting and valuable relationships. Before a client ever walks into your office, they've already experienced your practice. They've felt the tone of your emails, navigated your intake forms, and tested the responsiveness of your systems. Every one of those interactions says something: "You're safe here," or "Good luck figuring this out." That's why business decisions in counseling are clinical as well as operational.

Professionalism is the foundation. Not the stiff, scripted professionalism, but the kind that communicates reliability, boundaries, and care. How you manage your time, return phone calls, handle payments, or send reminders creates a rhythm that clients come to rely on. This structure is more than helpful—it's healing. Consistency, clear expectations, and respectful communication are linked to stronger therapeutic alliances, better client outcomes, and increased trust (Ackerman & Hilsenroth, 2001; Del Re et al., 2021). When our systems are clean and intentional, clients feel it. Their sense of comfort and safety starts long before the session.

Doing good business is also an ethical act. It means aligning your policies with your values because ethics don't stop at confidentiality and informed consent. Being ethical extends to how you run your calendar, how you price your services, and how you communicate across differences. If you value accessibility, your intake process shouldn't be a literacy test. If you value cultural responsiveness, it should be obvious in your space, language, and partnerships (Summers & Nelson, 2022). Business, at its best, becomes the invisible container that makes the work of counseling possible.

This chapter explores how to root your counseling business in professionalism, clarity, and care. Your presence, systems, and relationships shape your reputation and build a practice that communicates trust even when you're not in the room. Doing good business requires more than impressing people. It requires being a dependable and steady professional for your clients and colleagues.

## Professionalism in Counseling

Professionalism is what turns a practice into a place of healing. Business cards and a polished logo are part of that, but it's the consistent, day-to-day rhythm that builds trust. In counseling, one of the products you are selling is the relationship. When clients pay for your time, they're investing in your reliability, boundaries, and presence. Research has confirmed that when counselors demonstrate predictability and consistency, the therapeutic alliance and retention improve significantly (Ackerman & Hilsenroth, 2001; Del Re et al., 2021).

At its core, professionalism is about structure and follow-through. You must be on time for sessions, return calls, complete notes, send referrals, and manage paperwork. The latter may feel like small administrative tasks, but each one communicates your care. When you're prompt, organized, and prepared, clients feel it. These qualities send the message that you value your clients' time and that you are committed to showing up for those relationships.

Professionalism also lives in your administrative systems. Clean records, user-friendly scheduling, and transparent policies are the invisible signals that let people know they're in capable hands. If you believe in equity, your fees and access models should reflect that. If you value transparency, your documentation and onboarding processes should make that clear. Being consistent and following through on your mission creates alignment between your values and your operations (Wheeler & Bertram, 2019).

Professionalism extends beyond your policy manual and your interactions with clients and colleagues; it's also evinced in how you perform when no one is watching. Professionalism can be displayed in the tone of your emails, the calm in your voice when a client is dysregulated, and the respect you show colleagues in everyday interactions. It includes the courage to say no, the humility to consult, and the clarity to enforce your own boundaries (Hakim, 2022).

Professionalism also shows up in how you honor your limits. It's knowing when to pause before saying yes, when to ask for help instead of pretending you have it all figured out, and when to refer a client because it's in *their* best interest, not your ego. It's having the courage to admit, "This might be outside my scope," and the humility to bring in support. Boundaries are the structure that keeps your practice, your sanity, and your clients safe.

In counseling, we talk a lot about presence, attunement, and safety, but those things don't exist in a vacuum. They rest on the backbone of professionalism. It's what creates the container for everything else. If you want to build a practice that lasts, start by honoring the invisible agreements: the tone, the structure, the consistency, and the trust that holds it all together.

## Effective Communication Skills

If professionalism is the structure of your business, communication is its voice. How you speak, write, and respond, even outside the counseling room, either reinforces trust or erodes it. You can have the cleanest systems and strongest ethics, but if your tone is reactive or your timing is inconsistent, clients and colleagues won't feel safe. Research has shown that clear and timely communication is one of the most consistent predictors of client satisfaction and retention (Norcross & Lambert, 2019; Del Re et al., 2021).

Counselors are trained to listen deeply and communicate with empathy in session, but business communication asks something different. It requires more clarity than exploration. Whether you're solo, in a group practice, or part of an agency, the way you communicate about logistics like scheduling, payment, policies, or referrals matters just as much as how you listen in the room.

Start with responsiveness. When a client reaches out, a colleague asks for a consult, or an insurance representative needs documentation, the timing and tone of your reply says everything. Responding within 24–48 hours is both polite and a reflection of your reliability. A warm, auto-reply message, like "I respond to non-urgent messages within 48 hours, Monday through Thursday," sets expectations without overextending yourself. These small policies do big relational work. They communicate respect, containment, and safety (Ladmanová et al., 2021).

Your forms and onboarding materials are another major part of your communication system. They should be clean, readable, and accessible, especially for clients who are neurodiverse, stressed, or coming from marginalized communities. Use plain language, avoid jargon, and check that your reading level is appropriate for your audience (Mcinnes & Haglund, 2011). To ensure your materials stay sharp, institute quarterly audits. Read your intake paperwork out loud. Ask a colleague to review the frequently asked questions page of your website or your policies. Use a readability checker to scan for clarity.

Conflict is another area where communication makes or breaks your professionalism. Cancellations, late payments, or policy violations don't need to lead to drama, but they do require clarity. Most of us were trained to handle clinical ruptures, not business ones, but you can borrow the same intentional process to navigate both: Name the pattern, explain the impact, and hold the boundary. For example, you can say, "I noticed we've had a few missed sessions recently. This impacts our ability to maintain progress and affects my schedule. Per our policy, no-shows are subject to a fee. Let's talk about how to prevent this going forward." Your tone should be calm, firm, and kind, not apologetic, punitive, or avoidant. Clear communication is part of client care.

Don't overlook your digital footprint. Your website, Google Business profile, and social media accounts speak for you when you're not available to speak for yourself. Make sure your biographies are up to date, your hours are accurate, and your tone is aligned with your values. A study found that counselor websites with clear language, a welcoming tone, and transparent policies significantly improved initial engagement and client trust (Sillence et al., 2007). Before posting anything online, ask yourself: "Would I be comfortable with a client or supervisor reading this out of context?" If the answer is no, don't post it.

Finally, create a habit of reflecting on your communication the same way you reflect on your clinical work. Discern if your messages are reactive or grounded, if you are bringing clarity or confusion, and if your tone is aligned with how you want to be known. If certain situations, like no-shows, difficult clients, or declining offers, trip you up, consider writing scripts in advance. It saves emotional labor and reduces the risk of miscommunication. Professional communication isn't limited to using polished language. It requires consistency, kindness, and clarity. When it's done well, your business becomes an extension of your therapeutic presence, a seamless part of the care you provide.

### Networking and Collaboration

Networking is crucial to building relationships that last. It's less "elevator speech" and more "let's collaborate." When done with intention, networking helps you find community, earn trust, and create opportunities for referrals, co-presentations, supervision, and support (Mellin et al., 2011). Whether in person or online, meaningful networking requires consistency and value. Join a continuing education group, contribute to an email newsletter, or engage in a values-aligned Facebook group or Slack channel. Research has shown that digital spaces now provide faster, more inclusive access to mentorship and collaboration, especially across geographic and identity boundaries (Rousmaniere, 2014). Keep in mind, your focus should not be on gaining popularity. Your strongest professional relationships may not come from big names, but from the colleagues sitting next to you in class, supervision, or your first job. Don't just network upward; network sideways. Show up, offer support, and share the microphone. That's where real growth and real business start.

## Building a Good Reputation

When we were around 16, we were already long used to Dad's rhythms. We'd be doing our own thing, hanging out at home after school or training, but as soon as we heard his truck and trailer pull into the driveway, we dropped everything. That was the routine. We would help back in the trailer, move tools, or swap out what he didn't need tomorrow with what he did. We were already professional soccer players at that point, working our way up the Olympic Development Program, but we weren't about to remind Dad of that. When he got home, we went to work.

Now, as fathers ourselves, we understand something our dad modeled without ever saying it: sometimes you have to create spaces for conversations to happen. Those driveway tool swaps taught us empathic listening, how to reflect content and feelings, and how to confront illogical beliefs with steadiness and clarity.

One evening, after wrapping up, Dad sat on the tailgate and said he'd pick us up around 1 p.m. the next day to go to a job site. When he pulled up, we got in, but the energy in the truck was different than usual—it was quiet and focused.

"I want y'all to come with me and watch me fire someone," he said. "Stay in the truck. Keep the window cracked. Just listen to how I talk to him."

We were stunned, but we agreed.

We pulled up to the site, and Dad got out and walked straight up to a crew member we'd known our whole lives. It was his brother, our uncle. We won't share much about what followed, but if you've ever wondered where our style of confrontation comes from, it's that day. Our father was calm, direct, and respectful, but unflinching.

When Dad got back in the truck, he asked, "What did y'all learn?"

Julius, without missing a beat, said, "Don't hire my brother."

After getting smacked by everyone in the truck, we had one of the best conversations of our lives. We talked about reputation, not just as a business asset, but as a survival tool. Dad said his reputation was how people decided to work with him, vouch for him, and even protect him. As African American boys in a rural Southern town, he reminded us that our futures, and sometimes our safety, could hinge on whether people trusted our name.

In this field, your reputation is your business. A strong one is built over time through consistent care, follow-through, and professionalism. It can unravel quickly with a missed email, a mishandled termination, or one offhand comment in a staff meeting. Reputation is less about how visible you are and more about how consistently you show up. It's what people say about you when you're not in the room, and whether clients and colleagues trust your name enough to send someone your way (American Psychological Association, 2017).

Reputation starts with competence, but it's sustained through humility, accountability, and generosity. You don't have to be everywhere or do everything, but when you show up, show up well. Follow through.

Be consultable. Own your mistakes. Elevate others. As Flückiger et al. (2018) found, the most respected counselors are those who blend strong clinical skills with openness and integrity. One way to keep in touch with your reputation is to ask two colleagues twice a year: "What do I do well professionally, and what should I watch out for?" Doing so is not fishing for praise; it anchors your practice in awareness. Your reputation as a counselor is personal and clinical. It impacts referrals, collaborations, and trust. In this profession, trust is everything.

## Contributing to the Community

If professionalism is how we show up and communicate, building a good reputation is how we advertise ourselves, and networking is how we connect, then community contribution is how we stay rooted. Counseling doesn't have to be confined to counseling rooms. When we step outside of those rooms, we serve individuals, and we shift systems.

### Why Community Work Matters

Our profession has always been tied to social change. From school reform to labor rights, early counselors showed up where people were struggling—not just to listen, but to advocate (Toporek et al., 2009). That legacy continues when counselors speak at local events, volunteer with re-entry programs, or mentor students in underserved areas. Community work extends your reach and sharpens your skills. Summers and Nelson (2022) found that counselors involved in community-based efforts reported stronger cultural competence, deeper clinical stamina, and greater client trust. Similarly, researchers have shown that community engagement enhances both counselor development and burnout prevention (Wilson, 2016; Lewis et al., 2011). When we step into our communities, we become more attuned, more accessible, and more effective.

### What Community Contribution Can Look Like

Community contribution doesn't necessarily dictate starting a nonprofit or donating your weekends. Community impact can start with small, intentional steps.

- **Pro bono or sliding-scale work:** A portion of your caseload offered at reduced rates increases access, but only works when supported by clear policies and boundaries (Knapp & VandeCreek, 2008).

- **Educational outreach:** Speak at a school. Host a workshop at a local business. Run a Q&A at a library. Visibility reduces stigma and builds bridges.
- **Mentorship:** Supervise an associate or host an intern. Giving back through mentorship deepens the profession's bench and keeps wisdom circulating (Borders et al., 2014).
- **Board service:** Join your local counseling association or a community board aligned with your values. Clinicians bring lived expertise that can inform policies from the inside.
- **Partnerships:** Don't work in isolation. Collaborate with shelters, clinics, schools, or grassroots groups already doing the work. Community impact multiplies through relationships.

### *Keeping It Sustainable*

Good intentions burn out fast without structure. Start with one cause you care about and one consistent way to show up. Build that work into your business model: Set aside a monthly time block, rotate interns into local placements, or donate a small percentage of your earnings to a mental health cause. As Roncoroni and Tucker (2024) noted, counselors who link activism and service into their workflow are more likely to sustain both. Try building a Community Engagement Calendar to simply plan and track your impact. Schedule one outreach or service event per quarter, and jot down outcomes or takeaways. It keeps you accountable and reminds you that impact isn't always measured in sessions billed.

### *Measuring the Intangible*

We're trained to think in charts and treatment plans, but community work doesn't always show up in metrics. Sometimes, success is a student who considers counseling as a career because you spoke at their school. Sometimes, it's a pastor who refers a grieving family to you because of a talk you gave. These moments matter, and they often ripple further than you will ever see (Tierney et al., 2025). Counseling happens outside the office, too, in classrooms, barbershops, churches, shelters, and community halls. You can be part of the wave that brings it there.

## The Legacy of Good Business

Every time you return a phone call, send a thoughtful email, document a session with care, or collaborate with a colleague, you're shaping the reputation of the profession. When you mentor someone, show up to a board meeting, or say "no" to something that misaligns with your values, you're doing business. Counselors are often trained to think of their impact in one-hour increments, session by session, week by week. But your impact compounds, just like investments. A reputation built with integrity gains interest over time. A practice run with compassion and clarity becomes a magnet for good clients, good partnerships, and good opportunities.

## The Counselor as a Community Fixture

The best counselors are pillars of their communities. They're the names people whisper when someone's in crisis, the guest speakers at schools and churches, and the supervisors who shape the next generation. Your business is your platform. It's how you amplify what matters most to you. It's how you create safety for your clients and structure for yourself. Done well, it becomes a part of your community's healing fabric. That's bigger than a business—that's legacy.

## What to Keep in Mind as You Grow

Growth is measured in scale, reach, and depth. Not every counselor wants to build a group practice or speak on stages, but every counselor should want to grow their competence, their confidence, and their capacity to serve well. That kind of growth shows up in the small, consistent habits that shape your work every day.

- Stay organized, so your clients don't carry the weight of your chaos.
- Stay ethical, so your colleagues know they can trust your name in the room.
- Stay clear, so your expectations are known before they're violated.
- Stay generous, not just with your time, but with your presence.
- Stay teachable, because the moment you think you've arrived, you stop growing.

## Systems Create Freedom

The more you commit to structure, the more space you create for joy, rest, and creativity. Think of systems not as cages, but as organizational containers that protect your time and your peace. They keep your work manageable and prevent burnout. Structure turns your business into a living ecosystem, not just a hustle. If you want to be here for the long haul, take your systems seriously. Automate where you can, delegate the tasks that drain you, review your policies regularly, charge what sustains you, and document like your license depends on it (because it does). Don't forget to make room for your own humanity inside the process.

## A Final Word from Us

We didn't write this book because we had everything figured out. We wrote it because time and time again, we met good counselors caught in systems that didn't teach them how to build, protect, or grow the kind of careers they imagined. These were smart, compassionate people who were stuck, not because they lacked heart, but because they lacked the tools and resources they needed. We decided to write the kind of book we wish someone had handed us years ago. We sought to offer a blueprint. Being a great clinician and a savvy business owner are twin strengths, rather than opposing goals. You don't have to trade your ethics for excellence. You don't have to sacrifice your peace to make a living. You can be grounded in your values and unapologetic about your worth. Let your practice mirror your values. Let your business honor your boundaries. Let your growth point toward your purpose. In this field, doing good business isn't just possible, it's necessary. It's time to get started.

# References

Ackerman, S. J., & Hilsenroth, M. J. (2001). A review of therapist characteristics and techniques negatively impacting the therapeutic alliance. *Psychotherapy: Theory, Research, Practice, Training, 38*(2), 171–185. https://doi.org/10.1037/0033-3204.38.2.171

American Psychological Association. (2017). Ethical principles of psychologists and code of conduct (2002, amended effective June 1, 2010, and January 1, 2017). https://www.apa.org/ethics/code

Borders, L. D., Glosoff, H. L., Welfare, L. E., Hays, D. G., DeKruyf, L., Fernando, D. M., & Page, B. (2014). Best practices in clinical supervision: Evolution of a counseling specialty. *The Clinical Supervisor, 33*(1), 26–44. https://doi.org/10.1080/07325223.2014.905225

Del Re, A. C., Flückiger, C., Horvath, A. O., & Wampold, B. E. (2021). Examining therapist effects in the alliance–outcome relationship: A multilevel meta-analysis. *Journal of Consulting and Clinical Psychology, 89*(5), 371–383. https://doi.org/10.1037/ccp0000637

Flückiger, C., Del Re, A. C., Wampold, B. E., & Horvath, A. O. (2018). The alliance in adult psychotherapy: A meta-analytic synthesis. *Psychotherapy, 55*(4), 316–340. https://doi.org/10.1037/pst0000172

Hakim, A. B. (2022). *Assessing the relationship between the supervisory environment, job satisfaction, and burnout among new counseling professionals* [Doctoral dissertation, Capella University]. ProQuest Dissertations & Theses.

Knapp, S., & VandeCreek, L. (2008). The ethics of advertising, billing, and finances in psychotherapy. *Journal of Clinical Psychology, 64*(5), 613–625. https://doi.org/10.1002/jclp.20475

Ladmanová, M., Řiháček, T., & Timulak, L. (2021). Client-identified impacts of helpful and hindering events in psychotherapy: A qualitative meta-analysis. *Psychotherapy Research, 32*(6), 723–735. https://doi.org/10.1080/10503307.2021.2003885

Lewis, J. A., Ratts, M. J., Paladino, D. A., & Toporek, R. L. (2011). Social justice counseling and advocacy: Developing new leadership roles and competencies. *Journal for Social Action in Counseling & Psychology, 3*(1), 5–16. https://doi.org/10.33043/JSACP.3.1.5-16

Mcinnes, N., & Haglund, B. J. A. (2011). Readability of online health information: Implications for health literacy. *Informatics for Health and Social Care, 36*(4), 173–189. https://doi.org/10.3109/17538157.2010.542529

Mellin, E. A., Hunt, B., & Nichols, L. M. (2011). Counselor professional identity: Findings and implications. *Journal of Counseling and Development, 89*(2), 140–147. https://doi.org/10.1002/j.1556-6678.2011.tb00071.x

Norcross, J. C., & Lambert, M. J. (Eds.). (2019). *Psychotherapy relationships that work: Evidence-based therapist contributions* (3rd ed.). Oxford University Press.

Lewis, J. A., Ratts, M. J., Paladino, D. A., & Toporek, R. L. (2011). Social justice counseling and advocacy: Developing new leadership roles and competencies. *Journal for Social Action in Counseling and Psychology, 3*(1), 5–16. https://doi.org/10.33043/JSACP.3.1.5-16

Roncoroni, J., & Tucker, C. M. (2024). Radical healing community-based participatory research to eliminate health disparities. *The Counseling Psychologist, 52*(4), 551–580. https://doi.org/10.1177/00110000241234311

Rousmaniere, T. (2014). Using technology to enhance clinical supervision and training. In C. E. Watkins, Jr. & D. L. Milne (Eds.), *The Wiley international handbook of clinical supervision* (pp. 204–237). Wiley Blackwell. https://doi.org/10.1002/9781118846360.ch9

Sillence, E., Briggs, P., Harris, P. R., & Fishwick, L. (2007). How do patients evaluate and make use of online health information? *Social Science and Medicine, 64*(9), 1853–1862. https://doi.org/10.1016/j.socscimed.2007.01.012

Summers, L. M., & Nelson, L. (Eds.). (2022). *Multicultural counseling: Responding with cultural humility, empathy, and advocacy*. Springer Publishing Company.

Tierney, W. M., McNamee, C., Harris, S. S., & Strakowski, S. M. (2025). Community-based mental health improvement initiatives: A narrative review and Indiana case study. *Population Health Management, 28*(1), 31–36. https://doi.org/10.1089/pop.2024.0153

Toporek, R. L., Lewis, J. A., & Crethar, H. C. (2009). Promoting systemic change through the ACA Advocacy Competencies. *Journal of Counseling and Development, 87*(3), 260–268. https://doi.org/10.1002/j.1556-6678.2009.tb00105.x

Wheeler, A. M., & Bertram, B. (2019). *The counselor and the law: A guide to legal and ethical practice* (8th ed.). American Counseling Association.

Wilson, F. (2016). Identifying, preventing, and addressing job burnout and vicarious burnout for social work professionals. *Journal of Evidence-Informed Social Work, 13*(5), 479–483. https://doi.org/10.1080/23761407.2016.1166856

# Conclusion
*Putting It Together*

Counseling is more than a calling. It's a profession, a business, and a livelihood. The work now is holding all of it—your clinical skills, your heart for the work, and your growing business mindset—in your hands.

Early in our careers, we were doing deeply meaningful work in the counseling room. Behind the scenes, we were scrambling to chase down late payments, cover rent with credit cards, and file taxes in a panic. We weren't failing because we didn't care enough. We cared so much it nearly broke us. What we lacked was structure. We didn't need to scale back our compassion; we needed a bigger and sturdier container to hold it. That's where the business side came in for us. We finally got our billing system in order, and our clients stopped losing time sorting through errors. We organized our calendars and were able to stop showing up tired and distracted. We charged what our work was worth and we no longer had to work later just to stay afloat. Our paperwork was solid, and we slept better knowing we were covered. Those weren't just logistical wins. They were clinical ones. When our practice ran well, we could be fully present with our clients.

Good counseling and good business rely on each other. One delivers the healing, the other makes sure that healing is sustainable. Take what you've learned—how to listen, how to intervene, how to support someone through crisis—and pair it with the tools we've explored in this book: pricing, marketing, supervision, retirement planning. If you're ever unsure about how much to lean into the business side, decide what kind of example you want to set. Someone is always watching, whether it's your supervisees, your clients, your family, or your future self. Build something they'd be proud to follow.

## Developing a Comprehensive Business Plan

For counselors, a business plan is not a formality. It's a framework for decision-making, growth, and long-term alignment with your values.

Think of your business plan as a mirror and a map. It shows you where you are right now, and where you want to go. It forces you to be specific about what you offer, who you serve, how you charge, and what you want your future to look like. These are the core elements that every counselor's business plan should include.

- **Mission:** Why does your practice exist? Who do you serve? What values guide your work? How do you want to be remembered? A clear mission keeps your focus steady when opportunities start pulling you in too many directions.
- **Services:** What exactly are you offering: individual counseling, couples work, group counseling, supervision, workshops, or consulting? Each service should have its own pricing, schedule, and audience.
- **Finances:** Map out your income goals, expenses, and pricing strategy. What do you need to earn each month to live, save, and reinvest in your business? Identify both fixed and variable costs, and don't undervalue your work.
- **Operations:** Plan for the administrative side of your practice. How will you handle scheduling, billing, record-keeping, and technology? What systems or tools will keep things organized? Write this section as if you're onboarding your future self or your first hire.
- **Marketing:** Where will your referrals come from? How will potential clients find you? Will you focus on SEO, social media, networking, or community workshops? Marketing creates visibility and helps your practice develop a consistent voice.
- **Risk management:** What happens if you get sick, move, or experience sudden growth? What insurance coverage and legal structure protect your assets? A strong plan should make your business safer, not just more profitable.
- **Vision:** Where do you want your practice to be in five years? Will you measure success beyond income based on balance, impact, or creative freedom? Your business plan should evolve with you. Revisit it each year, refine it, and let it guide your decisions when the path feels uncertain.

Your business plan is more than paperwork. It's your blueprint for building a practice that takes care of others and takes care of you.

## Reflecting on Personal and Professional Growth

Growth in this field is earned through mistakes, breakthroughs, and moments that bend you into someone wiser. That's why reflection matters—not as a soft ending, but as a vital reckoning. The longer you practice, the more you start to realize how much your business is a reflection of your inner life. Your boundaries, your fears, your hopes, and your beliefs about worth and work show up in your systems, your fees, your scheduling, and your supervision. That reflection offers opportunity. The more honest you are about your growth edges, the stronger your business becomes.

In a 2017 study, Wilkinson et al. found that self-reflection among mental health practitioners was significantly correlated with reduced burnout and increased empathy. Another study by West et al. (2016) emphasized that structured reflection was key to physician and counselor resilience. Utilize this advice and reflect on your work. Ask yourself:

- When do I feel most clear and confident in my career?
- What patterns keep surfacing in my stress or overwhelm?
- Who am I becoming in the way I run this business?

Reflection also demands gratitude. Look at how far you've come. Remember the version of you who didn't know how to bill insurance, who felt sick raising fees, or who believed leadership was for someone else. That person started you on this journey. If you're reading this with a mix of pride and panic, welcome to the party. You are allowed to be unsure. You are allowed to revise. Growth requires presence. There is no final arrival, but there is deep peace in knowing you're doing the work with intention.

## Setting Goals and Strategies for the Future

If you have written and executed your business plan, congratulations. Maybe you have a thriving counseling business, and you're not sure what to do next. Your job doesn't stop when you've met your goals. Revisit the vision you wrote in your business plan. Has it come to pass? Is there more you want to do? What else do you want to achieve?

The final stretch of building a business grounded in counseling values is knowing how to grow it with clarity and intention. In this profession, our growth goals must be rooted in who we are, who we serve, and how we want to live.

## Break Big Goals Into Small, Repeatable Actions

Once you've clarified (and, perhaps, expanded) your vision in your business plan, reverse-engineer your goals. Do you want to reduce your caseload by 20% and raise your rates by next year? Start by mapping out your monthly income needs and identifying one training or credential that can justify the shift. Is it time to hire an assistant? Set a 90-day goal to define the role, research payroll systems, and test your budget with a mock salary. Small, repeated steps build infrastructure. Use systems like SMART goals (Specific, Measurable, Achievable, Relevant, and Time-bound) to structure your strategy. It's not about hustle. It's about rhythm.

## Track Progress with Compassion, Not Criticism

The best strategic thinkers aren't the most aggressive. They're the most self-aware. Build quarterly check-ins for your goals. Figure out what has been working and what hasn't, and reflect on whether your context and values have changed. Make tracking visual in the form of a dashboard, a spreadsheet, or a journal. Keep your goals where you can see them. Celebrate what you hit. Revise what no longer fits. Research done by Morisano et al. (2010) showed that goal-setting interventions that incorporate reflective journaling significantly improve long-term achievement and personal satisfaction. When you write your goals and revisit them reflectively, you're more likely to keep moving forward.

## Strategize for More Than Money

While financial sustainability is essential, so is setting goals for leadership, rest, mentorship, and creativity. Set goals to train your first intern, take a 10-day vacation without checking email, speak at a local conference, or build a grief group in your community. Business goals that nurture your spirit are just as strategic as those that pad your income.

## Expect to Evolve

The goals that fit you now may not fit you in five years. It's natural to grow and evolve in your personal life, and your professional life is no different in that regard. Where have your needs changed? What impact do you want to make next? One of the biggest predictors of long-term success is adaptability. Counselors who thrive over decades aren't those who found the perfect niche and stuck to it without blinking. They're

Conclusion

the ones who stayed anchored in their values while adjusting their business model to new needs, new seasons, and new dreams.

## Strategic Planning Map

It can be overwhelming to name goals without knowing how exactly to achieve them. That's where this strategic planning map comes in. This keeps you focused when things get loud, messy, or overwhelming. Use the prompts below to design your year with purpose.

> **Strategic Planning Map**
>
> *Top Three Professional Priorities*
>
> What needs your attention the most? This could include:
>
> - Increasing your caseload with your ideal clients
> - Launching a supervision track
> - Publishing your first blog post or newsletter
> - Restructuring your pricing for sustainability
>
> Keep it focused. These should be actions or behaviors that move the needle—not just busywork.
>
> *Top Three Personal Wellness Priorities*
>
> Your practice can't be healthy if you're not. What wellness habits support your energy and presence? This could include:
>
> - Weekly unplugged time
> - Monthly counseling or peer consultation
> - Committing to your sleep schedule or fitness routine
> - Protecting a no-client Friday
>
> Be honest here. Wellness helps prevent burnout.
>
> *One New System or Tool to Implement*
>
> What's one tool or workflow that could make your business smoother? This could include:
>
> (continued)

- Switching to an electronic health record system
- Automating reminders or intake forms
- Creating a referral tracker
- Using a scheduling app that syncs with your calendar

Start small. Pick one that reduces friction for you and your clients.

### One Risk to Take

Growth doesn't happen without discomfort. What's one stretch move you've been avoiding? This could include:

- Raising your rates
- Teaching your first workshop
- Pitching yourself to speak at a conference
- Hiring someone for admin support

Risk doesn't always mean danger. Sometimes, it just means taking a small step outside of your comfort zone.

### One Colleague to Teach You or Collaborate With You

You're not meant to do this alone. Choose someone you admire or want to build with. They could be:

- A trusted peer with whom you've been meaning to reconnect
- A mentor or supervisor whose business approach you respect
- A friend who teaches continuing education units or runs a successful group practice

Reach out. Ask a question. Share your goal. Collaboration multiplies momentum.

### One Way to Give Back

How will you invest in the field, your community, or your colleagues? This could include:

(continued)

- Offering sliding-scale spots for a local nonprofit
- Mentoring a new graduate
- Running a free group for underserved folks
- Writing something that helps another counselor breathe easier

Giving back reminds you of why you started. It keeps the work rooted in meaning.

Following this map ensures that you remain intentional with your energy, your time, and your growth. Let it guide your decisions, especially when the pressure builds or the doubt creeps in.

As our grandpa Bishop MJ Bernard would say before leaving the cookout, "Welp, that's me, y'all." You have spent this book sharpening your clinical skills, building your business mindset, and reimagining what it means to be both a healer and an entrepreneur. Now it's time to live it. Move forward. Forget about perfection. Instead, focus on presence. Build what only you can build. Serve clients only you can serve. Let your business become an extension of your purpose, one ethical, well-crafted decision at a time.

## References

Morisano, D., Hirsh, J. B., Peterson, J. B., Pihl, R. O., & Shore, B. M. (2010). Setting, elaborating, and reflecting on personal goals improves academic performance. *Journal of Applied Psychology, 95*(2), 255–264. https://doi.org/10.1037/a0018478

West, C. P., Dyrbye, L. N., Erwin, P. J., & Shanafelt, T. D. (2016). Interventions to prevent and reduce physician burnout: A systematic review and meta-analysis. *The Lancet, 388*(10057), 2272–2281. https://doi.org/10.1016/S0140-6736(16)31279-X

Wilkinson, H., Whittington, R., Perry, L., & Eames, C. (2017). Examining the relationship between burnout and empathy in healthcare professionals: A systematic review. *Burnout Research, 6*, 18–29. https://doi.org/10.1016/j.burn.2017.06.003

# About the Authors

**Dr. Julius A. Austin** is a Licensed Professional Counselor Supervisor and an Assistant Professor in the Counseling Program at the University of Louisiana at Lafayette. He is also in private practice in Lafayette, Louisiana. He holds a Ph.D in Counselor Education and Supervision from the University of Wyoming. He is an avid speaker at counseling conferences around the country, and was the 2021 American Counseling Association Conference Keynote Speaker. He is a co-author of *Counselor Self-Care, Surviving and Thriving in your Counseling Program, Doing Counseling: Developing Your Clinical Skills and Style,* and *The Counselor Educator's Guide: Practical In-Class Strategies and Activities.*

**Dr. Jude T. Austin, II**, is a Licensed Professional Counselor Supervisor, and a Licensed Marriage and Family Therapist Supervisor. He is an Associate Professor in the Master of Arts in Counseling Program at the University of Mary Hardin-Baylor and serves as Program Coordinator for the Clinical Mental Health Counseling track. He is also in private practice in Belton, Texas. He holds a PhD in Counselor Education and Supervision from the University of Wyoming. He consistently speaks at counseling conferences around the country, and was the 2021 American Counseling Association Conference Keynote Speaker. He is a co-author of *Counselor Self-Care, Surviving and Thriving in your Counseling Program, Doing Counseling: Developing Your Clinical Skills and Style,* and *The Counselor Educator's Guide: Practical In-Class Strategies and Activities.*

www.ingramcontent.com/pod-product-compliance
Lightning Source LLC
Jackson TN
JSHW082042150126
96745JS00007B/5